INSTRUCTOR'S MANUAL

Using QuickBooks Pro® FOR ACCOUNTING 2005

Glenn Owen

Allan Hancock College

University of California at Santa Barbara

THOMSON

SOUTH-WESTERN

Australia · Canada · Mexico · Singapore · Spain · United Kingdom · United States

THOMSON

SOUTH-WESTERN

Instructor's Manual to accompany Using QuickBooks Pro 2005 for Accounting
Glenn Owen

VP/Editorial Director:
Jack W. Calhoun

Publisher:
Rob Dewey

Acquisitions Editor:
Matt Filimonov

Associate Developmental Editor:
Allison Rolfes

Marketing Manager:
Chris McNamee

Production Project Manager:
Stephanie Schempp

Senior Manufacturing Coordinator:
Doug Wilke

Production House:
DPS Associates, Inc.

Printer:
Globus
Minster, OH

Art Director:
Bethany Casey

Cover Designer:
Beckmeyer Design, Cincinnati

Cover Images:
© PhotoDisc, Inc.

Thomson Higher Education
5191 Natorp Boulevard
Mason, OH 45040
USA

Table of Contents

To the Instructor

OVERVIEW

Using QuickBooks Pro® 2004 for Accounting is designed for a variety of courses. You can use it as a stand-alone text for courses that teach students how to use QuickBooks only. You can also use it with a core accounting textbook that provides the basic accounting concepts; in this case *QuickBooks* reinforces the accounting concepts presented in the core text. But no matter how you use this text, it will help students learn how to use QuickBooks in a step-by-step way. This textbook encourages students to use the QuickBooks Help facility; context-sensitive help is a major feature of QuickBooks and use of this feature helps students build critical-thinking and problem-solving skills. Furthermore, *some* of the Practice assignments at the end of the chapters ask students to go a little beyond what they actually did in the chapter.

TROUBLESHOOTING TIPS

1. <u>Payroll tax tables</u> All of the text and solution material was created without using tax tables, with the exception of rock.qbw. If your students are using a version of the tax tables their answers for payroll tax liabilities and payroll expenses *may* be different from those provided in this set of solutions. Once again a warning about these potential differences may preempt student confusion.

2. Dates QuickBooks is *very* date sensitive. Thus, students will often make errors when they record transactions if they enter the default or system date. Using the system date will result in incorrect reports. Note that transactions for the Phoenix Systems and Central Coast Cellular assignments are all 2003. Transactions for Ocean View Flowers, Sarah Duncan, CPA, and Sports City assignments are all dated in 2004. Transactions for Pacific Brew are all dated 2006. Transactions for Century Kitchens are all dated 2007. **Please remind all of your students to enter correct dates so they will produce correct reports.**

3. Disk Space Managing disk space could be a problem for students. If you provide students with data disks, they should be instructed to copy the files one at a time as needed to a blank formatted "working" disk. This will insure that enough space is available on the disk for QuickBooks to temporarily store other data. This will also keep the original data files unchanged in case students need to start over.

4. Saving QuickBooks saves data automatically. In other words, students do not have to manually save a data file. This is different from most other software applications, such as spreadsheets and word processing programs, which students might have used in previous courses. *Remind students that with QuickBooks their data is always automatically saved and that they should back up their data whenever possible.*

5. Backing Up Data In QuickBooks backing up a file from the hard drive to the disk is a straightforward process. But if the student is backing up a QuickBooks data file stored on a disk, the process is not so easy. *Do not use the QuickBooks backup and restore process to back up a data file on a disk.* Instead, tell students to make disk-to-disk copies using the Windows Explorer. Also make sure that when they make disk-to-disk copies that they have exited QuickBooks and, thus, closed the QuickBooks data file. Otherwise they may lose data.

6. Web Pages Currently these pages contain the Internet Assignments that appear in the Assignments at the end of each chapter in the book. As instructors provide feedback on this textbook, those ideas, tips, corrections, and other helpful material will be posted at *http://owen.swlearning.com.*

7. Figures Some solutions in this *Instructor's Manual* are figures of reports and other printouts. You will find all of these figures for each chapter collected together at the *end* of each chapter in this *Instructor's Manual.*

If you have questions about the features, use, and/or installation of QuickBooks itself, please contact Intuit Inc. at its customer support line 1-888-222-7276 or at its website *http://www.intuit.com.*

If you have comments to make about this textbook, please contact me at the following address:

Glenn Owen at *gowen@hancockcollege.edu*

I hope your students enjoy using this textbook and that you reap the benefits that teaching QuickBooks provides.

1

Getting Started with QuickBooks

Chapter 1 is designed to help students get a top-down view of QuickBooks as a user-oriented accounting program. This chapter is divided into five sessions, which students can work through on their own. In Session 1 students learn—in an interactive way—basic QuickBooks terminology, basic file management with QuickBooks, navigation techniques, and other essential skills such as printing and correcting mistakes. Sessions 2, 3, 4, and 5 give students a quick overview of how to create balance sheets, income statements, cash flow statements, and supporting reports using QuickBooks.

SESSION 1 AN INTERACTIVE TOUR OF QUICKBOOKS

Session 1 Questions

1. QuickBooks is used as an automated accounting information system that can help describe an entity's financial position and operating results. Like any accounting system, QuickBooks can be used as an information tool to help make better decisions and help facilitate business record keeping and management. QuickBooks can be used to invoice customers, maintain receivables, pay bills, maintain accounts payable, track inventory, and create purchase orders.

2. QuickBooks's four basic features are lists, forms, registers, and reports and graphs.

3. Lists are used to manage names and related information on such things as customers, vendors, employees, inventory, and accounts, to name a few.

4. Forms are used to record business activities such as a sale on account (customer invoice), a purchase (vendor bill), or a payment (check).

5. The customer invoice, vendor bill, and check are three forms used in QuickBooks.

6. Registers are used in QuickBooks to summarize all financial activity for specific balance sheet accounts such as checking, accounts receivable, inventory, and accounts payable.

7. Reports and graphs are used to present financial position and operating results of a company in a way that makes business decision-making easier.

8. Navigators provide quick access to commonly used activities and reports.

9. In order to be printed in QuickBooks, a report must first be created using the Reports menu, then printed with the Print button on the Button bar.

10. Several help features are available in QuickBooks. The main QuickBooks Help area is accessed via the main menu and provides a table of contents, find, and index modes. "How do I" information buttons are another help feature that provide context-sensitive help. Small Business by Quicken.com also provides help such as feature articles and answers to frequently asked questions (FAQs).

Session 1 Assignments

1. Working with Files: Opening, Closing, and Printing—see Figure 1.1 *[Note: You will find all solution figures for this chapter at the end of the chapter, beginning on page 17.]*

2. Practice Using the QuickBooks Help Menu

    a. See Figure 1.2.

    b. See Figure 1.3.

    c. See Figure 1.3a.

    d. See Figure 1.3b.

3. For each item of inventory, this report shows quantity on hand, average cost, and asset value.

4. Internet assignments and related solutions are found at *http://owen.swlearning.com.*

Session 1   Case Problems

1. Accessing Inventory Data

   a. n/a

   b. n/a

   c. Base double door double drawer.

   d. At that date there were 3 units on hand.

   e. At that date the average cost was $480.

   f. See Figure 1.4.

[Note: You will find all solution figures for this chapter at the end of the chapter, beginning on page 17.]

2. Accessing Sales Data

   a. n/a

   b. n/a

   c. J Wilson was billed $12,480.

   d. S Gomez was billed for planning and design.

   e. Century billed customers $37,995.

   f. See Figure 1.5.

SESSION 2   PREPARING A BALANCE SHEET USING QUICKBOOKS

Session 2   Questions

1. QuickBooks has four preset Balance Sheet reports: Standard, Comparison, Summary, and Itemized.

2. QuickBooks provides many time period alternatives for the balance sheet, including today, this week, last

   month, etc.

3. To create a balance sheet for a date other than the system date you must either enter a new date in the As of edit

   box in the Balance Sheet window or select an alternate time period in the Dates edit box.

4. To generate a balance sheet in QuickBooks do the following: 1. Click Reports from the available menus.

   2. Click Company & Financial from the sub menu shown. 3. Choose either Standard, Comparison, Summary, or

   Itemized from the sub menu provided.

5. To reformat the columns of a balance sheet click and hold the mouse over the small diamond-shaped symbols to the right or left of any column and drag to the right or left to increase or decrease the column's width.

6. Two different types of transactions are found in an Accounts Receivable Transaction by Account report: invoice and payment. The first represents the billing of a customer, the second the receipt of payment on account from that customer.

7. QuickZoom can provide more information from a balance sheet by providing detail which underlies a particular account balance. For instance, QuickZoom can be used to view transactions which support the Accounts Receivable account.

8. A manager might use the QuickZoom feature to view transactions which underlie the Cash account. In this case, the QuickZoom result identifies all transactions for the period that created the ending balance reported in the balance sheet.

9. A QuickBooks report can be modified in five ways: 1. Report dates can be changed. 2. From/To dates can be changed. 3. Report Basis can be either Accrual or Cash. 4. Columns can be changed from totals only to week, month, quarter, etc. 5. Other columns can be added, such as previous period, previous year, etc.

10. You can add a column entitled % of column, which describes what percentage each asset, liability, and owners' equity account was of the total assets amount, using the Modify Report button on the balance sheet.

Session 2   Assignments

1. Creating a Summary & Standard Balance Sheet as of 1/31/2007
   a. See Figure 1.6. *[Note: You will find all solution figures for this chapter at the end of the chapter.]*
   b. See Figure 1.7.

2. Investigating the Balance Sheet Using QuickZoom
   a. n/a
   b. n/a
   c. See Figure 1.8.
   d. See Figure 1.8a.

3. Internet Assignments and related solutions are found at *http://owen.swlearning.com*.

4. See Figure 1.8.b.

Session 2 Case Problem

[Note: You will find all solution figures for this chapter at the end of the chapter.]

1.   See Figure 1.9.

2.   See Figure 1.10.

3.   See Figure 1.11.

4.   See Figure 1.12.

5.   See Figure 1.13.

SESSION 3 PREPARING AN INCOME STATEMENT USING QUICKBOOKS

Session 3 Questions

1.   QuickBooks has ten preset formats for an income statement. The first three are Standard, YTD Comparison, and

     Prev Year Comparison.

2.   QuickBooks provides many time period alternatives for the income statement including today, this week, last

     month, etc.

3.   To create an income statement for a date other than the system date you must either enter a new date in the As of

     edit box in the Income Statement window or select an alternate time period in the Dates edit box.

4.   To generate an income statement in QuickBooks do the following: 1. Click Reports from the available menus.

     2. Click Company & Financial from the sub menu shown. 3. Choose one of the preset formats from the sub

     menu provided.

5.   To reformat the columns of a comparative income statement click and hold the mouse over the small diamond-

     shaped symbols to the right or left of any column and drag to the right or left to increase or decrease the

     column's width.

6.   To include comparative information on an income statement do the following: 1. Create a standard income

     statement. 2. Click the Modify Report button on the button toolbar. 3. Change the columns drop-down edit box

     and select an appropriate comparative column (such as month, week, etc.). 4. Change the From and To edit

     boxes to reflect the appropriate period you want reported on the comparative income statement. 5. Click OK.

7. QuickZoom can provide more information from an income statement by providing detail that underlies a particular account balance. For instance, QuickZoom can be used to view transactions which support the sales account.

8. A manager might use the QuickZoom feature to view transactions which underlie the sales account. In this case the QuickZoom result identifies all sales transactions for the period which created the balances reported in the income statement.

9. A QuickBooks report can be modified in five ways: 1. Report dates can be changed. 2. From/To dates can be changed. 3. Report Basis can be either Accrual or Cash. 4. Columns can be changed from totals only to week, month, quarter, etc. 5. Other columns, such as previous period, previous year, etc., can be added.

10. Using the Modify Reports button on the income statement you can add a column on the income statement entitled % of income that describes what percentage each revenue and expense account was of total income. (Remember, QuickBooks uses the term *income* instead of revenues.)

Session 3   Assignments

1. Preparing an income statement for Century Kitchens

    a. See Figure 1.14.

    b. See Figure 1.15. This income statement was modified using a right page layout and changing the report title to income statement.

2. Investigating the Century Kitchens Income Statement using QuickZoom

    a. n/a

    b. n/a

    c. Home Depot.

    d. Check 119.

3. Internet assignments and related solutions are found at *http://owen.swlearning.com.*

4. Modifying an income statement

    a. n/a

    b. n/a

    c. n/a

    d. See Figure 1.16.

Session 3 Case Problem

1. n/a

2. See Figure 1.17.

3. See Figure 1.18.

4. See Figure 1.19.

SESSION 4   PREPARING A STATEMENT OF CASH FLOWS USING QUICKBOOKS

Session 4 Questions

1. QuickBooks provides two reports for reporting cash flow: the statement of cash flow and forecast.

2. To create a statement of cash flows click Cash Flow from the Reports menu, click Company & Financial, then click Statement of Cash Flows.

3. To create a statement of cash flows for a period other than the one ending with the current system date of the computer, change the From and To dates in the Report window.

4. The first three periods of time that QuickBooks provides for a statement of cash flows are All, Today, and This Week. Others, such as Fiscal Year-to-date, Last Month, etc., are available.

5. The three sections of the statement of cash flows are operating activities, investing activities, and financing activities.

6. The statement of cash flow operating section created by QuickBooks starts with net income followed by adjustments to reconcile net income to net cash provided by operations. Some of these adjustments are increases or decreases during the period to accounts receivable, inventory, accounts payable, payroll liabilities, sales tax payable, etc.

7. The one adjustment necessary to reconcile net income to cash provided by operations which was not initially a part of the Rock Castle statement of cash flows was to accumulated depreciation. These accounts were initially included as adjustments to investing activities.

8. The steps necessary to make changes in the statement of cash flows report layout to properly reflect the adjustments necessary to reconcile net income to cash provided by operations are as follows: 1. Click the Classify cash button on the statement of cash flows report. 2. Click the Classify cash button in the Preferences window. 3. Change the classification of each accumulated depreciation account from investing activities to operating activities.

9. The QuickZoom feature of QuickBooks does not provide the same help in the statement of cash flows as it does in the income statement. This feature allows you to look at the underlying transactions which created the changes (some increasing, some decreasing) in the statement of cash flows, not the net changes.

10. To format and print a statement of cash flows: 1. Change the header by clicking Modify Reports, then select the Header/Footer tab and formatting (such as without cents, etc.) by clicking the Fonts & Numbers tab. 2. Click Print from the statement of cash flows window. 3. Click Print in the Print Reports window.

Session 4 Assignments

1. Preparing a statement of cash flows. See Figure 1.20.

2. Internet assignments and related solutions are found at *http://owen.swlearning.com*.

Session 4 Case Problem

1. n/a

2. See Figure 1.21 for the Statement of Cash Flows for 1/1/04 to 1/31/04.

3. See Figure 1.22 for the Statement of Cash Flows for 1/1/04 to 1/31/04 without cents.

SESSION 5   CREATING SUPPORTING REPORTS TO HELP MAKE BUSINESS DECISIONS

Session 5 Questions

1. The Reports menu provides you access to supporting reports.

2. The Accounts Receivable Aging report provides information on each customer's account balance, such as if balances are current or past due, if they are past due how old they are, and total balances receivable from all customers by date.

3. Two examples of transactions appearing in an Accounts Receivable Aging QuickZoom report would be invoices and payments.

4. A payment history can help explain how payments on account were allocated to invoices for each customer, thereby explaining the nature of balances owed.

5. An inventory valuation summary lists all items on hand as of a specific date and provides information on quantity, average cost, and asset value.

6. Two examples of transactions appearing in an Inventory Summary QuickZoom report would be invoices and inventory adjustments.

7. An accounts payable aging report provides information on each vendor's accounts payable balance, such as if balances are current or past due, if they are past due how old they are, and total balances payable to all vendors by date.

8. Two examples of transactions appearing in an Accounts Payable Aging QuickZoom report would be bills and checks.

9. The Print Reports dialog box gives you the option to print to the printer or to a file, print with a portrait or landscape orientation, print all or just some pages of a report, and print a report to fit to one page wide.

10. Supporting reports can be generated for any date desired by changing the From and/or To dates or by specifying a different date description in the Dates drop-down list (last month, last quarter, etc.). One example might be the creation of a vendor balance summary report for the current and previous month.

Session 5 Assignments

1. Creating Supporting Reports for Century Kitchens

   a. See Figure 1.23 for the Customer Balance Summary report. The largest customer receivable other than R Coe is from J Wilson. Wilson owes Century Kitchens $12,030.00 from Invoice 1004 for cabinets and installation.

   b. See Figure 1.24 for the Aging of Accounts Receivable report. The only past due item was invoice 1002 to R Coe. This invoice was due 1/19/07 and was for kitchen upgrade planning and design.

   c. See Figure 1.25 for the Aging of Accounts Payable report. The largest vendor liability was to Thomasville Cabinets. This liability was from one bill dated 2/16/07 for cabinets on the I Bowen job and was due 2/26/07.

   d. See Figure 1.26 for an inventory valuation summary. Item 1014, Wall Angle, is the item with the largest asset cost ($1,620.00) with a retail value of $1,875.00.

2. Creating More Supporting Reports

   a. See Figure 1.27 for the Customer Balance Summary report. Invoice 1008 created this receivable. Monroe was invoiced for cabinets and cabinet installation with terms of net 15.

   b. See Figure 1.28 for the Aging of Accounts Receivable report. Invoice 1015 created this receivable. Summer was invoiced for 30 hours of design and planning with terms of net 15.

   c. See Figure 1.29 for the Aging of Accounts Payable report. This payable is represented by one bill dated 1/22/07 for cabinets for customer A Monroe with terms of net 15.

   d. See Figure 1.30 for the Inventory Valuation Summary. There were no items of inventory on hand at this date.

3. Internet assignments and related solutions are found at *http://owen.swlearning.com.*

Session 5 Case Problem

1. n/a

2. See Figure 1.31. Evelyn Walker Real Estate has the largest balance receivable ($4,865) which is represented by Invoices 2, 4, and 11. All three are current with amounts due for a radio commercial, press release, and promotion work. Paulson has the next largest receivable ($1,950) which is represented by Invoice 10. This invoice is also current with an amount due for a television commercial and film.

3. See Figure 1.32. KCOY TV has the largest balance payable ($2,500) represented by a bill received 1/10/04 for TV commercial spots. Rex's Film Supply has the next largest payable ($1,270) which is represented by two bills, one dated 1/12/04 for 100 rolls of regular film, the other dated 1/29/04 for 150 rolls of regular film.

4. See Figure 1.33. The most recent purchase of film was from Rex's Film Supply. 150 rolls of film were purchased at a cost of $5.50 each.

Solution Figures for Chapter 1

Figure 1.1

Century Kitchens
Open Invoices

Type	Date	Num	P. O.#	Terms	Due Date	Aging	Open Balance
A Monroe							
Invoice	2/15/2007	1008		Net 15	3/2/2007	29	13,535.00
Invoice	3/30/2007	1019		Net 15	4/14/2007		4,960.00
Total A Monroe							18,495.00
B Scaggs							
Invoice	3/30/2007	1016		Net 15	4/14/2007		16,045.00
Total B Scaggs							16,045.00
I Bowen							
Invoice	3/30/2007	1017		Net 15	4/14/2007		3,960.00
Total I Bowen							3,960.00
J Summer							
Invoice	2/28/2007	1015		Net 15	3/15/2007	16	2,250.00
Invoice	3/30/2007	1018		Net 15	4/14/2007		10,560.00
Total J Summer							12,810.00
R Coe							
Invoice	1/31/2007	1005		Net 15	2/15/2007	44	12,765.00
Total R Coe							12,765.00
R Rose							
Invoice	2/28/2007	1014		Net 15	3/15/2007	16	4,500.00
Total R Rose							4,500.00
G Gomez							
Invoice	2/20/2007	1010		Net 15	3/7/2007	24	2,300.00
Invoice	2/28/2007	1012		Net 15	3/15/2007	16	5,120.00
Total S Gomez							7,420.00
TOTAL							**75,995.00**

Figure 1.2

Changing the date range of a report

All reports have a preset or "default" date range. You can change the date range to cover a different period of time.

In some editions of QuickBooks, you cannot modify the date range for a report. For example, you can modify the date range of the Income Tax Preparation report only in the QuickBooks Accountant Edition.

To change the date range for a report

1. Display the report you want to modify.
2. In the report window buttonbar, define the date range to use:
   - To use a different date range, select one of the ranges shown on the Dates drop-down list.

     What do the different date ranges mean?
   - To change to a period of time not specified by one of the preset ranges, click the calendars to change the dates shown in the From and To fields. When the calendar appears, click the arrows to display the month you want, then click the day of the month.

Related topics

- Getting the most out of a report

  Do you need more information? Try the Support Center.

  Did this Help topic provide you with the information you needed?

  Requires an Internet connection.

Figure 1.3

Adding a customer

If you are new to QuickBooks

You can add new customers to the list at any time. QuickBooks uses the list to hold information about the people and companies to whom you sell your products and services.

> You can quickly add a list of customers by entering only the customer's name, and, if they currently owe you money, their opening balance information. Then click Next and enter the next customer's name.

To add a customer

1. From the Lists menu, choose Customer:Job List.
2. From the Customer:Job menu button, choose New.
3. In the Customer field, enter the name of the customer as you'd like it to appear on your Customer:Job list. For example, if the customer is Joan Green and you want the list to show last names first, enter Green, Joan.
4. If you have an outstanding balance for this customer, enter the Opening balance and "as of" information.

   Are you entering the correct opening balance?

   > You can quickly add a list of customers by entering only the customer's name, and, if they currently owe you money, their opening balance information. Then click Next and enter the next customer's name.

   > If you are going to set up jobs for this customer, do not enter an opening balance. QuickBooks
   will calculate and track the overall balance for this customer from the balances you enter for the individual jobs.
5. Complete the Address Info, Additional Info, and Payment Info tabs.
6. Click Next to save the customer information and close the window.

   Or

   Click OK to save the customer information and close the window.

Related topics

- You make a lot of sales and you want to keep your Costomer:Job list short?
- What if a customer is also a vendor?
- Adding a vendor
- Printing a list
- Merging similar list entries
- Keeping notes about a customer or job
- Using names and addresses in a form letter

> Do you need more information? Try the Support Center.

Did this Help topic provide you with the information you needed?

Requires an Internet connection.

Figure 1.3a

Calculating payroll taxes without a subscription to one of the Intuit Payroll Services

What we recommend

Intuit strongly recommends that you sign up for one of the Intuit Payroll Services to make sure that you have the most current tax tables available. In addition to providing current tax tables, the payroll services provide additional features that take the worry out of doing your payroll.

If you prefer to calculate your payroll taxes manually

If you don't sign up for one of the Intuit Payroll Services, QuickBooks won't calculate your payroll taxes or provide payroll tax forms. You will have to calculate your payroll taxes manually and enter them for each paycheck.

Before you start

Set your company file to manual payroll setting. (This is a one-time task.)

1. From the Employees menu, choose Payroll Services and then choose Set Up Payroll.
2. Click Choose a payroll option.
3. Scroll to the bottom of the page, and in the paragraph that begins, "If you don't want to use an Intuit Payroll Service…," click Learn more.
4. Click "I choose to manually calculate payroll taxes."

Payroll tax information for the federal, state, and local agencies can change at various times throughout the tax year. To avoid penalties, be sure to consult your tax agencies often for any changes.

Prepare your payroll

Follow these steps to prepare your payroll in QuickBooks:

1. Contact the IRS, your state tax agency, and your professional tax advisor to get the most recent payroll tax information:
    *   Tax tables, including mid-year tax changes that can affect your payroll
    *   Wage base limits on taxes such as FUTA
    *   The frequency with which you pay your payroll taxes. (The frequency can change from year to year, depending on certain conditions in your company.)
2. For each pay period, use the information you gather in Step 1 to calculate the current and year-to-date federal and state tax information for each employee.
    Without a subscription to one of the Intuit Payroll Services, QuickBooks inserts a zero-tax amount for each payroll item associated with a tax. You must replace the zero-tax amounts with the appropriate tax for each paycheck.
3. Pay your payroll taxes using the tax schedules provided by the IRS and your state or local tax agency.

Do you need more information? Try the Support Center.

Did this Help topic provide you with the information you needed?

Requires an Internet connection.

Figure 1.3b

Using the chart of accounts

How do I display this list?

What you store in this list
The chart of accounts contains a complete list of your business's accounts and their balances. You use it to track how much money your company has, how much money it owes, how much money is coming in, and how much is going out. To open the register of any balance sheet account (except Retained Earnings), double-click it. To display a QuickReport of transactions for any income or expense account, double-click it.

Managing your accounts
Use the Account menu button at the bottom of the list to add, edit, or delete accounts. You can make an account inactive, sort the list in alphabetical order, print the list, and more.

◇Construction
　　◇Discounts given
　　◇Labor

| Account ▾ | Activities ▾ | Reports ▾ |

Other menu buttons allow you to choose Activities and Reports related to the list.

Columns and options in this list
Name/Type
Balance
Include inactive

Related topics

■ What is the chart of accounts?

■ Descriptions of account types

■ Exporting the chart of accounts

Do you need more information? Try the Support Center.

Did this Help topic provide you with the information you needed?

　Yes　　No

Requires an Internet connection.

Figure 1.4

Century Kitchens
Inventory Valuation Summary
As of January 28, 2007

Item Description	On Hand	Avg Cost	Asset Value	% of Tot As...	Sales Price	Retail Value	% of Tot Re...
Inventory							
1001 Base Double Door	2	440.00	880.00	4.6%	550.00	1,100.00	4.6%
1002 Base Single Door	3	400.00	1,200.00	6.2%	500.00	1,500.00	6.3%
1003 Base Double Door Double Drawer	6	480.00	2,880.00	14.9%	600.00	3,600.00	15%
1004 Base Double Door with Tray	4	440.00	1,760.00	9.1%	550.00	2,200.00	9.2%
1005 Base Oven Cabinet	2	240.00	480.00	2.5%	300.00	600.00	2.5%
1006 Base Lattice	4	320.00	1,280.00	6.6%	400.00	1,600.00	6.7%
1007 Pantry	6	520.00	3,120.00	16.1%	650.00	3,900.00	16.3%
1008 Chopping Block Table	1	360.00	360.00	1.9%	450.00	450.00	1.9%
1009 Easy Reach Corner	1	600.00	600.00	3.1%	750.00	750.00	3.1%
1010 Wall MV Cabinet	0	480.00	0.00	0%	600.00	0.00	0%
1011 Wall Refrigerator	2	240.00	480.000	2.5%	300.00	600.00	2.5%
1012 Sink/Range Base	3	320.00	960.00	5%	400.00	1,200.00	5%
1013 Wall Double Door	2	360.00	720.00	3.7%	450.00	900.00	3.8%
1014 Wall Angle	5	540.00	2,700.00	14%	625.00	3,125.00	13.1%
1015 Wall Blind Corner	3	640.00	1,920.00	9.9%	800.00	2,400.00	10%
1016 High Wall End Angle	0	200.00	0.00	0%	250.00	0.00	0%
1017 Peninsula Base	0	500.00	0.00	0%	625.00	0.00	0%
2001 Granite Counter	0	50.00	0.00	0%	70.00	0.00	0%
2002 Silestone	0	45.00	0.00	0%	65.00	0.00	0%
2003 Corian	0	40.00	0.00	0%	60.00	0.00	0%
Total Inventory	44		19,340.00	100.00%		23,925.00	100.00%
TOTAL	**44**		**19,340.00**	**100.00%**		**23,925.00**	**100.00%**

Figure 1.5

Century Kitchens
Sales by Customer Detail
January 2007

Type	Date	Num	Memo	Name	Item	Qty	Sales Price	Amount	Balance
A Monroe									
Invoice	1/9/2007	1003	Kitchen remo...	A Monroe	Planning ...	8	75.00	600.00	600.00
Invoice	1/9/2007	1003	Meet with client	A Monroe	Planning ...	2	75.00	150.00	750.00
Total A Monroe								750.00	750.00
I Bowen									
Invoice	1/31/2007	1006	Planning and ...	I Bowen	Planning ...	66	75.00	4,950.00	4,950.00
Total I Bowen								4,950.00	4,950.00
J Wilson									
Invoice	1/2/2007	1001	Plan and desi...	J Wilson	Planning ...	6	75.00	450.00	450.00
Invoice	1/30/2007	1004		J Wilson	Install ca...	8	80.00	640.00	1,090.00
Invoice	1/30/2007	1004		J Wilson	Install ca...	8	80.00	640.00	1,730.00
Invoice	1/30/2007	1004		J Wilson	Install ca...	8	80.00	640.00	2,370.00
Invoice	1/30/2007	1004		J Wilson	Install ca...	8	80.00	640.00	3,010.00
Invoice	1/30/2007	1004		J Wilson	Install ca...	2	80.00	160.00	3,170.00
Invoice	1/30/2007	1004		J Wilson	Install ca...	8	80.00	640.00	3,810.00
Invoice	1/30/2007	1004		J Wilson	Install ca...	8	80.00	640.00	4,450.00
Invoice	1/30/2007	1004		J Wilson	Install ca...	4	80.00	320.00	4,770.00
Invoice	1/30/2007	1004		J Wilson	Install ca...	8	80.00	640.00	5,410.00
Invoice	1/30/2007	1004		J Wilson	Install ca...	4	80.00	320.00	5,730.00
Invoice	1/30/2007	1004		J Wilson	Install ca...	5	80.00	400.00	6,130.00
Invoice	1/30/2007	1004		J Wilson	Install ca...	5	80.00	400.00	6,530.00
Invoice	1/30/2007	1004		J Wilson	Install ca...	5	80.00	400.00	6,930.00
Invoice	1/30/2007	1004	Base Double ...	J Wilson	1003	3	600.00	1,800.00	8,730.00
Invoice	1/30/2007	1004	Base Oven C....	J Wilson	1005	1	300.00	300.00	9,030.00
Invoice	1/30/2007	1004	Wall Refriger...	J Wilson	1011	1	300.00	300.00	9,330.00
Invoice	1/30/2007	1004	Wall Blind Co...	J Wilson	1015	1	800.00	800.00	10,130.00
Invoice	1/30/2007	1004	Base Lattice	J Wilson	1006	1	400.00	400.00	10,530.00
Invoice	1/30/2007	1004	Wall Double ...	J Wilson	1012	3	400.00	1,200.00	11,730.00
Invoice	1/30/2007	1004	Easy Reach ...	J Wilson	1009	1	750.00	750.00	12,480.00
Total J Wilson								12,480.00	12,480.00
R Coe									
Invoice	1/4/2007	1002	Kitchen Upgr...	R Coe	Planning ...	7	75.00	525.00	525.00
Invoice	1/31/2007	1005	Wall Blind Co...	R Coe	1015	2	800.00	1,600.00	2,125.00
Invoice	1/31/2007	1005	Wall Refriger...	R Coe	1011	1	300.00	300.00	2,425.00
Invoice	1/31/2007	1005	Base Double ...	R Coe	1001	2	550.00	1,100.00	3,525.00
Invoice	1/31/2007	1005	Base Single ...	R Coe	1002	3	500.00	1,500.00	5,025.00
Invoice	1/31/2007	1005	Base Double ...	R Coe	1004	1	550.00	550.00	5,575.00
Invoice	1/31/2007	1005	Wall Angle	R Coe	1014	2	625.00	1,250.00	6,825.00
Invoice	1/31/2007	1005	Wall Double ...	R Coe	1013	2	450.00	900.00	7,725.00
Invoice	1/31/2007	1005	Pantry	R Coe	1007	4	650.00	2,600.00	10,325.00
Invoice	1/31/2007	1005		R Coe	Install ca...	8	80.00	640.00	10,965.00
Invoice	1/31/2007	1005		R Coe	Install ca...	4	80.00	320.00	11,285.00
Invoice	1/31/2007	1005		R Coe	Install ca...	3	80.00	240.00	11,525.00
Invoice	1/31/2007	1005		R Coe	Install ca...	8	80.00	640.00	12,165.00

Figure 1.5 (continued)

Century Kitchens
Sales by Customer Detail
January 2007

Type	Date	Num	Memo	Name	Item	Qty	Sales Price	Amount	Balance
Invoice	1/31/2007	1005		R Coe	Install ca...	3	80.00	240.00	12,405.00
Invoice	1/31/2007	1005		R Coe	Install ca...	8	80.00	640.00	13,045.00
Invoice	1/31/2007	1005		R Coe	Install ca...	2	80.00	160.00	13,205.00
Invoice	1/31/2007	1005		R Coe	Install ca...	8	80.00	640.00	13,845.00
Invoice	1/31/2007	1005		R Coe	Install ca...	8	80.00	640.00	14,485.00
Invoice	1/31/2007	1005		R Coe	Install ca...	8	80.00	640.00	15,125.00
Invoice	1/31/2007	1005		R Coe	Install ca...	8	80.00	640.00	15,765.00
Total R Coe								15,765.00	15,765.00
S Gomez									
Invoice	1/31/2007	1007	Planning and ...	S Gomez	Planning ...	54	75.00	4,050.00	4,050.00
Total S Gomez								4,050.00	4,050.00
TOTAL								**37,995.00**	**37,995.00**

Figure 1.6

($ in 1,000's)

Century Kitchens
Summary Balance Sheet
As of January 31, 2007

	Jan 31, 07
ASSETS	
Current Assets	
Checking/Savings	48
Accounts Receivable	37
Other Current Assets	7
Total Current Assets	92
Fixed Assets	49
TOTAL ASSETS	**141**
LIABILITIES & EQUITY	
Liabilities	
Current Liabilities	
Accounts Payable	7
Other Current Liabilities	5
Total Current Liabilities	12
Total Liabilities	12
Equity	129
TOTAL LIABILITIES & EQUITY	**141**

Figure 1.7

Century Kitchens
Balance Sheet
As of January 31, 2007

	Jan. 31, '07
ASSETS	
Current Assets	
Checking/Savings	
Checking	48
Total Checking/Savings	48
Accounts Receivable	
Accounts Receivable	37
Total Accounts Receivable	37
Other Current Assets	
Inventory Assets	7
Total Other Current Assets	7
Total Current Assets	92
Fixed Assets	
Equipment	
Original Cost	50
Depreciation	−1
Total Equipment	49
Total Fixed Assets	49
TOTAL ASSETS	**141**
LIABILITIES & EQUITY	
Liabilities	
Current Liabilities	
Accounts Payable	
Accounts Payable	7
Total Accounts Payable	7
Other Current Liabilities	
Payroll Liabilities	5
Total Other Current Liabilities	5
Total Current Liabilities	12
Total Liabilities	12
Equity	
Capital Stock	125
Net Income	4
Total Equity	129
TOTAL LIABILITIES & EQUITY	**141**

Figure 1.8

Century Kitchens
Transactions by Account
As of January 31, 2007

Type	Date	Num	Name	Memo	Clr	Split	Amount	Balance
Accounts Receivable								12,555.00
Invoice	1/31/2007	1005	R Coe			–SPLIT–	15,240.00	27,795.00
Invoice	1/31/2007	1006	I Bowen			Design and Pl...	4,950.00	32,745.00
Invoice	1/31/2007	1007	S Gomez			Design and Pl...	4,050.00	36,795.00
Total Accounts Receivable							24,240.00	36,795.00
TOTAL							**24,240.00**	**36,795.00**

Figure 1.8a

Century Kitchens

1836 55th Street Southwest
Naples, FL 34116

Invoice

Date	Invoice #
1/31/2007	1005

Bill To
R Coe 1223 Forest Ave Naples, FL 34102-5442

P.O. No.	Terms	Project
	Net 15	

Quantity	Description	Rate	Amount
2	Wall Blind Corner	800.00	1,600.00
1	Wall Refrigerator	300.00	300.00
2	Base Double Door	550.00	1,100.00
3	Base Single Door	500.00	1,500.00
1	Base Double Door with Tray	550.00	550.00
2	Wall Angle	625.00	1,250.00
2	Wall Double Door	450.00	900.00
4	Pantry	650.00	2,600.00
	Total Reimbursable Expenses		5,440.00

| | | **Total** | $15,240.00 |

Figure 1.8b

Century Kitchens
Comparative Balance Sheet
As of February 28, 2007

	Jan 31, 07	% of Column	Feb 28, 07	% of Column
ASSETS				
Current Assets				
Checking/Savings	48	34%	22	14%
Accounts Receivable	37	26%	66	41%
Other Current Assets	7	5%	25	16%
Total Current Assets	92	65%	113	70%
Fixed Assets	49	35%	48	30%
TOTAL ASSETS	141	100%	161	100%
LIABILITIES & EQUITY				
Liabilities				
Current Liabilities				
Accounts Payable	7	5%	14	9%
Other Current Liabilities	5	3%	9	6%
Total Current Liabilities	12	8%	23	14%
Total Liabilities	12	8%	23	14%
Equity	129	92%	138	86%
TOTAL LIABILITIES & EQUITY	141	100%	161	100%

Figure 1.9

Jennings & Associates (KJ01cp)
Balance Sheet
As of December 31, 2003

	Dec 31, '03
ASSETS	
Current Assets	
Checking/Savings	
First Valley Savings & Loan	1,000.00
Union Bank Checking	2,590.00
Total Checking/Savings	3,590.00
Accounts Receivable	
Accounts Receivable	3,250.00
Total Accounts Receivable	3,250.00
Total Current Assets	6,840.00
Fixed Assets	
Computer Equipment	
Depreciation	-1,000.00
Original Cost	4,000.00
Total Computer Equipment	3,000.00
Furniture	
Depreciation	-500.00
Original Cost	2,500.00
Total Furniture	2,000.00
Total Fixed Assets	5,000.00
TOTAL ASSETS	**11,840.00**
LIABILITIES & EQUITY	
Liabilities	
Current Liabilities	
Accounts Payable	
Accounts Payable	1,000.00
Total Accounts Payable	1,000.00
Total Current Liabilities	1,000.00
Long Term Liabilities	
Bank of San Martin	5,000.00
Total Long Term Liabilities	5,000.00
Total Liabilities	6,000.00
Equity	
Opening Bal Equity	3,590.00
Net Income	2,250.00
Total Equity	5,840.00
TOTAL LIABILITIES & EQUITY	**11,840.00**

Figure 1.10

Jennings & Associates (KJ01cp)
Balance Sheet
As of January 31, 2004

	Jan 31, '04
ASSETS	
Current Assets	
Checking/Savings	
First Valley Savings & Loan	1,500.00
Union Bank Checking	158.94
Total Checking/Savings	1,658.94
Accounts Receivable	
Accounts Receivable	11,902.50
Total Accounts Receivable	11,902.50
Other Current Assets	
Interest Receivable	41.17
Inventory Asset	972.84
Prepaid Insurance	2,200.00
Total Other Current Assets	3,214.01
Total Current Assets	16,775.45
Fixed Assets	
Computer Equipment	
Depreciation	-1,083.33
Original Cost	4,000.00
Total Computer Equipment	2,916.67
Furniture	
Depreciation	-541.67
Original Cost	2,500.00
Total Furniture	1,958.33
Total Fixed Assets	4,875.00
TOTAL ASSETS	**21,650.45**
LIABILITIES & EQUITY	
Liabilities	
Current Liabilities	
Accounts Payable	
Accounts Payable	6,184.00
Total Accounts Payable	6,184.00
Other Current Liabilities	
Payroll Liabilities	3,712.38
Total Other Current Liabilities	3,712.38
Total Current Liabilities	9,896.38
Long Term Liabilities	
Bank of San Martin	5,000.00
Total Long Term Liabilities	5,000.00
Total Liabilities	14,896.38
Equity	
Opening Bal Equity	3,590.00
Retained Earnings	2,250.00
Net Income	914.07
Total Equity	6,754.07
TOTAL LIABILITIES & EQUITY	**21,650.45**

Figure 1.11

Jennings & Associates (KJ01cp)
Transaction Detail by Account
January 2004

Type	Date	Num	Name	Memo	Clr	Split	Amount	Balance
First Valley Savings & Loan								
Check	1/31/04	1265	First Valley Savings...			Union Bank C...	500.00	500.00
Total First Valley Savings & Loan							500.00	500.00
Union Bank Checking								
Payment	1/3/04	337	AAA Appliance			Accounts Rec...	100.00	100.00
Payment	1/6/04	1002	Fancy Yogurt Co.			Accounts Rec...	500.00	600.00
Bill Pmt -Check	1/6/04	1251	Frank Mendez Prop...	Opening bala...		Accounts Pay...	-700.00	-100.00
Bill Pmt -Check	1/6/04	1252	General Telephone	Opening bala...		Accounts Pay...	-75.00	-175.00
Bill Pmt -Check	1/6/04	1253	On-Time Copy Shop	Opening bala...		Accounts Pay...	-125.00	-300.00
Payment	1/15/04	150	Sally's Fabrics			Accounts Rec...	200.00	-100.00
Paycheck	1/15/04	1258	Cheryl P Boudreau			-SPLIT-	-876.40	-976.40
Paycheck	1/15/04	1259	Diane A Murphy			-SPLIT-	-918.40	-1,894.80
Paycheck	1/15/04	1260	Kelly A Jennings			-SPLIT-	-1,359.73	-3,254.53
Payment	1/15/04	215	Bob and Mary Schultz			Accounts Rec...	800.00	-2,454.53
Check	1/18/04	1256	US Post Office			Postage and...	-62.00	-2,516.53
Check	1/18/04	1257	Chef Ricks	Opening bala...		Practice Devel...	-35.00	-2,551.53
Bill Pmt -Check	1/20/04	1254	Pacific Electric Co.	Opening bala...		Accounts Pay...	-35.00	-2,586.53
Bill Pmt -Check	1/20/04	1255	So. Cal Gas			Accounts Pay...	-65.00	-2,651.53
Payment	1/20/04	659	AAA Appliance			Accounts Rec...	275.00	-2,376.53
Payment	1/21/04	2251	Ray's Chevron			Accounts Rec...	75.00	-2,301.53
Payment	1/21/04	850	Evelyn Walker Real...			Accounts Rec...	700.00	-1,601.53
Payment	1/28/04	852	Sally's Fabrics			Accounts Rec...	4,375.00	2,773.47
Payment	1/29/04		Paulson			Accounts Rec...	600.00	3,373.47
Payment	1/31/04	455	Big 10			Accounts Rec...	250.00	3,623.47
Paycheck	1/31/04	1261	Cheryl P Boudreau			-SPLIT-	-876.40	2,747.07
Paycheck	1/31/04	1262	Diane A Murphy			-SPLIT-	-918.40	1,828.67
Paycheck	1/31/04	1263	Kelly A Jennings			-SPLIT-	-1,359.73	468.94
Check	1/31/04	1264	Walker Insurance Co.			Prepaid Insura...	-2,400.00	-1,931.06
Check	1/31/04	1265	First Valley Savings...			First Valley Sa...	-500.00	-2,431.06
Total Union Bank Checking							-2,431.06	-2,431.06
Accounts Receivable								
Payment	1/3/04	337	AAA Appliance			Union Bank C...	-100.00	-100.00
Payment	1/6/04	1002	Fancy Yogurt Co.			Union Bank C...	-500.00	-600.00
Invoice	1/10/04	1	Bob and Mary Schultz			-SPLIT-	300.00	-300.00
Invoice	1/12/04	2	Evelyn Walker Real...			-SPLIT-	390.00	90.00
Payment	1/15/04	150	Sally's Fabrics			Union Bank C...	-200.00	-110.00
Payment	1/15/04	215	Bob and Mary Schultz			Union Bank C...	-800.00	-910.00
Invoice	1/18/04	3	Yaskar Farms			-SPLIT-	1,612.50	702.50
Payment	1/20/04	659	AAA Appliance			Union Bank C...	-275.00	427.50
Payment	1/21/04	2251	Ray's Chevron			Union Bank C...	-75.00	352.50
Payment	1/21/04	850	Evelyn Walker Real...			Union Bank C...	-700.00	-347.50
Invoice	1/22/04	4	Evelyn Walker Real...			-SPLIT-	200.00	-147.50
Invoice	1/23/04	5	Big 10			-SPLIT-	325.00	177.50
Invoice	1/25/04	6	AAA Appliance			-SPLIT-	25.00	202.50
Invoice	1/28/04	7	Sally's Fabrics			-SPLIT-	4,375.00	4,577.50
Payment	1/28/04	852	Sally's Fabrics			Union Bank C...	-4,375.00	202.50
Payment	1/29/2004		Paulson			Union Bank C...	-600.00	-397.50
Invoice	1/31/2004	8	Ray's Chevron			-SPLIT-	650.00	252.50
Invoice	1/31/2004	9	Fancy Yogurt Co.			-SPLIT-	1,562.50	1,815.00
Invoive	1/31/2004	10	Paulson			-SPLIT-	1,950.00	3,765.00

Figure 1.12

Jennings & Associates (KJ01cp)
Summary Balance Sheet

($ in 1,000's)   As of January 31, 2004

	Jan 31, '04
ASSETS	
Current Assets	
Checking/Savings	2
Accounts Receivable	12
Other Current Assets	3
Total Current Assets	17
Fixed Assets	5
TOTAL ASSETS	**22**
LIABILITIES & EQUITY	
Liabilities	
Current Liabilities	
Accounts Payable	6
Other Current Liabilities	4
Total Current Liabilities	10
Long Term Liabilities	5
Total Liabilities	15
Equity	7
TOTAL LIABILITIES & EQUITY	**22**

Figure 1.13

Jennings & Associates (KJ01cp)
Transactions by Account
As of January 31, 2004

Type	Date	Num	Name	Memo	Clr	Split	Amount	Balance
Accounts Payable								1,000.00
Bill Pmt -Check	1/6/2004	1251	Frank Mendez Properties	Opening balance		Union Bank Checking	-700.00	300.00
Bill Pmt -Check	1/6/2004	1252	General Telephone	Opening balance		Union Bank Checking	-75.00	225.00
Bill Pmt -Check	1/6/2004	1253	On-Time Copy Shop	Opening balance		Union Bank Checking	-125.00	100.00
Bill	1/8/2004		Frank Mendez Properties			Rent	700.00	800.00
Bill	1/8/2004		KCRQ Radio			Radio Spots	750.00	1,550.00
Bill	1/9/2004		San Martin Water District			Water	57.00	1,607.00
Bill	1/9/2004		Walker Insurance Co.			Liability Insurance	175.00	1,782.00
Bill	1/10/2004		KCOY TV			TV Commercial Spots	2,500.00	4,282.00
Bill	1/11/2004		Pacific Electric Co.			Gas and Electric	45.00	4,327.00
Bill	1/12/2004		Rex's Film Supply			Inventory Asset	445.00	4,772.00
Bill	1/13/2004		General Telephone			Telephone	89.00	4,861.00
Bill	1/13/2004		On-Time Copy Shop			-SPLIT-	100.00	4,961.00
Bill	1/18/2004		Phoenix Computers			Computer Repairs	95.00	5,056.00
Bill	1/18/2004		Federal Express			Postage and Delivery	47.00	5,103.00
Bill Pmt -Check	1/20/2004	1254	Pacific Electric Co.	Opening balance		Union Bank Checking	-35.00	5,068.00
Bill Pmt -Check	1/20/2004	1255	So. Cal Gas	Opening balance		Union Bank Checking	-65.00	5,003.00
Bill	1/22/2004		So. Cal Gas			Gas and Electric	55.00	5,058.00
Bill	1/27/2004		Banks Office Supply			Office Supplies	26.00	5,084.00
Bill	1/29/2004		Rex's Film Supply			Inventory Asset	825.00	5,909.00
Bill	1/30/2004		Owen & Owen			Legal Fees	275.00	6,184.00
Total Accounts Payable							5,184.00	6,184.00
TOTAL							**5,184.00**	**6,184.00**

Figure 1.14

Century Kitchens
Comparative Income Statements
February 2007

	Feb 07	Jan 07	$ Change	% Change
Ordinary Income/Expense				
Income				
Cabinets	26,300	15,350	10,950	71%
Installation	15,360	11,920	3,440	29%
Design and Planning	8,175	10,725	−2,550	−24%
Total Income	**49,835**	**37,995**	**11,840**	**31%**
Cost of Goods Sold				
Cost of Goods Sold	21,200	12,360	8,840	72%
Total COGS	21,200	12,360	8,840	72%
Gross Profit	28,635	25,635	3,000	12%
Expense				
Building Supplies	675	165	510	309%
Depreciation Expense	833	833	0	0%
Insurance	800	0	800	100%
Payroll Expenses	14,216	16,591	−2,375	−14%
Rent	3,500	3,500	0	0%
Utilities	375	165	210	127%
Total Expense	20,399	21,255	−855	−4%
Net Ordinary Income	8,236	4,380	3,855	88%
Net Income	**8,236**	**4,380**	**3,855**	**88%**

Figure 1.15

Century Kitchens
Income Statement
January 2007

	Jan 07
Ordinary Income/Expense	
Income	
Cabinets	15,350.00
Installation	11,920.00
Design and Planning	10,725.00
Total Income	37,995.00
Cost of Goods Sold	
Cost of Goods Sold	12,360.00
Total COGS	12,360.00
Gross Profit	25,635.00
Expense	
Building Supplies	165.00
Depreciation Expense	833.33
Payroll Expenses	16,591.30
Rent	3,500.00
Utilities	165.00
Total Expense	21,254.63
Net Ordinary Income	4,380.37
Net Income	**4,380.37**

Figure 1.16

Century Kitchen
Comparative Income Statement
March, 2007

	Mar 07	Jan - Mar 07	% YTD
Ordinary Income/Expense			
Income			
Counter Top	4,160	4,160	100%
Cabinets	19,300	60,950	32%
Installation	11,240	38,520	29%
Design and Planning	825	19,725	4%
Total Income	35,525	123,355	29%
Cost of Goods Sold			
Cost of Goods Sold	18,400	51,960	35%
Total COGS	18,400	51,960	35%
Gross Profit	17,125	71,395	24%
Expense			
Building Supplies	690	1,530	45%
Depreciation Expense	833	2,500	33%
Insurance	400	1,200	33%
Payroll Expenses	13,598	44,405	31%
Rent	3,500	10,500	33%
Utilities	375	915	41%
Total Expense	19,396	61,050	32%
Net Ordinary Income	−2,271	10,345	−22%
Net Income	**−2,271**	**10,345**	**−22%**

Figure 1.17

Jennings & Associates (KJ01cp)
Profit and Loss
January 2004

	Jan 04
Ordinary Income/Expense	
Income	
Fee Income	
Film	450.00
Magazine	600.00
Press Release	225.00
Promotion	4,275.00
Radio	2,177.50
Television	8,050.00
Total Fee Income	15,777.50
Total Income	15,777.50
Gross Profit	15,777.50
Expense	
Depreciation Expense	125.00
Equipment Rental	75.00
Film expenses	297.16
Insurance	
Liability Insurance	375.00
Total Insurance	375.00
Office Supplies	26.00
Payroll Expenses	10,021.44
Postage and Delivery	109.00
Practice Development	35.00
Printing and Reproduction	25.00
Professional Fees	
Legal Fees	275.00
Total Professional Fees	275.00
Radio Spots	0.00
Rent	700.00
Repairs	
Computer Repairs	95.00
Total Repairs	95.00
Telephone	89.00
TV Commercial Spots	2,500.00
Utilities	
Gas and Electric	100.00
Water	57.00
Total Utilities	157.00
Total Expense	14,904.60
Net Ordinary Income	872.90
Other Income/Expense	
Other Income	
Interest Income	41.17
Total Other Income	41.17
Net Other Income	41.17
Net Income	**914.07**

Figure 1.18

Jennings & Associates (KJ01cp)
Income Statement
January 2004

	Jan 04
Ordinary Income/Expense	
Income	
Fee Income	
Film	450
Magazine	600
Press Release	225
Promotion	4,275
Radio	2,178
Television	8,050
Total Fee Income	15,778
Total Income	15,778
Gross Profit	15,778
Expense	
Depreciation Expense	125
Equipment Rental	75
Film expenses	297
Insurance	
Liability Insurance	375
Total Insurance	375
Office Supplies	26
Payroll Expenses	10,021
Postage and Delivery	109
Practice Development	35
Printing and Reproduction	25
Professional Fees	
Legal Fees	275
Total Professional Fees	275
Radio Spots	0
Rent	700
Repairs	
Computer Repairs	95
Total Repairs	95
Telephone	89
TV Commercial Spots	2,500
Utilities	
Gas and Electric	100
Water	57
Total Utilities	157
Total Expense	14,905
Net Ordinary Income	873
Other Income/Expense	
Other Income	
Interest Income	41
Total Other Income	41
Net Other Income	41
Net Income	**914**

Figure 1.19

Jennings & Associates (KJ01cp)
Income Statement
January 2004

	Jan 04	% of Income
Ordinary Income/Expense		
Income		
Fee Income		
Film	450	3%
Magazine	600	4%
Press Release	225	1%
Promotion	4,275	27%
Radio	2,178	14%
Television	8,050	51%
Total Fee Income	15,778	100%
Total Income	15,778	100%
Gross Profit	15,778	100%
Expense		
Depreciation Expense	125	1%
Equipment Rental	75	0%
Film expenses	297	2%
Insurance		
Liability Insurance	375	2%
Total Insurance	375	2%
Office Supplies	26	0%
Payroll Expenses	10,021	64%
Postage and Delivery	109	1%
Practice Development	35	0%
Printing and Reproduction	25	0%
Professional Fees		
Legal Fees	275	2%
Total Professional Fees	275	2%
Radio Spots	0	0%
Rent	700	4%
Repairs		
Computer Repairs	95	1%
Total Repairs	95	1%
Telephone	89	1%
TV Commercial Spots	2,500	16%
Utilities		
Gas and Electric	100	1%
Water	57	0%
Total Utilities	157	1%
Total Expense	14,905	94%
Net Ordinary Income	873	6%
Other Income/Expense		
Other Income		
Interest Income	41	0%
Total Other Income	41	0%
Net Other Income	41	0%
Net Income	914	6%

Figure 1.20

Century Kitchens
Statement of Cash Flows
January 2007

	Jan 07
OPERATING ACTIVITIES	
Net Income	4,380
Adjustments to reconcile Net Income to net cash provided by operations:	
Accounts Receivable	−36,795
Inventory Asset	−6,980
Equipment:Depreciation	833
Accounts Payable	6,980
Payroll Liabilities	4,771
Net cash provided by Operating Activities	−26,811
INVESTING ACTIVITIES	
Equipment:Original Cost	−50,000
Net cash provided by Investing Activities	−50,000
FINANCING ACTIVITIES	
Capital Stock	125,000
Net cash provided by Financing Activities	125,000
Net cash increase for period	48,189
Cash at end of period	**48,189**

Figure 1.21

Jennings & Associated (KJ01cp)
Statement of Cash Flows
January 2004

	Jan 04
OPERATING ACTIVITIES	
Net Income	914.07
Adjustments to reconcile Net Income to net cash provided by operations:	
Accounts Receivable	−8,652.50
Interest Receivable	−41.17
Inventory Asset	−972.84
Prepaid Insurance	−2,200.00
Computer Equipment:Depreciation	83.33
Furniture:Depreciation	41.67
Accounts Payable	5,184.00
Payroll Liabilities	3,712.38
Net cash provided by Operating Activities	−1,931.06
Net cash increase for period	−1,931.06
Cash at beginning of period	3,590.00
Cash at end of period	**1,658.94**

Figure 1.22

Jennings & Associated (KJ01cp)
Statement of Cash Flows
January 2004

	Jan 04
OPERATING ACTIVITIES	
Net Income	914
Adjustments to reconcile Net Income	
to net cash provided by operations:	
Accounts Receivable	−8,653
Interest Receivable	−41
Inventory Asset	−973
Prepaid Insurance	−2,200
Computer Equipment:Depreciation	83
Furniture:Depreciation	42
Accounts Payable	5,184
Payroll Liabilities	3,712
Net cash provided by Operating Activities	−1,931
Net cash increase for period	−1,931
Cash at beginning of period	3,590
Cash at end of period	**1,659**

Figure 1.23

Century Kitchens
Customer Balance Summary
As of January 31, 2007

	Jan 31, 07
I Bowen	4,950.00
J Wilson	12,030.00
R Coe	15,765.00
S Gomez	4,050.00
TOTAL	**36,795.00**

Figure 1.24

Century Kitchens
A/R Aging Summary
As of January 31, 2007

	Current	1 - 30	31 − 60	61 - 90	> 90	TOTAL
I Bowen	4,950.00	0.00	0.00	0.00	0.00	4,950.00
J Wilson	12,030.00	0.00	0.00	0.00	0.00	12,030.00
R Coe	15,240.00	525.00	0.00	0.00	0.00	15,765.00
S Gomez	4,050.00	0.00	0.00	0.00	0.00	4,050.00
TOTAL	**36,270.00**	**525.00**	**0.00**	**0.00**	**00.00**	**36,795.00**

Figure 1.25

Century Kitchens
A/P Aging Summary
As of February 28, 2007

	Current	1 – 30	31 - 60	61 - 90	> 90	TOTAL
Kraft Maid	6,600.00	0.00	0.00	0.00	0.00	6,600.00
Thomasville Cabinets	0.00	7,620.00	0.00	0.00	0.00	7,620.00
TOTAL	**6,600.00**	**7,620.00**	**0.00**	**0.00**	**0.00**	**14,220.00**

Figure 1.26

Century Kitchens
Inventory Valuation Summary
As of January 31, 2007

Item Description	On Hand	Avg Cost	Asset Value	% of Tot As...	Sales Price	Retail Value	% of Tot Re...
Inventory							
1001 Base Double Door	0	440.00	0.00	0%	550.00	0.00	0%
1002 Base Single Door	0	400.00	0.00	0%	500.00	0.00	0%
1003 Base Double Door ...	3	480.00	1,440.00	20.6%	600.00	1,800.00	21%
1004 Base Double Door ...	3	440.00	1,320.00	18.9%	550.00	1,650.00	19.2%
1005 Base Oven Cabinet	1	240.00	240.00	3.4%	300.00	300.00	3.5%
1006 Base Lattice	3	320.00	960.00	13.8%	400.00	1,200.00	14%
1007 Pantry	2	520.00	1,040.00	14.9%	650.00	1,300.00	15.2%
1008 Chopping Block Ta...	1	360.00	360.00	5.2%	450.00	450.00	5.2%
1009 Easy Reach Corner	0	600.00	0.00	0%	750.00	0.00	0%
1010 Wall MV Cabinet	0	480.00	0.00	0%	600.00	0.00	0%
1011 Wall Refrigerator	0	240.00	0.00	0%	300.00	0.00	0%
1012 Sink/Range Base	0	320.00	0.00	0%	400.00	0.00	0%
1013 Wall Double Door	0	360.00	0.00	0%	450.00	0.00	0%
1014 Wall Angle	3	540.00	1,620.00	23.2%	625.00	1,875.00	21.9%
1015 Wall Blind Corner	0	640.00	0.00	0%	800.00	0.00	0%
1016 High Wall End Angle	0	200.00	0.00	0%	250.00	0.00	0%
1017 Peninsula Base	0	500.00	0.00	0%	625.00	0.00	0%
2001 Granite Counter	0	50.00	0.00	0%	70.00	0.00	0%
2002 Silestone	0	45.00	0.00	0%	65.00	0.00	0%
2003 Corian	0	40.00	0.00	0%	60.00	0.00	0%
Total Inventory	16		6,980.00	100.00%		8,575.00	100.00%
TOTAL	**16**		**6,980.00**	**100.00%**		**8,575.00**	**100.00%**

Figure 1.27

Century Kitchens
Customer Balance Summary
As of February 28, 2007

	Feb 28, 07
A Monroe	13,535.00
B Scaggs	1,425.00
I Bowen	13,705.00
J Summer	2,250.00
J Wilson	7,030.00
R Coe	15,765.00
R Rose	4,500.00
S Gomez	7,420.00
TOTAL	**65,630.00**

Figure 1.28

Century Kitchens
A/R Aging Summary
As of February 28, 2007

	Current	1 - 30	31 - 60	61 - 90	> 90	TOTAL
A Monroe	13,535.00	0.00	0.00	0.00	0.00	13,535.00
B Scaggs	1,425.00	0.00	0.00	0.00	0.00	1,425.00
I Bowen	13,705.00	0.00	0.00	0.00	0.00	13,705.00
J Summer	2,250.00	0.00	0.00	0.00	0.00	2,250.00
J Wilson	0.00	7,030.00	0.00	0.00	0.00	7,030.00
R Coe	0.00	15,240.00	525.00	0.00	0.00	15,765.00
R Rose	4,500.00	0.00	0.00	0.00	0.00	4,500.00
S Gomez	7,420.00	0.00	0.00	0.00	0.00	7,420.00
TOTAL	**42,835.00**	**22,270.00**	**525.00**	**0.00**	**0.00**	**65,630.00**

Figure 1.29

Century Kitchens
A/P Aging Summary
As of January 31, 2007

	Current	1 - 30	31 - 60	61 - 90	> 90	TOTAL
Kraft Maid	6,980.00	0.00	0.00	0.00	0.00	6,980.00
TOTAL	6,980.00	0.00	0.00	0.00	0.00	6,980.00

Figure 1.30

Century Kitchens
Inventory Valuation Summary
As of February 28, 2007

Item Description	On Hand	Avg Cost	Asset Value	% of Tot Asset	Sales Price	Retail Value	% of Tot Re....
Inventory							
1001 Base Double Door	0	440.00	0.00	0%	550.00	0.00	0%
1002 Base Single Door	3	400.00	1,200.00	10.2%	500.00	1,500.00	9.5%
1003 Base Double Door...	2	480.00	960.00	8.1%	600.00	1,200.00	7.6%
1004 Base Double Door...	0	440.00	0.00	0%	550.00	0.00	0%
1005 Base Oven Cabinet	0	240.00	0.00	0%	300.00	0.00	0%
1006 Base Lattice	3	320.00	960.00	8.1%	400.00	1,200.00	7.6%
1007 Pantry	0	520.00	0.00	0%	650.00	0.00	0%
1008 Chopping Block Ta...	1	360.00	360.00	3.1%	450.00	450.00	2.8%
1009 Easy Reach Corner	0	600.00	0.00	0%	750.00	0.00	0%
1010 Wall MV Cabinet	0	480.00	0.00	0%	600.00	0.00	0%
1011 Wall Refrigerator	0	240.00	0.00	0%	300.00	0.00	0%
1012 Sink/Range Base	5	320.00	1,600.00	13.6%	400.00	2,000.00	12.6%
1013 Wall Double Door	0	360.00	0.00	0%	450.00	0.00	0%
1014 Wall Angle	1	540.00	540.00	4.6%	625.00	625.00	3.9%
1015 Wall Blind Corner	0	640.00	0.00	0%	800.00	0.00	0%
1016 High Wall End Angle	0	200.00	0.00	0%	250.00	0.00	0%
1017 Peninsula Base	0	500.00	0.00	0%	625.00	0.00	0%
2001 Granite Counter	45	50.00	2,250.00	19.1%	70.00	3,150.00	19.9%
2002 Silestone	65	45.00	2,925.00	24.8%	65.00	4,225.00	26.7%
2003 Corian	25	40.00	1,000.00	8.5%	60.00	1,500.00	9.5%
Total Inventory	150		11,795.00	100.00%		15,850.00	100.00%
TOTAL	**150**		**11,795.00**	**100.00%**		**15,850.00**	**100.00%**

Figure 1.31

Jennings & Associates (KJ01cp)
A/R Aging Summary
As of January 31, 2004

	Current	1 - 30	31 - 60	61 - 90	> 90	TOTAL
Big 10	325.00	0.00	0.00	0.00	0.00	325.00
Evelyn Walker Real Estate	4,865.00	0.00	0.00	0.00	0.00	4,865.00
Fancy Yogurt Co.	1,562.50	0.00	0.00	0.00	0.00	1,562.50
Paulson	1,950.00	0.00	0.00	0.00	0.00	1,950.00
Ray's Chevron	650.00	0.00	75.00	0.00	0.00	725.00
Sally's Fabrics	862.50	0.00	0.00	0.00	0.00	862.50
Yaskar Farms	1,612.50	0.00	0.00	0.00	0.00	1,612.50
TOTAL	11,827.50	0.00	75.00	0.00	0.00	11,902.50

Figure 1.32

Jennings & Associates (KJ01cp)
A/P Aging Summary
As of January 31, 2004

	Current	1 - 30	31 - 60	61 - 90	> 90	TOTAL
Banks Office Supply	26.00	0.00	0.00	0.00	0.00	26.00
Federal Express	47.00	0.00	0.00	0.00	0.00	47.00
Frank Mendez Properties	700.00	0.00	0.00	0.00	0.00	700.00
General Telephone	89.00	0.00	0.00	0.00	0.00	89.00
KCOY TV	2,500.00	0.00	0.00	0.00	0.00	2,500.00
KCRQ Radio	750.00	0.00	0.00	0.00	0.00	750.00
On-Time Copy Shop	100.00	0.00	0.00	0.00	0.00	100.00
Owen & Owen	275.00	0.00	0.00	0.00	0.00	275.00
Pacific Electric Co.	0.00	45.00	0.00	0.00	0.00	45.00
Phoenix Computers	95.00	0.00	0.00	0.00	0.00	95.00
Rex's Film Supply	1,270.00	0.00	0.00	0.00	0.00	1,270.00
San Martin Water District	0.00	57.00	0.00	0.00	0.00	57.00
So. Cal Gas	55.00	0.00	0.00	0.00	0.00	55.00
Walker Insurance Co.	0.00	175.00	0.00	0.00	0.00	175.00
TOTAL	5,907.00	277.00	0.00	0.00	0.00	6,184.00

Figure 1.33

Jennings & Associates (KJ01cp)
Inventory Valuation Summary
As of January 31, 2004

Item Description	On Hand	Avg Cost	Asset Value	% of Tot Asset	Sales Price	Retail Value	% of Tot Retail
Inventory							
Film Film	190	5.12	972.84	100%	7.50	1,425.00	100%
Film HQ High Quality Film	0	15.00	0.00	0%	25.00	0.00	0%
Total Inventory	190		972.84	100.00%		1,425.00	100.00%
TOTAL	**190**		**972.84**	**100.00%**		**1,425.00**	**100.00%**

2

Setting Up Your Business's
Accounting System

In Chapter 2 students learn how to create a new company file and add new customers, vendors, employees, accounts, and items to lists. This effort should reinforce the systems nature of accounting and, in doing so, help students grasp the various steps involved in setting up a business.

Chapter 2   Questions

1. To create a new QuickBooks company file you may use the EasyStep Interview process or skip the EasyStep Interview and answer a few questions instead. The EasyStep Interview process provides a step-by-step guided series of questions that you can answer to help you choose various QuickBooks features. The alternative process requires you to enter basic company information, establish a set of accounts, provide sales tax information, and determine a file name.

2. The EasyStep Interview requires more time than the alternative method. If you wish to start quickly and add a minimal amount of information, the alternative method is your best choice. If you have some time and appropriate information the EasyStep Interview method is preferable.

3. Explanation of terms:

    Customer—anyone to whom you sell a product or provide a service.

    Vendor—anyone you purchase a product from or receive service from other than an employee.

    Employee—anyone you employ and who is subject to employment taxes.

Chart of accounts—a list of accounts where accounting information is maintained.

Item—a service or product.

4. Payment terms available in the Additional Information tab of the New Customer window include 1% 10 net 30,

    2% 10 net 30, due upon receipt, net 15, net 30, and net 60. (Note: These terms are not always available. In the

    consulting company established in Chapter 2 the terms listed above were available. If you selected [No type]

    when asked about a standard chart of accounts, no term choices are provided.)

5. A service item in QuickBooks represents a service provided, usually at an hourly rate. An inventory part item is

    usually a product which has been purchased from another manufacturer for resale, or a product manufactured

    and sold. The New Item window for service items requires a rate (usually hourly) while an inventory part item

    requires information about the product's cost, cost of goods sold account, preferred vendor, sales price,

    inventory asset account, and occasionally information on the quantity on hand and total value.

6. The Chart of Accounts list identifies 15 different types of accounts: cash, accounts receivable, other current

    asset, fixed asset, other asset, accounts payable, credit cards, other current liability, long term liability, equity,

    income, cost of goods sold, expense, other income, and other expense.

7. An employee might be subject to the following federal taxes: Federal Income Tax, FUTA, Social Security, and

    Medicare.

8. Filing status options available in the Payroll Set-up window include: Single, Married, Head of Household, and

    Don't Withhold for federal. State options include Single, Head of Household, Don't Withhold, and two options

    for Married: one income and two income.

9. Pay period options available in the Payroll Set-up window include daily, weekly, biweekly, semimonthly,

    monthly, quarterly, and yearly.

10. Entering a new item in the Item List requires you to specify an account where income will be recorded. If the

    account you want to specify doesn't currently exist, QuickBooks allows you to set up the account "on the fly."

    A message appears, indicating that the account specified doesn't exist and then asks if you would like to set up a

    new account or cancel. If you choose to set up a new account a New Account window appears. Once you

    provide the data for the new account, QuickBooks returns you to the New Item window.

Chapter 2   Assignments

1. Adding More Information to Phoenix Systems Consulting, Inc.

    a. See the updated Customer List in Figure 2.1. *[Note: Solution figures for Chapter 2 begin on page 55.]*

    b. See the updated Vendor List in Figure 2.2.

    c. See the updated Employee List in Figure 2.3.

    d. See the updated Chart of Accounts list in Figure 2.4.

    e. See the updated Item List in Figure 2.5.

2. Creating a New Company: Central Coast Cellular

    a.–g. n/a

    h. • See the Customer List in Figure 2.6.

        • See the Vendor List in Figure 2.7.

        • See the Employee List in Figure 2.8.

        • See the Chart of Accounts in Figure 2.9.

        • See the Item List in Figure 2.10.

3. Creating a New Company: Nashua AutoMarket

    a. n/a

    b. See the Customer List in Figure 2.11.

    c. See the Vendor List in Figure 2.12.

    d. See the Employee List in Figure 2.13.

    e. See the Chart of Accounts list in Figure 2.14.

    f. See the Item List in Figure 2.15.

4. Internet assignments and related solutions are found at *http://owen.swlearning.com.*

Chapter 2   Case Problems

1. Ocean View Flowers

    a. See the Customer List in Figure 2.16.

    b. See the Vendor List in Figure 2.17.

   c. See the Employee List in Figure 2.18.

   d. See the Chart of Accounts in Figure 2.19.

2. Jennings & Associates—The EasyStep Interview

(***Warning to Instructors:*** This case is included for purposes of completeness. Be forewarned, the nature of the EasyStep Interview is very detailed. Some questions will probably be beyond students' current level of understanding. Student solutions may be different from the following, since students were allowed to answer some EasyStep questions on their own. The purpose of this assignment is to give students experience with the EasyStep Interview. The specific output produced is less important than the experience of working through the interview.)

   a. See the Standard Balance Sheet in Figure 2.20.

   b. See the Customer List in Figure 2.21.

   c. See the Vendor List in Figure 2.22.

   d. See item list in Figure 2.23.

   e. See the Employee List in Figure 2.24.

   f. See the Chart of Accounts list in Figure 2.25.

3. Jennings & Associates—Skipping the EasyStep Interview

Same as 2 above.

Solution Figures for Chapter 2

Figure 2.1

Customer: Job List

Customer	Jdesign		
Company	Jdesign	**Phone**	408-555-3483
Contact	John F Gomez		
Bill To	Jdesign	**Ship To**	Jdesign
	John F Gomez		John F Gomez
	235 Ridgefield Place		235 Ridgefield Place
	Fremont, CA 95110		Fremont, CA 95110
Balance	0.00	**Type**	Corporate
Credit Limit	5,000.00	**Pmt Terms**	2% 10 Net 30
		Sales Tax Code	Tax
Rep	PAG		

Customer	Los Gatos School District		
Company	Los Gatos School District	**Phone**	408-555-9788
Contact	Francis L Cahn		
Bill To	Los Gatos School District	**Ship To**	Los Gatos School District
	Francis L Cahn		Francis L Cahn
	1000 Apple Farm Rd.		1000 Apple Farm Rd.
	Los Gatos, CA 95110		Los Gatos, CA 95110
Balance	0.00	**Type**	Corporate
Credit Limit	10,000.00	**Pmt Terms**	Net 30
		Sales Tax Code	Tax
Rep	PAG		

Customer	Netscape		
Company	Netscape Corporation	**Phone**	408-555-3697
Contact	Fred G Mendall	**Fax**	408-555-4585
Bill To	Netscape Corporation	**Ship To**	Netscape Corporation
	Fred G Mendall		Fred G Mendall
	1000 Stevens Creek Blvd.		1000 Stevens Creek Blvd.
	Cupertino, CA 95014		Cupertino, CA 95014
Balance	0.00	**Type**	Corporate
Credit Limit	15,000.00	**Pmt Terms**	2% 10 Net 30
		Sales Tax Code	Tax

Figure 2.2

Vendor List

Vendor	Apple Computer		
Company Name	Apple Computer, Inc.	**Phone**	408-555-9787
Contact	Barry G Franks		
Address	Apple Computer, Inc.	**Type**	Manufacturer
	Barry G Franks	**Tax ID**	77-6841257
	One Corporate Way	**Cred. Lim.**	3,000.00
	Cupertino, CA 95110	**Balance**	0.00
Vendor	Bank of California		
Address	Bank of California		
		Balance	0.00
Vendor	Bengal Drives, Inc		
Company Name	Bengal Drives, Inc	**Phone**	805-555-8777
Contact	Kelly Sweenie		
Address	Bengal Drives, Inc	**Type**	Manufacturer
	Kelly Sweenie	**Tax ID**	77-1487125
	4500 Rucker Rd.	**Cred. Lim.**	8,000.00
	Santa Barbara, CA 93103	**Balance**	0.00
Vendor	EDD		
Address	EDD		
		Balance	0.00
Vendor	IBM		
Company Name	IBM	**Phone**	808-555-7788
Contact	Paula A Pounder	**Fax**	808-555-3697
Address	IBM	**Type**	1099 contractor
	Paula A Pounder	**Tax ID**	77-6187459
	39992 Rancheras Blvd.	**Cred. Lim.**	50,000.00
	Palo Alto, CA 95015	**Balance**	0.00
Vendor	State Board of Equalization		
Address	State Board of Equalization		
		Balance	0.00

Figure 2.3

Employee List

Employee	Casey K Nicks	**SS No.**	566-79-3511

Type	Regular
Phone	408-555-1287

Address	Casey K Nicks	**Hired**	01/01/03
	345 Ocean View Dr.		
	Santa Cruz, CA 95888	**Salary**	60,000.00

Accrual	**Rate**	**Accrued**	**Limit**	**Used**	**By Year/Period**	**Reset Hrs**
Sick	0.00	0.00		0.00	Y	N
Vacation	0.00	0.00		0.00	Y	N

	FUTA:	**Soc. Sec.:**	**Medicare:**	**SDI**	**SUI**	**AEIC**
Subject To	Y	Y	Y	Y	Y	N

Withholding	**Allowances**	**Extra**	**Status**	**State Lived**	**State Worked**
Federal	0	0.00	Married		
State	0	0.00	Married (one income)	CA	CA

Earnings

Name	**Hour/Annual Rate**
Salary	60,000.00

Addition, Deduction, Commission, Company Contributions

Name	**Amount**	**Limit**

Employee	Kylie W Patrick	**SS No.**	426-85-6974

Type	Regular
Phone	408-555-3050

Address	Kylie W Patrick	**Hired**	01/01/03
	10101 Wildway		
	San Jose, CA 95822		

Accrual	**Rate**	**Accrued**	**Limit**	**Used**	**By Year/Period**	**Reset Hrs**
Sick	0.00	0.00		0.00	Y	N
Vacation	0.00	0.00		0.00	Y	N

	FUTA:	**Soc. Sec.:**	**Medicare:**	**SDI**	**SUI**	**AEIC**
Subject To	Y	Y	Y	Y	Y	N

Withholding	**Allowances**	**Extra**	**Status**	**State Lived**	**State Worked**
Federal	0	0.00	Head of Household		
State	0	0.00	Head of Household	CA	CA

Earnings

Name	**Hour/Annual Rate**
Clerical	7.50

Addition, Deduction, Commission, Company Contributions

Name	**Amount**	**Limit**

Figure 2.3 (Concluded)

Employee List

Employee	Paul A Gates			**SS No.**		645-98-7393	
Type	Regular						
Phone	808-555-6874						
Address	Paul A Gates			**Hired**		01/01/03	
	12 Ridgeview Lane						
	Los Gatos, CA 95004			**Salary**		50,000.00	

Accrual	**Rate**	**Accrued**	**Limit**	**Used**	**By Year/Period**	**Reset Hrs**
Sick	0.00	0.00		0.00	Y	N
Vacation	0.00	0.00		0.00	Y	N

	FUTA:	**Soc. Sec.:**	**Medicare:**	**SDI**	**SUI**	**AEIC**
Subject To	Y	Y	Y	Y	Y	N

Withholding	**Allowances**	**Extra**	**Status**	**State Lived**	**State Worked**
Federal	0	0.00	Married		
State	0	0.00	Married (two incomes)	CA	CA

Earnings

Name	**Hour/Annual Rate**
Salary	50,000.00

Addition, Deduction, Commission, Company Contributions

Name	**Amount**	**Limit**

Figure 2.4

Chart of Accounts

Account	Type	Income Tax Line
Bank of Cupertino	Bank	<Unassigned>
Accounts Receivable	Accounts Receivable	<Unassigned>
Employee Advances	Other Current Asset	<Unassigned>
Inventory Asset	Other Current Asset	<Unassigned>
Investments	Other Current Asset	<Unassigned>
Prepaid Insurance	Other Current Asset	<Unassigned>
Prepaid Rent	Other Current Asset	<Unassigned>
Undeposited Funds	Other Current Asset	<Unassigned>
Accounts Payable	Accounts Payable	<Unassigned>
Payroll Liabilities	Other Current Liability	<Unassigned>
Sales Tax Payable	Other Current Liability	<Unassigned>
Short-Term Debt	Other Current Liability	<Unassigned>
Unearned Revenue	Other Current Liability	<Unassigned>
Long-Term Debt	Long Term Liability	<Unassigned>
Capital Stock	Equity	<Unassigned>
Opening Bal Equity	Equity	<Unassigned>
Retained Earnings	Equity	<Unassigned>
Computer Add-ons	Income	<Unassigned>
Computer Sales	Income	<Unassigned>
Consulting Income	Income	Income: Gross receipts or sales
Maintenance & Repairs	Income	<Unassigned>
Other Regular Income	Income	Income: Gross receipts or sales
Parts income	Income	<Unassigned>
Reimbursed Expenses	Income	Income: Gross receipts or sales
Uncategorized Income	Income	<Unassigned>
Cost of Goods Sold	Cost of Goods Sold	<Unassigned>
Automobile Expense	Expense	Deductions: Other deductions
Bank Service Charges	Expense	Deductions: Other deductions
Cash Discounts	Expense	<Unassigned>
Contributions	Expense	Deductions: Charitable contributions
Depreciation Expense	Expense	B/S-Assets: Accumulated depreciation
Dues and Subscriptions	Expense	Deductions: Other deductions
Equipment Rental	Expense	Deductions: Other deductions
Insurance	Expense	Deductions: Other deductions
Disability Insurance	Expense	Deductions: Other deductions
Liability Insurance	Expense	Deductions: Other deductions
Work Comp	Expense	Deductions: Other deductions
Interest Expense	Expense	Deductions: Interest expense
Finance Charge	Expense	Deductions: Interest expense
Loan Interest	Expense	Deductions: Interest expense
Mortgage	Expense	<Unassigned>
Licenses and Permits	Expense	<Unassigned>
Miscellaneous	Expense	Deductions: Other deductions

Figure 2.4 (Concluded)

Chart of Accounts

Account	Type	Income Tax Line
Office Supplies	Expense	Deductions: Other deductions
Outside Services	Expense	<Unassigned>
Payroll Expenses	Expense	<Unassigned>
Postage and Delivery	Expense	Deductions: Other deductions
Printing and Reproduction	Expense	Deductions: Other deductions
Professional Fees	Expense	Deductions: Other deductions
Accounting	Expense	Deductions: Other deductions
Legal Fees	Expense	Deductions: Other deductions
Rent	Expense	Deductions: Rents
Repairs	Expense	Deductions: Repairs and maintenance
Building Repairs	Expense	Deductions: Repairs and maintenance
Computer Repairs	Expense	Deductions: Repairs and maintenance
Equipment Repairs	Expense	Deductions: Repairs and maintenance
Janitorial Exp	Expense	Deductions: Repairs and maintenance
Taxes	Expense	Deductions: Other miscellaneous taxes
Federal	Expense	Deductions: State taxes
Local	Expense	Deductions: Other miscellaneous taxes
Property	Expense	Deductions: Local property taxes
State	Expense	Deductions: State taxes
Telephone	Expense	Deductions: Other deductions
Travel & Ent	Expense	<Unassigned>
Entertainment	Expense	Deductions: Meals and entertainment
Meals	Expense	Deductions: Meals and entertainment
Travel	Expense	<Unassigned>
Uncategorized Expenses	Expense	<Unassigned>
Utilities	Expense	Deductions: Other deductions
Gas and Electric	Expense	Deductions: Other deductions
Water	Expense	Deductions: Other deductions
Investment Income	Other Income	<Unassigned>
Interest Revenue	Other Income	Income: Interest income
Other Income	Other Income	Income: Other income
Other Expenses	Other Expense	Deductions: Other deductions
Purchase Orders	Non-Posting	<Unassigned>

Figure 2.5

Item List

Item Name/Num…	Installation	**Type**	Service
Description	Installation of computer add-ons		
Price	45.00	Taxable	
Account	Maintenance & Repairs		

Item Name/Num…	Maintenance	**Type**	Service
Description	Monthly maintenance fee		
Price	50.00	Taxable	
Account	Maintenance & Repairs		

Item Name/Num…	1 gig HD	**Type**	Inventory Part	
Description	1,000mb Bengal Hard Disk			
Price	550.00	Taxable		
Inventory Asset	Inventory Asset	**Unit Cost**		450.00
Account	Computer Add-ons	**Avg. Cost**		450.00
COGS Account	Cost of Goods Sold	**Total Value**		0
		Preferred Vendor	Bengal Drives, Inc.	
Qty On Hand	0	**On Purch Order** 0	**On Sales Order**	0

Item Name/Num…	586-100	**Type**	Inventory Part	
Description	Phoenix Pentium Computer - 100 mhz			
Price	1,800.00	Taxable		
Inventory Asset	Inventory Asset	**Unit Cost**		1,500.00
Account	Computer Sales	**Avg. Cost**		1,500.00
COGS Account	Cost of Goods Sold	**Total Value**		0.00
		Preferred Vendor	IBM	
Qty On Hand	0	**On Purch Order** 0	**On Sales Order**	0

Item Name/Num…	800mb HD	**Type**	Inventory Part	
Description	800mb Bengal Hard Disk			
Price	300.00	Taxable		
Inventory Asset	Inventory Asset	**Unit Cost**		250.00
Account	Computer Add-ons	**Avg. Cost**		250.00
COGS Account	Cost of Goods Sold	**Total Value**		0.00
		Preferred Vendor	Bengal Drives	
Qty On Hand	0	**On Purch Order** 0	**On Sales Order**	0

Figure 2.5 (Concluded)

Item List

Item Name/Num...	Sales Tax	**Type**	Sales Tax Item
Description	Sales Tax		
Price		7.5%	
Account	Sales Tax Payable		

Figure 2.6

Customer: Job List

Customer	City of San Luis Obispo		
Company	City of San Luis Obispo	**Phone**	805 781-7100
Contact	Robert Preston		
Bill To	City of San Luis Obispo	**Ship To**	City of San Luis Obispo
	Robert Preston		Robert Preston
	990 Palm Street		990 Palm Street
	San Luis Obispo, CA 93401		San Luis Obispo, CA 93401
Balance	0.00		
		Pmt Terms	Net 30
		Sales Tax Code	Tax

Customer	Sterling Hotels Corporation		
Company	Sterling Hotels Corporation	**Phone**	805 546-9388
Contact	Monica Flowers		
Bill To	Sterling Hotels Corporation	**Ship To**	Sterling Hotels Corporation
	Monica Flowers		Monica Flowers
	4115 Broad Street, Suite B-1		4115 Broad Street, Suite B-1
	San Luis Obispo, CA, 93401		San Luis Obispo, CA 93401
Balance	0.00		
		Pmt Terms	Net 30
		Sales Tax Code	Tax

Customer	Tribune		
Company	Tribune	**Phone**	805 781-7800
Contact	Sara Miles		
Bill To	Tribune	**Ship To**	Tribune
	Sara Miles		Sara Miles
	3825 S. Higuera St.		3825 S. Higuera St.
	San Luis Obispo, CA 93401		San Luis Obispo, CA 93401
Balance	0.00		
		Pmt Terms	Net 30
		Sales Tax Code	Tax

Figure 2.7

Vendor List

Vendor	Employment Development Department (EDD)		
Address	Employment Development Department (EDD)		
		Balance	0.00

Vendor	Ericsson, Inc.		
Company Name	Ericsson, Inc.	**Phone**	972 583-0000
Contact	Monty Python		
Address	Ericsson, Inc.		
	Monty Python		
	740 East Campbell Road		
	Richardson, TX 75081	**Balance**	0.00

Vendor	Nokia Mobile Phones		
Company Name	Nokia Mobile Phones	**Phone**	818 876-6000
Contact	Brandy Parker		
Address	Nokia Mobile Phones		
	Brandy Parker		
	23621 Park Sorrento Road Suite 101		
	Calabasas, CA 91302	**Balance**	0.00

Vendor	State Board of Equalization		
Address	State Board of Equalization		
		Balance	0.00

Vendor	Verizon Communications		
Company Name	Verizon Communications	**Phone**	972 507-5000
Contact	Francisco Rojas		
Address	Verizon Communications		
	Francisco Rojas		
	1255 Corporate Drive		
	Irving, Texas 75038	**Balance**	0.00

Figure 2.8

Employee List

Employee	Alex Rodriguez			**SS No.**	487-98-1374	
Type	Regular					
Phone	805-555-1579					
Address	Alex Rodriguez			**Hired**	01/01/03	
	1480 Monterey St.					
	San Luis Obispo, CA 93401			**Salary**	48,000.00	

Accrual	**Rate**	**Accrued**	**Limit**	**Used**	**By Year/Period**	**Reset Hrs**
Sick	0:00	0:00		0:00	Y	N
Vacation	0:00	0:00		0:00	Y	N

	FUTA:	**Soc. Sec.:**	**Medicare:**	**SDI**	**SUI**	**AEIC**
Subject To	Y	Y	Y	Y	Y	N

Withholding	**Allowances**	**Extra**	**Status**	**State Lived**	**State Worked**
Federal	0	0.00	Married		
State	0	0.00	Married (one income)	CA	CA

Earnings

Name	**Hour/Annual Rate**
Salary	48,000.00

Addition, Deduction, Commission, Company Contributions

Name	**Amount**	**Limit**

Employee	Jay Bruner			**SS No.**	578-94-3154	
Type	Regular					
Phone	805-555-7894					
Address	Jay Bruner			**Hired**	01/01/03	
	552 Olive St.					
	San Luis Obispo, CA 93401			**Salary**	36,000.00	

Accrual	**Rate**	**Accrued**	**Limit**	**Used**	**By Year/Period**	**Reset Hrs**
Sick	0:00	0:00		0:00	Y	N
Vacation	0:00	0:00		0:00	Y	N

	FUTA:	**Soc. Sec.:**	**Medicare:**	**SDI**	**SUI**	**AEIC**
Subject To	Y	Y	Y	Y	Y	N

Withholding	**Allowances**	**Extra**	**Status**	**State Lived**	**State Worked**
Federal	0	0.00	Single		
State	0	0.00	Single	CA	CA

Earnings

Name	**Hour/Annual Rate**
Salary	36,000.00

Addition, Deduction, Commission, Company Contributions

Name	**Amount**	**Limit**

Figure 2.8
(Concluded)

Employee List

Employee	Megan Paulson		**SS No.**	547-31-5974
Type	Regular			
Phone	805-555-4489			
Address	Megan Paulson		**Hired**	01/01/03
	400 Beach St.			
	San Luis Obispo, CA 93401			

Accrual	**Rate**	**Accrued**	**Limit**	**Used**	**By Year/Period**	**Reset Hrs**
Sick	0:00	0:00		0:00	Y	N
Vacation	0:00	0:00		0:00	Y	N

	FUTA:	**Soc. Sec.:**	**Medicare:**	**SDI**	**SUI**	**AEIC**
Subject To	Y	Y	Y	Y	Y	N

Withholding	**Allowances**	**Extra**	**Status**	**State Lived**	**State Worked**
Federal	0	0.00	Married		
State	0	0.00	Married (two incomes)	CA	CA

Earnings

Name	Hour/Annual Rate
Hourly	12.00

Addition, Deduction, Commission, Company Contributions

Name	Amount	Limit

Figure 2.9

Chart of Accounts

Account	Type
Checking	Bank
Accounts Receivable	Accounts Receivable
Inventory Asset	Other Current Asset
Payroll Liabilities	Other Current Liability
Sales Tax Payable	Other Current Liability
Opening Bal Equity	Equity
Retained Earnings	Equity
Consulting	Income
Freight Income	Income
Phone Rentals	Income
Phone Sales	Income
Reimbursed Expenses	Income
Resale Discounts	Income
Resale Income	Income
Sales	Income
Sales Discounts	Income
Cost of Goods Sold	Cost of Goods Sold
Automobile Expense	Expense
Bank Service Charges	Expense
Cash Discounts	Expense
Contributions	Expense
Depreciation Expense	Expense
Dues and Subscriptions	Expense
Equipment Rental	Expense
Filing Fees	Expense
Franchise Fees	Expense
Insurance	Expense
Disability Insurance	Expense
Liability Insurance	Expense
Interest Expense	Expense
Finance Charge	Expense
Loan Interest	Expense
Mortgage	Expense
Licenses and Permits	Expense
Miscellaneous	Expense
Payroll Expenses	Expense
Postage and Delivery	Expense
Printing and Reproduction	Expense
Professional Fees	Expense
Accounting	Expense
Legal Fees	Expense
Rent	Expense
Repairs	Expense
Building Repairs	Expense
Computer Repairs	Expense
Equipment Repairs	Expense
Storage	Expense

Figure 2.9
(Concluded)

Chart of Accounts

Account	Type
Supplies	Expense
Marketing	Expense
Office	Expense
Taxes	Expense
Federal	Expense
Local	Expense
Property	Expense
State	Expense
Telephone	Expense
Travel & Ent	Expense
Entertainment	Expense
Meals	Expense
Travel	Expense
Utilities	Expense
Gas and Electric	Expense
Water	Expense
Interest Income	Other Income
Other Income	Other Income
Other Expenses	Other Expense

Figure 2.10

Item List

Item Name/Nu...	Consulting Services	**Type**	Service		
Description	Consulting Services				
Price	95.00	**Taxable**			
Account	Consulting				

Item Name/Nu...	Ericsson LX588	**Type**	Inventory Part		
Description	Ericsson LX588				
Price	85.00	**Taxable**			
Inventory Asset	Inventory Asset	**Unit Cost**			50.00
Account	Phone Sales	**Avg. Cost**			50.00
COGS Account	Cost of Goods Sold	**Total Value**			0.00
		Preferred Vendor	Ericsson, Inc.		
Qty On Hand	0	**On Purch Ord...**	0	**On Sales Order**	0

Item Name/Nu...	Ericsson T19LX	**Type**	Inventory Part		
Description	Ericsson T19LX				
Price	100.00	**Taxable**			
Inventory Asset	Inventory Asset	**Unit Cost**			75.00
Account	Phone Sales	**Avg. Cost**			75.00
COGS Account	Cost of Goods Sold	**Total Value**			0.00
		Preferred Vendor	Ericsson, Inc.		
Qty On Hand	0	**On Purch Ord...**	0	**On Sales Order**	0

Item Name/Nu...	Nokia 3285	**Type**	Inventory Part		
Description	Nokia 3285				
Price	300.00	**Taxable**			
Inventory Asset	Inventory Asset	**Unit Cost**			200.00
Account	Phone Sales	**Avg. Cost**			200.00
COGS Account	Cost of Goods Sold	**Total Value**			0.00
		Preferred Vendor	Nokia Mobile Phones		
Qty On Hand	0	**On Purch Order**	0.00		

Figure 2.10
(Concluded)

Item List

Item Name/Nu...	Nokia 8290	**Type**	Inventory Part
Description	Nokia 8290		
Price	225.00	Taxable	
Inventory Asset	Inventory Asset	**Unit Cost**	150.00
Account	Phone Sales	**Avg. Cost**	150.00
COGS Account	Cost of Goods Sold	**Total Value**	0.00
		Preferred Vendor	Nokia Mobile Phones
Qty On Hand	0	**On Purch Order** 0	**On Sales Order** 0

Item Name/Nu...	Nokia 8890	**Type**	Inventory Part
Description	Nokia 8890		
Price	250.00	Taxable	
Inventory Asset	Inventory Asset	**Unit Cost**	175.00
Account	Phone Sales	**Avg. Cost**	175.00
COGS Account	Cost of Goods Sold	**Total Value**	0.00
		Preferred Vendor	Nokia Mobile Phones
Qty On Hand	0	**On Purch Order** 0	**On Sales Order** 0

Item Name/Num...	Sales Tax	**Type**	Sales Tax Item
Description	Sales Tax		
Price	8.0%		
Account	Sales Tax Payable		

Figure 2.11

Customer: Job List

Customer	Diaz-Cruz Automotive		
Company	Diaz-Cruz Automotive	**Phone**	222-321-4456
Contact	John J. Jones		
Bill To	Diaz-Cruz Automotive	**Ship To**	Diaz-Cruz Automotive
	9396 Maryland Lane		9396 Maryland Lane
	Pensacola, FL 99999		Pensacola, FL 99999
Balance	0.00		
Credit Limit	1,000.00	**Pmt Terms**	Net 30 days

Figure 2.12

Vendor List

Vendor	Missoula Auto Supply		
Company Name	Missoula Auto Supply	**Phone**	333-334-1212
Contact	Robert S. Smith	**Fax**	333-334-1215
Address	Missoula Auto Supply		
	Robert S. Smith	**Tax ID**	33-8888888
	2231 Hawks Rd.	**Cred. Lim.**	5,000.00
	Billings, MT 99999	**Balance**	0.00

Figure 2.13

Employee List

Employee	William P Biaggi			**SS No.**		232-40-1199
Initials	Regular					
Phone	222-333-3334					
Address	William P Biaggi			**Hired**		07/23/2002
	2023 Lane					
	Reno, NV 99999			**Salary**		22,000.00

Accrual	**Rate**	**Accrued**	**Limit**	**Used By Year/Period**	**Reset Hrs**
Sick	0:00	0:00		0:00 Y	N
Vacation	0:00	0:00		0:00 Y	N

	FUTA:	**Soc.Sec.:**	**Medicare:**	**SDI:**	**SUI:**	**AEIC:**
Subject To	Y	Y	Y	N	Y	N

Withholding	**Allowances**	**Extra**	**Status**	**State Lived**	**State Worked**
Federal	0	0.00	Single		
State	0	0.00			NV

Earnings

Name	**Hourly/Annual Rate**
Salary	22,000.00

Addition, Deduction, Commission, Company Contributions

Name	**Amount**	**Limit**

Figure 2.14

Chart of Accounts

Account	Type
Union Checking	Bank
Payroll Liabilities	Other Current Liability
Opening Bal Equity	Equity
Retained Earnings	Equity
Product Sales	Income
Freight Income	Income
Reimbursement Expenses	Income
Resale Discounts	Income
Resale Income	Income
Sales	Income
Sales Discounts	Income
Cost of Goods Sold	Cost of Goods Sold
Automobile Expense	Expense
Bank Service Charges	Expense
Cash Discounts	Expense
Contributions	Expense
Depreciation Expense	Expense
Dues and Subscriptions	Expense
Equipment Rental	Expense
Filing Fees	Expense
Franchise Fees	Expense
Insurance	Expense
Disability Insurance	Expense
Liability Insurance	Expense
Interest Expense	Expense
Finance Charge	Expense
Loan Interest	Expense
Mortgage	Expense
Licenses and Permits	Expense
Miscellaneous	Expense
Payroll Expenses	Expense
Postage and Delivery	Expense
Printing and Reproduction	Expense
Professional Fees	Expense
Accounting	Expense
Legal Fees	Expense
Rent	Expense
Repairs	Expense
Building Repairs	Expense
Computer Repairs	Expense
Equipment Repairs	Expense
Storage	Expense
Supplies	Expense
Marketing	Expense

Figure 2.14 (Concluded)

Chart of Accounts

Account	**Type**
Office	Expense
Taxes	Expense
Federal	Expense
Local	Expense
Property	Expense
State	Expense
Telephone	Expense
Travel & Ent	Expense
Entertainment	Expense
Meals	Expense
Travel	Expense
Utilities	Expense
Gas and Electric	Expense
Water	Expense
Interest Income	Other Income
Other Income	Other Income
Other Expenses	Other Expense

Figure 2.15

Item List

Item Name/Num...	Bumper 100	**Type**	Inventory Part	
Description	Blazer Bumper 1996			
Price	400.00			
Inventory Asset	Inventory Asset	**Unit Cost**		300.00
Account	Product Sales	**Avg. Cost**		300.00
COGS Account	Cost of Goods Sold	**Total Value**		0.00
		Preferred Vendor	Missoula Auto Supply	
Qty On Hand	0	**On Purch Order** 0	**On Sales Order**	0

Figure 2.16

Customer: Job List

Customer	California Beauties		
Company	California Beauties		
Contact	Farrah Faucet		
Bill To	California Beauties	**Ship To**	California Beauties
	Farrah Faucet		Farrah Faucet
	239 Hyde Street		239 Hyde Street
	San Francisco, CA 95114		San Francisco, CA 95114
Balance	0.00		
		Pmt Terms	2% 10 Net 30

Customer	Eastern Scents		
Company	Eastern Scents		
Contact	Nick Giovanni		
Bill To	Eastern Scents	**Ship To**	Eastern Scents
	Nick Giovanni		Nick Giovanni
	938 42nd St.		938 42nd St.
	New York, NY 10054		New York, NY 10054
Balance	0.00		
		Pmt Terms	2% 10 Net 30

Customer	FTD		
Company	FTD		
Contact	Beverly Rose		
Bill To	FTD	**Ship To**	FTD
	Beverly Rose		Beverly Rose
	2033 Lakewood Dr.		2033 Lakewood Dr.
	Chicago, IL 60601		Chicago, IL 60601
Balance	0.00		
		Pmt Terms	Net 30

Customer	Latin Ladies		
Company	Latin Ladies		
Contact	Juan Valdez		
Bill To	Latin Ladies	**Ship To**	Latin Ladies
	Juan Valdez		Juan Valdez
	209 Zona Rosa		209 Zona Rosa
	Mexico City, Mexico		Mexico City, Mexico
Balance	0.00		
		Pmt Terms	2% 10 Net 30

Figure 2.16 (Concluded)

Customer: Job List

Customer	Valley Florists			
Company	Valley Florists			
Contact	Sam Davies			
Bill To	Valley Florists	**Ship To**		Valley Florists
	Sam Davies			Sam Davies
	101 Main St.			101 Main St.
	Los Angeles, CA 90113			Los Angeles, CA 90113
Balance		0.00		
			Pmt Terms	2% 10 Net 30

Figure 2.17

Vendor List

Vendor	Brophy Bros. Farms		
Company Name	Brophy Bros. Farms		
Contact	Tim Beach		
Address	Brophy Bros. Farms		
	Tim Beach		
	90 East Hwy 246		
	Santa Barbara, CA 93101	**Balance**	0.00
Vendor	EDD Employment Development Dept		
Address	EDD Employment Development Dept		
		Balance	0.00
Vendor	Hawaiian Farms		
Company Name	Hawaiian Farms		
Contact	Mahalo Baise		
Address	Hawaiian Farms		
	Mahalo Baise		
	2893 1st Street		
	Honolulu, HI 05412	**Balance**	0.00
Vendor	Keenan's Pride		
Company Name	Keenan's Pride		
Contact	Kelly Keenan		
Address	Keenan's Pride		
	Kelly Keenan		
	10 East Betteravia		
	Santa Maria, CA 93454	**Balance**	0.00
Vendor	Princess Flowers		
Company Name	Princess Flowers		
Contact	Bonnie Sobieski		
Address	Princess Flowers		
	Bonnie Sobieski		
	92 West Way		
	Medford, OR 39282	**Balance**	0.00

Figure 2.17 (Concluded)

Vendor List

Vendor	Vordale Farms
Company Name	Vordale Farms
Contact	Donna Vordale
Address	Vordale Farms
	Donna Vordale
	62383 Lido Isle
	Newport, CA 90247

Balance   0.00

Figure 2.18

Employee List

Employee	Edward Thomas	SS No.	556-98-4125
Type	Regular		
Address	Edward Thomas	Hired	01/04/04
	1234 St. Andrews Way		
	Lompoc, CA 93436	Salary	70,000.00

Accrual	Rate	Accrued	Limit	Used	By Year/Period	Reset Hrs
Sick	0:00	0:00		0:00	Y	N
Vacation	0:00	0:00		0:00	Y	N

	FUTA:	Soc. Sec.:	Medicare:	SDI	SUI	AEIC
Subject To	Y	Y	Y	Y	Y	N

Withholding	Allowances	Extra	Status	State Lived	State Worked
Federal	0	0.00	Single		
State	0	0.00	Single	CA	CA

Earnings

Name	Hour/Annual Rate
Salary	70,000.00

Addition, Deduction, Commission, Company Contributions

Name	Amount	Limit

Employee	Kelly Gusland	SS No.	567-78-1334
Type	Regular		
Address	Kelly Gusland	Hired	01/04/2004
	203 B St.		
	Lompoc, CA 93436		

Accrual	Rate	Accrued	Limit	Used	By Year/Period	Reset Hrs
Sick	0:00	0:00		0:00	Y	N
Vacation	0:00	0:00		0:00	Y	N

	FUTA:	Soc. Sec.:	Medicare:	SDI	SUI	AEIC
Subject To	Y	Y	Y	Y	Y	N

Withholding	Allowances	Extra	Status	State Lived	State Worked
Federal	0	0.00	Single		
State	0	0.00	Single	CA	CA

Earnings

Name	Hour/Annual Rate
Hourly	15.00

Addition, Deduction, Commission, Company Contributions

Name	Amount	Limit

Figure 2.18 (Continued)

Employee List

Employee	Margie Coe		**SS No.**	654-85-1254	
Type	Regular				
Address	Margie Coe		**Hired**	01/04/04	
	2322 Courtney				
	Buellton, CA 93246				

Accrual	**Rate**	**Accrued**	**Limit**	**Used**	**By Year/Period**	**Reset Hrs**
Sick	0:00	0:00		0:00	Y	N
Vacation	0:00	0:00		0:00	Y	N

	FUTA:	**Soc. Sec.:**	**Medicare:**	**SDI**	**SUI**	**AEIC**
Subject To	Y	Y	Y	Y	Y	N

Withholding	**Allowances**	**Extra**	**Status**	**State Lived**	**State Worked**
Federal	0	0.00	Head of Household		
State	0	0.00	Head of Household	CA	CA

Earnings

Name	**Hour/Annual Rate**
Hourly	12.00

Addition, Deduction, Commission, Company Contributions

Name	**Amount**	**Limit**

Employee	Marie McAninch		**SS No.**	668-41-9578	
Type	Regular				
Address	Marie McAninch		**Hired**	01/04/04	
	1299 College Ave.				
	Santa Maria, CA 93454		**Salary**	60,000.00	

Accrual	**Rate**	**Accrued**	**Limit**	**Used**	**By Year/Period**	**Reset Hrs**
Sick	0:00	0:00		0:00	Y	N
Vacation	0:00	0:00		0:00	Y	N

	FUTA:	**Soc. Sec.:**	**Medicare:**	**SDI**	**SUI**	**AEIC**
Subject To	Y	Y	Y	Y	Y	N

Withholding	**Allowances**	**Extra**	**Status**	**State Lived**	**State Worked**
Federal	0	0.00	Married		
State	0	0.00	Married (two incomes)	CA	CA

Earnings

Name	**Hour/Annual Rate**
Salary	60,000.00

Addition, Deduction, Commission, Company Contributions

Name	**Amount**	**Limit**

Figure 2.18 (Concluded)

Employee List

Employee	Stan Comstock			**SS No.**	126-85-7843	

Type Regular

Address	Stan Comstock			**Hired**	01/04/04

383 Lemon St.

Lompoc, CA 93436   **Salary**   50,000.00

Accrual	**Rate**	**Accrued**	**Limit**	**Used**	**By Year/Period**	**Reset Hrs**
Sick	0:00	0:00		0:00	Y	N
Vacation	0:00	0:00		0:00	Y	N

	FUTA:	**Soc. Sec.:**	**Medicare:**	**SDI**	**SUI**	**AEIC**
Subject To	Y	Y	Y	Y	Y	N

Withholding	**Allowances**	**Extra**	**Status**	**State Lived**	**State Worked**
Federal	0	0.00	Married		
State	0	0.00	Married (one income)	CA	CA

Earnings

Name	**Hour/Annual Rate**
Salary	50,000.00

Addition, Deduction, Commission, Company Contributions

Name	**Amount**	**Limit**

Figure 2.19

Chart of Accounts

Account	Type
Union Checking	Bank
Payroll Liabilities	Other Current Liability
Opening Bal Equity	Equity
Retained Earnings	Equity
Freight Income	Income
Reimbursed Expenses	Income
Resale Discounts	Income
Resale Income	Income
Sales	Income
Sales Discounts	Income
Cost of Goods Sold	Cost of Goods Sold
Automobile Expense	Expense
Bank Service Charges	Expense
Cash Discounts	Expense
Contributions	Expense
Depreciation Expense	Expense
Dues and Subscriptions	Expense
Equipment Rental	Expense
Filing Fees	Expense
Franchise Fees	Expense
Insurance	Expense
Disability Insurance	Expense
Liability Insurance	Expense
Interest Expense	Expense
Finance Charge	Expense
Loan Interest	Expense
Mortgage	Expense
Licenses and Permits	Expense
Miscellaneous	Expense
Payroll Expenses	Expense
Postage and Delivery	Expense
Printing and Reproduction	Expense
Professional Fees	Expense
Accounting	Expense
Legal Fees	Expense
Rent	Expense
Repairs	Expense
Building Repairs	Expense
Computer Repairs	Expense
Equipment Repairs	Expense

Figure 2.19 (Concluded)

Chart of Accounts

Account	Type
Storage	Expense
Supplies	Expense
Marketing	Expense
Office	Expense
TaxesExpense	
Federal	Expense
Local	Expense
Property	Expense
State	Expense
Telephone	Expense
Travel & Ent	Expense
Entertainment	Expense
Meals	Expense
Travel	Expense
Utilities	Expense
Gas and Electric	Expense
Water	Expense
Interest Income	Other Income
Other Income	Other Income
Other Expenses	Other Expense

Figure 2.20

Jennings & Associates
Balance Sheet
As of January 1, 2004

	Jan 1, 04
ASSETS	
Current Assets	
Checking/Savings	
First Valley Savings & Loan	1,000.00
Union Bank Checking	2,590.00
Total Checking/Savings	3,590.00
Accounts Receivable	
Accounts Receivable	3,250.00
Total Accounts Receivable	3,250.00
Total Current Assets	6,840.00
Other Assets	
Computer Equipment	3,000.00
Furniture	2,000.00
Total Other Assets	5,000.00
TOTAL ASSETS	**11,840.00**
LIABILITIES & EQUITY	
Liabilities	
Current Liabilities	
Accounts Payable	
Accounts Payable	1,000.00
Total Accounts Payable	1,000.00
Total Current Liabilities	1,000.00
Long Term Liabilities	
Bank of San Martin	5,000.00
Total Long Term Liabilities	5,000.00
Total Liabilities	6,000.00
Equity	
Opening Bal Equity	3,590.00
Retained Earnings	2,250.00
Total Equity	5,840.00
TOTAL LIABILITIES & EQUITY	**11,840.00**

Figure 2.21

Customer: Job List

Customer	AAA Appliance		
Company	AAA Appliance Co.	**Phone**	901-123-4567
Contact	Jane E Seymor		
Bill To	AAA Appliance Co.	**Ship To**	AAA Appliance Co.
	Jane E Seymor		Jane E Seymor
	1034 Sycamore		1034 Sycamore
	San Martin, CA 93110	San Martin, CA 93110	
Balance	350.00		
		Pmt Terms	Net 30
		Sales Tax Code	Tax

Customer	Big 10 Sporting Goods		
Company	Big 10 Sporting Goods	**Phone**	901-234-5678
Contact	Sammy A Goodwin		
Bill To	Big 10 Sporting Goods	**Ship To**	Big 10 Sporting Goods
	Sammy A Goodwin		Sammy A Goodwin
	1003 A Street		1003 A Street
	San Martin, CA 93100	San Martin, CA 93100	
Balance	250.00		
		Pmt Terms	Net 30
		Sales Tax Code	Tax

Customer	Bob and Mary Schultz		
		Phone	901-345-6789
Company	Bob and Mary Schultz		
Bill To	Bob and Mary Schultz	**Ship To**	Bob A Schultz
	122 Garden St.		122 Garden St.
	San Martin, CA 93107	San Martin, CA 93107	
Balance	500.00		
		Pmt Terms	Net 30
		Sales Tax Code	Tax

Customer	Evelyn Walker Real Estate		
Company	Evelyn Walker Real Estate	**Phone**	901-456-7890
Contact	Nancy P Revlon		
Bill To	Evelyn Walker Real Estate	**Ship To**	Evelyn Walker Real Estate
	Nancy P Revlon		Nancy P Revlon

Figure 2.21 (Continued)

Customer: Job List

3233 Central	3233 Central
San Martin, CA 93107	San Martin, CA 93107

Balance   700.00

Pmt Terms   Net 30
Sales Tax Code   Non

Customer   Fancy Yogurt Co.
Company   Fancy Yogurt Co.   **Phone**   901-567-8900
Contact   Paul F Montoya
Bill To   Fancy Yogurt Co.   **Ship To**   Fancy Yogurt Co.
                Paul F Montoya   Paul F Montoya
                3299 Bonita Lane   3299 Bonita Lane
                San Martin, CA 93107   San Martin, CA 93107

Balance   500.00

Pmt Terms   Net 30
Sales Tax Code   Non

Customer   Paulsons Nursery
Company   Paulsons Nursery   **Phone**   901-678-9000
Contact   Robert J Paulson
Bill To   Paulsons Nursery   **Ship To**   Paulsons Nursery
                Robert J Paulson   Robert J Paulson
                100 Central   100 Central
                San Martin, CA 93110   San Martin, CA 93110

Balance   600.00

Pmt Terms   Net 30
Sales Tax Code   Non

Customer   Ray's Chevron
Company   Ray's Chevron   **Phone**   901-890-1111
Contact   Fanny J May
Bill To   Ray's Chevron   **Ship To**   Ray's Chevron
                Fanny J May   Fanny J May
                1990 Broadway   1990 Broadway
                San Martin, CA 93110   San Martin, CA 93110

Balance   150.00

Pmt Terms   Net 30
Sales Tax Code   Non

Figure 2.21 (Concluded)

Customer: Job List

Customer   Sally's Fabrics

Company   Sally's Fabrics   **Phone**   555-1587

Contact   Ray E Farray

Bill To   Sally's Fabrics   **Ship To**   Sally's Fabrics
                 Ray E Farray   Ray E Farray
                 900 West Laurel   900 West Laurel
                 San Martin, CA 93115   San Martin, CA 93115

Balance   200.00

                                                                   Pmt Terms   Net 30
                                                                   Sales Tax Code   Non

Rep   KAJ

Figure 2.22

Vendor List

Vendor	Banks Office Supply		
Company Name	Banks Office Supply		
Contact	Pamela Reese		
Address	Banks Office Supply	**Type**	Supplies
	Pamela Reese		
	1209 Oak Lane		
	San Martin, CA 93110	**Balance**	0.00

Vendor	EDD	**Type**	Tax Agency
Address	EDD	**Balance**	0.00

Vendor	Frank Mendez Properties		
Company Name	Frank Mendez Properties		
Contact	Frank Mendez		
Address	Frank Mendez Properties	**Type**	Consultant
	Frank Mendez		
	12400 Calle Real		
	San Martin, CA 93110	**Balance**	700.00

Vendor	General Telephone		
Company Name	General Telephone		
Address	General Telephone	**Type**	Supplies
	12100 North Main		
	San Martin, CA 93110		
		Balance	75.00

Vendor	On-Time Copy Shop		
Company Name	On-Time Copy Shop		
Contact	Jennifer Jacobs		
Address	On-Time Copy Shop	**Type**	Printing
	Jennifer Jacobs		
	3402 A Street		
	San Martin, CA 93110	**Balance**	125.00

Figure 2.22 (Concluded)

Vendor	Pacific Electric Company		
Company Name	Pacific Electric Company		
Address	Pacific Electric Company	**Type**	Supplies
	12000 North Main		
	San Martin, CA 93110		
		Balance	35.00

Vendor	Rex's Film Supply		
Company Name	Rex's Film Supply		
Address	Rex's Film Supply	**Type**	Supplies
	800 North Central Ave.		
	Suite F		
	San Martin, CA 93017	**Balance**	0.00

Vendor	So. Cal Gas		
Company Name	So. Cal Gas		
Contact	Kyle N Schultz		
Address	So. Cal Gas	**Type**	Supplies
	Kyle N Schultz		
	200 South Main		
	San Martin, CA 93110	**Balance**	65.00

Vendor	State Board of Equalization		
Address	State Board of Equalization	**Type**	Tax Agency
		Balance	0.00

Figure 2.23

Item List

Item Name/Num…	Film-High Quality	**Type**	Inventory Part	
Description	Film-High Quality			
Price	25.00	Taxable		
Inventory Asset	Inventory Asset	**Unit Cost**		15.00
Account	Film	**Avg. Cost**		15.00
COGS Account	Film expenses	**Total Value**		0.00
		Preferred Ven	Rex's Film Supply	
Qty On Hand	0	**On Purch Order** 0	**On Sales Order**	0

Item Name/Num…	Film-Regular	**Type**	Inventory Part	
Description	Film-Regular			
Price	7.50	Taxable		
Inventory Asset	Inventory Asset	**Unit Cost**		4.45
Account	Film	**Avg. Cost**		4.45
COGS Account	Film expenses	**Total Value**		0.00
		Preferred Vendor	Rex's Film Supply	
Qty On Hand	0	**On Purch Order** 0	**On Sales Order**	0

Item Name/Num…	Out of State	**Type**	Sales Tax Item
Description	Out-of-state sale, exempt from sales tax		
Price	0.0%		
Account	Sales Tax Payable		

Item Name/Num…	Sales Tax	**Type**	Sales Tax Item
Description	Tax		
Price	7.75%		
Account	Sales Tax Payable		

Figure 2.24

Employee List

Employee	Cheryl A Boudreau	**SS No.**	545-99-5512
Type	Regular		
Address	Cheryl A Boudreau	**Hired**	01/15/2004
	19090 Mockingbird Lane		
	San Martin, CA 93107		

Accrual	**Rate**	**Accrued**	**Limit**	**Used**	**By Year/Period**	**Reset Hrs**
Sick	0:00	0:00		0:00	Y	N
Vacation	0:00	0:00		0:00	Y	N

	FUTA:	**Soc. Sec.:**	**Medicare:**	**SDI**	**SUI**	**AEIC**
Subject To	Y	Y	Y	Y	Y	N

Withholding	**Allowances**	**Extra**	**Status**	**State Lived**	**State Worked**
Federal	0	0.00	Single		
State	0	0.00	Single	CA	CA

Earnings

Name	**Hourly/Annual Rate**
Hourly	15.00

Addition, Deduction, Commission, Company Contributions

Name	**Amount**	**Limit**

Employee	Diane Murphy	**SS No.**	556-89-9999
Type	Regular		
Address	Diane Murphy	**Hired**	01/01/2004
	455 Galaxy Rd.		
	San Martin, CA 93107		

Accrual	**Rate**	**Accrued**	**Limit**	**Used**	**By Year/Period**	**Reset Hrs**
Sick	0:00	0:00		0:00	Y	N
Vacation	0:00	0:00		0:00	Y	N

	FUTA:	**Soc. Sec.:**	**Medicare:**	**SDI**	**SUI**	**AEIC**
Subject To	Y	Y	Y	Y	Y	N

Withholding	**Allowances**	**Extra**	**Status**	**State Lived**	**State Worked**
Federal	0	0.00	Married		
State	0	0.00	Married (two incomes)	CA	CA

Earnings

Name	**Hourly/Annual Rate**
Hourly	15.00

Addition, Deduction, Commission, Company Contributions

Name	**Amount**	**Limit**

Figure 2.24 (Concluded)

Employee	Kelly Jennings		SS No.	854-60-7882
Type	Regular			
Address	Kelly Jennings		Hired	01/01/2004
	2333 Dire Straits Rd.			
	San Martin, CA 93107		Salary	48,000.00

Accrual	Rate	Accrued	Limit	Used	By Year/Period	Reset Hrs
Sick	0:00	0:00		0:00	Y	N
Vacation	0:00	0:00		0:00	Y	N

	FUTA:	Soc. Sec.:	Medicare:	SDI	SUI	AEIC
Subject To	Y	Y	Y	Y	Y	N

Withholding	Allowances	Extra	Status	State Lived	State Worked
Federal	0	0.00	Head of Household		
State	0	0.00	Head of Household	CA	CA

Earnings

Name	Hour/Annual Rate
Salary	48,000.00

Addition, Deduction, Commission, Company Contributions

Name	Amount	Limit

Figure 2.25

Chart of Accounts

Account	Type	Income Tax Line
First Valley Savings & Loan	Bank	<Unassigned>
Union Bank	Bank	<Unassigned>
Accounts Receivable	Accounts Receivable	<Unassigned>
Inventory Asset	Other Current Asset	<Unassigned>
Unbilled Client Costs	Other Current Asset	<Unassigned>
Computer Equipment	Other Asset	<Unassigned>
Furniture	Other Asset	<Unassigned>
Accounts Payable	Accounts Payable	<Unassigned>
Client Advance Payments	Other Current Liability	<Unassigned>
Payroll Liabilities	Other Current Liability	<Unassigned>
Sales Tax Payable	Other Current Liability	<Unassigned>
Bank of San Martin	Long Term Liability	<Unassigned>
Capital Stock	Equity	<Unassigned>
Opening Bal Equity	Equity	<Unassigned>
Retained Earnings	Equity	<Unassigned>
Fee Income	Income	Income: Gross receipts or sales
Events	Income	Income: Gross receipts or sales
Film	Income	<Unassigned>
Press Release	Income	Income: Gross receipts or sales
Reimbursed Expenses	Income	Income: Gross receipts or sales
Uncategorized Income	Income	<Unassigned>
Cost of Goods Sold	Cost of Goods Sold	<Unassigned>
Film Expenses	Cost of Goods Sold	<Unassigned>
Automobile Expense	Expense	Deductions: Other deductions
Bank Service Charges	Expense	Deductions: Other deductions
Cash Discounts	Expense	<Unassigned>
Contract Labor	Expense	<Unassigned>
Contributions	Expense	Deductions: Charitable contr...
Depreciation Expense	Expense	<Unassigned>
Dues and Subscriptions	Expense	Deductions: Other deductions
Equipment Rental	Expense	Deductions: Other deductions
Insurance	Expense	Deductions: Other deductions
Disability Insurance	Expense	Deductions: Other deductions
Liability Insurance	Expense	Deductions: Other deductions
Work Comp	Expense	Deductions: Other deductions

Figure 2.25 (Continued)

Account	Type	Income Tax Line
Interest Expense	Expense	Deductions: Interest expense
Finance Charge	Expense	Deductions: Interest expense
Loan Interest	Expense	Deductions: Interest expense
Mortgage	Expense	<Unassigned>
Licenses and Permits	Expense	Deductions: Licenses
Mechanical Prep	Expense	Deductions: Other deductions
Miscellaneous	Expense	Deductions: Other deductions
Office Supplies	Expense	Deductions: Other deductions
Payroll Expenses	Expense	<Unassigned>
Postage and Delivery	Expense	Deductions: Other deductions
Printing and Reproduction	Expense	Deductions: Other deductions
Professional Development	Expense	Deductions: Other deductions
Professional Fees	Expense	Deductions: Other deductions
Accounting	Expense	Deductions: Other deductions
Consulting	Expense	Deductions: Other deductions
Legal Fees	Expense	Deductions: Other deductions
Reference Materials	Expense	Deductions: Other deductions
Rent	Expense	Deductions: Rents
Repairs	Expense	Deductions: Repairs and mai...
Building Repairs	Expense	Deductions: Repairs and mai...
Computer Repairs	Expense	Deductions: Repairs and mai...
Equipment Repairs	Expense	Deductions: Repairs and mai..
Service Bureau	Expense	Deductions: Other deductions
Supplies	Expense	Deductions: Other deductions
Marketing	Expense	Deductions: Other deductions
Office	Expense	Deductions: Other deductions
Taxes	Expense	Deductions: Other misc. taxes
Federal	Expense	<Unassigned>
Local	Expense	Deductions: Other miscellan...
Property	Expense	Deductions: Local property ...
State	Expense	Deductions: State taxes
Telephone	Expense	Deductions: Other deductions
Travel & Ent	Expense	<Unassigned>
Entertainment	Expense	Deductions: Meals and entert...
Meals	Expense	Deductions: Meals and entert...
Travel	Expense	<Unassigned>

Chapter 2

Figure 2.25 (Concluded)

Account	Type	Income Tax Line
Uncategorized Expenses	Expense	<Unassigned>
Utilities	Expense	Deductions: Other deductions
Gas and Electric	Expense	Deductions: Other deductions
Water	Expense	Deductions: Other deductions
Interest Income	Other Income	Income: Interest income
Other Income	Other Income	Income: Other income
Other Expenses	Other Expense	Deductions: Other deductions

3

Cash-Oriented Business Activities

In Chapter 3 students learn how to record cash-oriented transactions classified as financing, investing, and operating activities. The concepts of operating, investing, and financing activities are emphasized in this chapter and these basic types of business activities are reinforced. This chapter focuses on cash transactions to introduce students to the accounting process. Additional transactions, including non-cash events, are covered in Chapter 4.

Chapter 3 Questions

1. Operating activities occur when the money obtained from financing activities and the long-term assets obtained from investing activities are applied either to purchase or produce goods and services for sale. Operating activities are substantially completed when goods are delivered or sold and when services are performed. Financing activities, on the other hand, are initiated when money or other resources are obtained from short-term non-trade creditors, long-term creditors, and owners. Financing activities are completed when amounts owed are repaid to or otherwise settled with these same creditors and owners. Investing activities are initiated when the money obtained from financing activities is applied to non-operating uses, such as buying investment securities and productive equipment. Investing activities are completed when the productive equipment or investment securities are sold.

2. The Make Deposits menu item is in the Banking menu, which opens the Make Deposit window.

3. To create a new account in QuickBooks:

    a. Open the Chart of Accounts window by clicking the Chart of Accounts item from the Company menu, Navigators list, or account icon.

    b. Click Account, then New.

    c. Select an account type (Cash, Accounts Receivable, etc.).

    d. Enter a name, description, and subaccount if appropriate.

4. To write a QuickBooks check:

    a. Open the Write Checks window by clicking the Write Checks item from the Banking menu or Navigators list or check icon.

    b. Select a bank account from the drop-down list.

    c. Enter the date, payee, amount, and account.

    d. Click Save & Close for a single check or Save & New to continue entering checks.

5. To create a purchase order in QuickBooks:

    a. Open the Purchase Order window by clicking the Create Purchase Orders item from the Vendors menu.

    b. Select a vendor from the drop-down list.

    c. Enter the date, PO number, items, and quantity.

    d. Click Save & Close for a single purchase order or Save & New to continue entering purchase orders.

6. To record the receipt and payment of inventory you can write a QuickBooks check:

    a. Open the Write Checks window by clicking the Write Checks item from the Banking menu or Navigators list.

    b. Select a bank account from the drop-down list.

    c. Enter the date, payee, amount, item, and quantity (enter this information after clicking the Items tab).

    d. Click Save & Close for a single check or Save & New to continue entering checks.

7. To record cash sales in QuickBooks:

    a. Open the Enter Cash Sales window by clicking the Enter Sales Receipts item from the Customers menu.

    b. Select a customer from the drop-down list.

    c. Enter the date, sale number, item, quantity.

    d. Select either Group with other undeposited funds or Deposit To.

    e.   If you selected Deposit To, select a bank account to deposit funds to from the drop-down list.

    f.   Click Save & Close for a single cash sale or Save & New to continue entering cash sales.

8.   To record the receipt of cash payments in QuickBooks:

    a.   Open the Receive Payments window by clicking the Receive Payments item from the Customers menu or Navigators list.

    b.   Select a customer from the drop-down list.

    c.   Enter the date, amount, and customer:job.

    d.   Select either Group with other undeposited funds or Deposit To.

    e.   If you selected Deposit To, select a bank account to deposit funds to from the drop-down list.

    f.   Match invoices and payments from the Outstanding Invoices/Statement Charges window (Match Discount Info if applicable).

    g.   Click Save & Close for a single payment or Save & New to continue entering payments.

9.   To record payroll in QuickBooks:

    a.   Open the Pay Employees window by clicking the Pay Employees menu item from the Employees menu or Navigators list.

    b.   Choose To be printed if appropriate.

    c.   Select a bank account from the drop-down list.

    d.   Enter the check date and pay period end date.

    e.   Select employees to pay.

    f.   Click Create to create the payroll information.

    g.   For each employee, enter hours (if hourly employee), related tax information and then click Create to enter payroll data.

    h.   When all employees' payroll data for the period is entered, click Leave in the Select Employees to Pay window.

10. All employee data originates from the information entered in the employee list.

Chapter 3   Assignments

1. Adding More Information to Phoenix Systems, Inc.

    a.   The completed Balance Sheet is shown in Figure 3.1. *[Solution figures for Chapter 3 begin on page 101.]*

    b.   The completed Income Statement is shown in Figure 3.2.

2. Adding more information to Central Coast Cellular.

    Items a.–l. have no output required.

    m.   Item *m* requires three outputs.
    *   The completed Profit & Loss statement is shown in Figure 3.3.
    *   The completed Balance Sheet is shown in Figure 3.4.
    *   The completed Transaction Report is shown in Figure 3.5.

3. Internet assignments and related solutions are found at *http://owen.swlearning.com.*

Chapter 3   Case Problems

1. Ocean View Flowers

    a.   The completed Balance Sheet is shown in Figure 3.6.

    b.   The completed Profit & Loss statement is shown in Figure 3.7.

    c.   The completed Transactions Report is shown in Figure 3.8.

2. Jennings & Associates—Cash-Oriented Activities

    a.   The completed Balance Sheet is shown in Figure 3.9.

    b.   The completed Profit & Loss statement is shown in Figure 3.10

Chapter 3   Comprehensive Problem 1—Sarah Duncan

1. The Custom Transaction Detail Report is shown in Figure 3.11.

2. The Standard Balance Sheet is shown in Figure 3.12.

3. The Standard Profit & Loss statement is shown in Figure 3.13.

4. The Statement of Cash Flows is shown in Figure 3.14.

Chapter 3 Comprehensive Problem 2—Pacific Brew

1.   The Chart of Accounts is shown in Figure 3.15.

2.   The Customer:Job List is shown in Figure 3.16.

3.   The Employee List is shown in Figure 3.17.

4.   The Item List is shown in Figure 3.18.

5.   The Vendor List is shown in Figure 3.19.

6.   The Customer Transaction Detail Report is shown in Figure 3.20.

7.   The Standard Balance Sheet is shown in Figure 3.21.

8.   The Standard Profit & Loss Statement is shown in Figure 3.22.

9.   The Statement of Cash Flows is shown in Figure 3.23.

Chapter 3 Comprehensive Problem 3—Sunset Spas

1.   n/a

2.   n/a

3.   n/a

4.   Lists:

   a.   The Chart of Accounts is shown in Figure 3.24.

   b.   The Customer: Job List is shown in Figure 3.25.

   c.   The Item List is shown in Figure 3.26.

   d.   The Vendor List is shown in Figure 3.27.

   e.   The Employee List is shown in Figure 3.28.

5.   Reports:

   a.   The Custom Transaction Detail Report is shown in Figure 3.29.

   b.   The Inventory Valuation Summary is shown in Figure 3.30.

   c.   The Summary Balance Sheet is shown in Figure 3.31.

   d.   The Standard Profit & Loss Statement is shown in Figure 3.32.

   e.   The Statement of Cash Flows is shown in Figure 3.33.

Solution Figures for Chapter 3

Figure 3.1

Phoenix Software 03CP
Balance Sheet
As of March 31, 2003

	Mar 31, '03
ASSETS	
Current Assets	
Checking/Savings	
Bank of Cupertino	28,318.78
Short-term Investments	8,000.00
Total Checking/Savings	36,318.78
Accounts Receivable	
Accounts Receivable	-9,000.00
Total Accounts Receivable	-9,000.00
Other Current Assets	
Inventory Asset	19,029.90
Investments	50,000.00
Prepaid Insurance	1,384.67
Prepaid Rent	1,600.00
Undeposited Funds	897.46
Total Other Current Assets	72,912.03
Total Current Assets	100,230.81
Fixed Assets	
Furniture	
Cost	3,756.44
Total Furniture	3,756.44
Computer Equipment	
Cost	6,750.00
Total Computer Equipment	6,750.00
Total Fixed Assets	10,506.44
TOTAL ASSETS	**110,737.25**
LIABILITIES & EQUITY	
Liabilities	
Current Liabilities	
Accounts Payable	
Accounts Payable	15,199.75
Total Accounts Payable	15,199.75
Other Current Liabilities	
Short-Term Debt	3,000.00
Payroll Liabilities	7,992.81
Sales Tax Payable	1,218.74
Total Other Current Liabilities	12,211.55
Total Current Liabilities	27,411.30
Long Term Liabilities	
Long-Term Debt	25,000.00
Total Long Term Liabilities	25,000.00
Total Liabilities	52,411.30
Equity	
Capital Stock	75,000.00
Net Income	-16,674.05
Total Equity	58,325.95
TOTAL LIABILITIES & EQUITY	**110,737.25**

Figure 3.2

Phoenix Software 03CP
Profit and Loss
January through March 2003

	Jan - Mar 03
Ordinary Income/Expense	
Income	
Computer Add-ons	1,100.00
Computer Sales	10,800.00
Consulting Income	3,750.00
Maintenance & Repairs	450.00
Parts income	149.85
Total Income	16,249.85
Cost of Goods Sold	
Cost of Goods Sold	10,019.85
Total COGS	10,019.85
Gross Profit	6,230.00
Expense	
Bank Service Charges	45.00
Payroll Expenses	22,859.05
Total Expense	22,904.05
Net Ordinary Income	-16,674.05
Net Income	**-16,674.05**

Figure 3.3

Central Coast Cellular
Profit & Loss
January 2003

	Jan 03
Ordinary Income/Expense	
Income	
Consulting	4,750.00
Phone Sales	2,125.00
Total Income	6,875.00
Cost of Goods Sold	
Cost of Goods Sold	1,250.00
Total COGS	1,250.00
Gross Profit	5,625.00
Expense	
Payroll Expenses	4,873.44
Rent	3,000.00
Total Expense	7,873.44
Net Ordinary Income	-2,248.44
Net Income	**-2,248.44**

Figure 3.4

Central Coast Cellular
Balance Sheet
As of January 17, 2003

	Jan 17, 03
ASSETS	
Current Assets	
Checking/Savings	
Checking	235,220.49
Total Checking/Savings	235,220.49
Accounts Receivable	
Accounts Receivable	-10,000.00
Total Accounts Receivable	-10,000.00
Other Current Assets	
Store Supplies	3,000.00
Inventory Asset	5,250.00
Short-term Investments	75,000.00
Total Other Current Assets	83,250.00
Total Current Assets	308,470.49
Fixed Assets	
Office Furniture	
Cost	20,000.00
Total Furniture	20,000.00
Total Fixed Assets	20,000.00
Other Assets	
Security Deposit	3,000.00
Total Other Assets	3,000.00
TOTAL ASSETS	331,470.49
LIABILITIES & EQUITY	
Liabilities	
Current Liabilities	
Accounts Payable	
Accounts Payable	6,500.00
Total Accounts Payable	6,500.00
Other Current Liabilities	
Payroll Liabilities	1,668.93
Sales Tax Payable	550.00
Total Other Current Liabilities	2,218.93
Total Current Liabilities	8,718.93
Long Term Liabilities	
Notes Payable	125,000.00
Total Long-Term Liabilities	125,000.00
Total Liabilities	133,718.93
Equity	
Common Stock	200,000.00
Net Income	-2,248.44
Total Equity	197,751.56
TOTAL LIABILITIES & EQUITY	**331,470.49**

Figure 3.5

Central Coast Cellular
Custom Transaction Detail Report
January 1-17, 2003

Type	Date	Num	Name	Memo	Account	Cir	Split	Amount	Balance
Jan 1 – 17, 03									
Deposit	1/3/2003		Van Morrison	Deposit	Checking		Common Stock	200,000.00	200,000.00
Deposit	1/3/2003		Van Morrison	25,000 shares	Common Stock		Checking	-200,000.00	0.00
Check	1/6/2003	3001	Schwab Investments		Checking		Short-term Inv...	-75,000.00	-75,000.00
Check	1/6/2003	3001	Schwab Investments		Short-term Investm...		Checking	75,000.00	0.00
Deposit	1/7/2003		Wells Fargo Bank	Deposit	Checking		Notes Payable	125,000.00	125,000.00
Deposit	1/7/2003		Wells Fargo Bank	5 yr, 8%	Notes Payable		Checking	-125,000.00	0.00
Check	1/8/2003	3002	Russco		Checking		Cost	-20,000.00	-20,000.00
Check	1/8/2003	3002	Russco		Cost		Checking	20,000.00	0.00
Check	1/10/2003	3003	Russco		Checking		Store Supplies	-3,000.00	-3,000.00
Check	1/10/2003	3003	Russco		Store Supplies		Checking	3,000.00	0.00
Check	1/13/2003	3004	Central Coast Leasi...	Rent - January	Checking		-SPLIT-	-6,000.00	-6,000.00
Check	1/13/2003	3004	Central Coast Leasi...	Rent - January	Rent		Checking	3,000.00	-3,000.00
Check	1/13/2003	3004	Central Coast Leasi...	Rent - January	Security Deposit		Checking	3,000.00	0.00
Payment	1/14/2003		City of San Luis Obi...	Adv pay...	Checking		Accounts Rec...	10,000.00	10,000.00
Payment	1/14/2003		City of San Luis Obi...	Adv pay...	Accounts Receivable		Checking	-10,000.00	0.00
Item Receipt	1/15/2003	PO101	Ericsson, Inc.	Received ite...	Accounts Payable		-SPLIT-	-6,500.00	-6,500.00
Item Receipt	1/15/2003	PO101	Ericsson, Inc.	Ericsson LX5...	Inventory Asset		Accounts Pay...	2,000.00	-4,500.00
Item Receipt	1/15/2003	PO101	Ericsson, Inc.	Ericsson T19...	Inventory Asset		Accounts Pay...	4,500.00	0.00
Sales Receipt	1/16/2003	501	Sterling Hotels Corp...		Checking		-SPLIT-	7,425.00	7,425.00
Sales Receipt	1/16/2003	501	Sterling Hotels Corp...	Consulting...	Consulting		Checking	-4,750.00	2,675.00
Sales Receipt	1/16/2003	501	Sterling Hotels Corp...	Ericsson LX5...	Phone Sales		Checking	-2,125.00	550.00
Sales Receipt	1/16/2003	501	Sterling Hotels Corp...	Ericsson LX5...	Inventory Asset		Checking	-1,250.00	-700.00
Sales Receipt	1/16/2003	501	Sterling Hotels Corp...	Ericsson LX5...	Cost of Goods Sold		Checking	1,250.00	550.00
Sales Receipt	1/16/2003	501	State Board of Equ...	Sales Tax	Sales Tax Payable		Checking	-550.00	0.00
Paycheck	1/17/2003	3005	Alex Rodriguez		Checking		-SPLIT-	-1,437.00	-1,437.00
Paycheck	1/17/2003	3005	Alex Rodriguez		Payroll Expenses		Checking	2,000.00	563.00
Paycheck	1/17/2003	3005	Alex Rodriguez		Payroll Liabilities		Checking	-300.00	263.00
Paycheck	1/17/2003	3005	Alex Rodriguez		Payroll Expenses		Checking	124.00	387.00
Paycheck	1/17/2003	3005	Alex Rodriguez		Payroll Liabilities		Checking	-124.00	263.00
Paycheck	1/17/2003	3005	Alex Rodriguez		Payroll Expenses		Checking	-125.00	139.00
Paycheck	1/17/2003	3005	Alex Rodriguez		Payroll Expenses		Checking	29.00	168.00
Paycheck	1/17/2003	3005	Alex Rodriguez		Payroll Liabilities		Checking	-29.00	139.00
Paycheck	1/17/2003	3005	Alex Rodriguez		Payroll Liabilities		Checking	-29.00	110.00
Paycheck	1/17/2003	3005	Alex Rodriguez		Payroll Expenses		Checking	6.40	116.40
Paycheck	1/17/2003	3005	Alex Rodriguez		Payroll Liabilities		Checking	-6.40	110.00
Paycheck	1/17/2003	3005	Alex Rodriguez		Payroll Liabilities		Checking	-100.00	10.00
Paycheck	1/17/2003	3005	Alex Rodriguez		Payroll Liabilities		Checking	-10.00	0.00
Paycheck	1/17/2003	3005	Alex Rodriguez		Payroll Liabilities		Checking	24.00	24.00
Paycheck	1/17/2003	3005	Alex Rodriguez		Payroll Liabilities		Checking	-24.00	0.00
Paycheck	1/17/2003	3005	Alex Rodriguez		Payroll Liabilities		Checking	2.00	2.00
Paycheck	1/17/2003	3005	Alex Rodriguez		Payroll Liabilities		Checking	-2.00	0.00
Paycheck	1/17/2003	3006	Jay Bruner		Checking		-SPLIT-	-1,077.75	-1,077.75
Paycheck	1/17/2003	3006	Jay Bruner		Payroll Expenses		Checking	1,500.00	422.25
Paycheck	1/17/2003	3006	Jay Bruner		Payroll Liabilities		Checking	-225.00	197.25
Paycheck	1/17/2003	3006	Jay Bruner		Payroll Expenses		Checking	93.00	290.25
Paycheck	1/17/2003	3006	Jay Bruner		Payroll Liabilities		Checking	-93.00	197.25
Paycheck	1/17/2003	3006	Jay Bruner		Payroll Liabilities		Checking	-93.00	104.25
Paycheck	1/17/2003	3006	Jay Bruner		Payroll Expenses		Checking	21.75	126.00

Figure 3.5
(Concluded)

Central Coast Cellular
Custom Transaction Detail Report
January 1-17, 2003

Type	Date	Num	Name	Memo	Account	Clr	Split	Amount	Balance
Paycheck	1/17/2003	3006	Jay Bruner		Payroll Liabilities		Checking	-21.75	104.25
Paycheck	1/17/2003	3006	Jay Bruner		Payroll Liabilities		Checking	-21.75	82.50
Paycheck	1/17/2003	3006	Jay Bruner		Payroll Expenses		Checking	4.80	87.30
Paycheck	1/17/2003	3006	Jay Bruner		Payroll Liabilities		Checking	-4.80	82.50
Paycheck	1/17/2003	3006	Jay Bruner		Payroll Liabilities		Checking	-75.00	7.50
Paycheck	1/17/2003	3006	Jay Bruner		Payroll Liabilities		Checking	-7.50	0.00
Paycheck	1/17/2003	3006	Jay Bruner		Payroll Expenses		Checking	18.00	18.00
Paycheck	1/17/2003	3006	Jay Bruner		Payroll Liabilities		Checking	-18.00	0.00
Paycheck	1/17/2003	3006	Jay Bruner		Payroll Liabilities		Checking	1.50	1.50
Paycheck	1/17/2003	3006	Jay Bruner		Payroll Liabilities		Checking	-1.50	0.00
Paycheck	1/17/2003	3007	Megan Paulson		Checking		-SPLIT-	-689.76	-689.76
Paycheck	1/17/2003	3007	Megan Paulson		Payroll Expenses		Checking	960.00	270.24
Paycheck	1/17/2003	3007	Megan Paulson		Payroll Liabilities		Checking	-144.00	126.24
Paycheck	1/17/2003	3007	Megan Paulson		Payroll Expenses		Checking	59.52	185.76
Paycheck	1/17/2003	3007	Megan Paulson		Payroll Liabilities		Checking	-59.52	126.24
Paycheck	1/17/2003	3007	Megan Paulson		Payroll Liabilities		Checking	-59.52	66.72
Paycheck	1/17/2003	3007	Megan Paulson		Payroll Expenses		Checking	13.92	80.64
Paycheck	1/17/2003	3007	Megan Paulson		Payroll Liabilities		Checking	-13.92	66.72
Paycheck	1/17/2003	3007	Megan Paulson		Payroll Liabilities		Checking	-13.92	52.80
Paycheck	1/17/2003	3007	Megan Paulson		Payroll Expenses		Checking	3.07	55.87
Paycheck	1/17/2003	3007	Megan Paulson		Payroll Liabilities		Checking	-3.07	52.80
Paycheck	1/17/2003	3007	Megan Paulson		Payroll Liabilities		Checking	-48.00	4.80
Paycheck	1/17/2003	3007	Megan Paulson		Payroll Liabilities		Checking	-4.80	0.00
Paycheck	1/17/2003	3007	Megan Paulson		Payroll Expenses		Checking	11.52	11.52
Paycheck	1/17/2003	3007	Megan Paulson		Payroll Liabilities		Checking	-11.52	0.00
Paycheck	1/17/2003	3007	Megan Paulson		Payroll Expenses		Checking	0.96	0.96
Paycheck	1/17/2003	3007	Megan Paulson		Payroll Liabilities		Checking	-0.96	0.00
Jan1 –17, 03								0.00	0.00

Figure 3.6

Ocean View Flowers
Balance Sheet
As of January 31, 2004

	Jan 31, 04
ASSETS	
Current Assets	
Checking/Savings	
Union Checking	70,862.94
Total Checking/Savings	70,862.94
Accounts Receivable	
Accounts Receivable	-5,000.00
Total Accounts Receivable	-5,000.00
Other Current Assets	
Inventory Asset	20,100.00
Office Supplies	1,500.00
Short-Term Investments	25,000.00
Total Other Current Assets	46,600.00
Total Current Assets	112,462.94
Fixed Assets	
Computer Equipment	
Cost	15,000.00
Total Computer Equipment	15,000.00
Office Equipment	
Cost	20,000.00
Total Office Equipment	20,000.00
Total Fixed Assets	35,000.00
TOTAL ASSETS	**147,462.94**
LIABILITIES & EQUITY	
Liabilities	
Current Liabilities	
Other Current Liabilities	
Payroll Liabilities	7,178.84
Total Other Current Liabilities	7,178.84
Total Current Liabilities	7,178.84
Long Term Liabilities	
Note Payable	50,000.00
Total Long-Term Liabilities	50,000.00
Total Liabilities	57,178.84
Equity	
Common Stock	100,000.00
Net Income	-9,715.90
Total Equity	90,284.10
TOTAL LIABILITIES & EQUITY	**147,462.94**

Figure 3.7

Ocean View Flowers
Profit and Loss
January 2004

	Jan 04
Ordinary Income/Expense	
Income	
Sales	
Daylilies	28,800.00
Total Sales	28,800.00
Total Income	28,800.00
Cost of Goods Sold	
Cost of Goods Sold	14,400.00
Total COGS	14,400.00
Gross Profit	14,400.00
Expense	
Payroll Expenses	20,215.90
Rent	3,000.00
Telephone	400.00
Utilities	
Gas and Electric	500.00
Total Utilities	500.00
Total Expense	24,115.90
Net Ordinary Income	-9,715.90
Net Income	**-9,715.90**

Figure 3.8

Ocean View Flowers
Transaction List by Date
January 2004

Type	Date	Num	Name	Memo	Account	Clr	Split	Amount
Jan '04								
Deposit	1/4/2004			Deposit	Union Checking		Common Stock	100,000.00
Deposit	1/6/2004			Deposit	Union Checking		Long-Term Note Payable	50,000.00
Check	1/8/2004				Union Checking		Short-term investments	-25,000.00
Check	1/11/2004	101	Prudent Investments		Union Checking		Cost	-20,000.00
Check	1/12/2004	102	Stateside Office Su...		Union Checking		Cost	-15,000.00
Paycheck	1/15/2004	103	Gateway Computers		Union Checking		-SPLIT-	-1,819.67
Paycheck	1/15/2004	104	Edward Thomas		Union Checking		-SPLIT-	-689.33
Paycheck	1/15/2004	105	Kelly Gusland		Union Checking		-SPLIT-	-699.33
Paycheck	1/15/2004	106	Margie Coe		Union Checking		-SPLIT-	-1,740.70
Check	1/15/2004	107	Marie McAninch		Union Checking		-SPLIT-	-1,565.67
Check	1/18/2004	108	Stan Comstock		Union Checking		-SPLIT-	-34,500.00
Check	1/20/2004	109	Brophy Bros. Farms		Union Checking		Office Supplies	-1,500.00
Cash Sale	1/22/2004	110	Stateside Office Su...		Union Checking		-SPLIT-	6,600.00
Cash Sale	1/25/2004	1	Valley Florists		Union Checking		-SPLIT-	22,200.00
Payment	1/28/2004	2	Eastern Scents		Union Checking		Accounts Receivable	5,000.00
Check	1/29/2004	111	FTD		Union Checking		Rent	-3,000.00
Check	1/29/2004	112	Hawaiian Farms		Union Checking		Utilities	-500.00
Check	1/29/2004	113	Edison Inc.		Union Checking		Telephone	-400.00
Paycheck	1/29/2004	114	GTE		Union Checking		-SPLIT-	-1,819.65
Paycheck	1/29/2004	115	Edward Thomas		Union Checking		-SPLIT-	-741.90
Paycheck	1/29/2004	116	Kelly Gusland		Union Checking		-SPLIT-	-654.42
Paycheck	1/29/2004	117	Margie Coe		Union Checking		-SPLIT-	-1,740.70
Paycheck	1/29/2004	118	Marie McAninch		Union Checking		-SPLIT-	-1,565.69
Jan '04			Stan Comstock					

Figure 3.9

Jennings & Associates (KJ03cp)
Balance Sheet
As of February 29, 2004

	Feb 29, '04
ASSETS	
Current Assets	
Checking/Savings	
First Valley Savings & Loan	63,275.00
Union Bank Checking	7,050.49
Total Checking/Savings	70,325.49
Accounts Receivable	
Accounts Receivable	9,902.50
Total Accounts Receivable	9,902.50
Other Current Assets	
Interest Receivable	41.17
Inventory Asset	832.79
Prepaid Insurance	2,200.00
Short-term investments	5,000.00
Total Other Current Assets	8,073.96
Total Current Assets	88,301.95
Fixed Assets	
Computer Equipment	
Accumulated Depreciation	-1,083.33
Cost	7,000.00
Total Computer Equipment	5,916.67
Furniture	
Accumulated Depreciation	-541.67
Cost	2,500.00
Total Furniture	1,958.33
Total Fixed Assets	7,875.00
TOTAL ASSETS	**96,176.95**
LIABILITIES & EQUITY	
Liabilities	
Current Liabilities	
Accounts Payable	
Accounts Payable	6,184.00
Total Accounts Payable	6,184.00
Other Current Liabilities	
Payroll Liabilities	6,694.08
Total Other Current Liabilities	6,694.08
Total Current Liabilities	12,878.08
Long Term Liabilities	
Bank of San Martin	5,000.00
Total Long Term Liabilities	5,000.00
Total Liabilities	17,878.08
Equity	
Capital Stock	70,000.00
Opening Bal Equity	3,590.00
Retained Earnings	2,250.00
Net Income	2,458.87
Total Equity	78,298.87
TOTAL LIABILITIES & EQUITY	**96,176.95**

Figure 3.10

Jennings & Associates (KJ03cp)
Profit & Loss
February 2004

	Feb 04
Ordinary Income/Expense	
Income	
Fee Income	
Film	440.00
Magazine	7,500.00
Promotion	3,325.00
Total Fee Income	11,265.00
Total Income	11,265.00
Gross Profit	11,265.00
Expense	
Film expenses	290.05
Office Supplies	75.00
Payroll Expenses	9,568.99
Total Expense	9,934.04
Net Ordinary Income	1,330.96
Net Income	**1,330.96**

Figure 3.11 Comprehensive Problem 1, Custom Transaction Detail Report, page 1

Sarah Duncan, CPA
Custom Transaction Detail Report
September 2004

Type	Date	Num	Name	Memo	Account	Clr	Split	Amount	Balance
Sep 04									
Deposit	9/1/2004	dep	Common Stock	From Sarah ...	Union Bank Checking		Common Stock	50,000.00	50,000.00
Deposit	9/1/2004	dep	Common Stock	From Sarah ...	Common Stock		Union Bank C...	-50,000.00	0.00
Check	9/4/2004	1001	Sam Sneed	Purchased F...	Union Bank Checking		Cost	-4,000.00	-4,000.00
Check	9/4/2004	1001	Sam Sneed	Purchased F...	Cost		Union Bank C...	4,000.00	0.00
Check	9/5/2004	1002	Dean Witter		Union Bank Checking		Investment - D...	-15,000.00	-15,000.00
Check	9/5/2004	1002	Dean Witter		Investment - Dean ...		Union Bank C...	15,000.00	0.00
Check	9/6/2004	1003	Wiser Realty	Rent, Last M...	Union Bank Checking		-SPLIT-	-3,000.00	-3,000.00
Check	9/6/2004	1003	Wiser Realty	First Months ...	Rent		Union Bank C...	1,000.00	-2,000.00
Check	9/6/2004	1003	Wiser Realty	Last Months ...	Prepaid Rent		Union Bank C...	1,000.00	-1,000.00
Check	9/6/2004	1003	Wiser Realty	Rent Security...	Security Deposit		Union Bank C...	1,000.00	0.00
Sales Receipt	9/8/2004	1	Valley Medical Group		Union Bank Checking		Individual Taxes	4,500.00	4,500.00
Sales Receipt	9/8/2004	1	Valley Medical Group	Income Tax ...	Individual Taxes		Union Bank C...	-4,500.00	0.00
Sales Receipt	9/11/2004	2	Pactuco, Inc	Auditing	Union Bank Checking		Audit	6,000.00	6,000.00
Sales Receipt	9/11/2004	2	Pactuco, Inc		Audit		Union Bank C...	-6,000.00	0.00
Deposit	9/13/2004		Celite Corporation	Deposit	Union Bank Checking		Customer Dep...	5,000.00	5,000.00
Deposit	9/13/2004		Celite Corporation	Advance pay...	Customer Deposits		Union Bank C...	-5,000.00	0.00
Deposit	9/20/2004		Wells Fargo Bank	Wells Fargo...	Union Bank Checking		Loan -Wells F...	3,000.00	3,000.00
Deposit	9/20/2004		Wells Fargo Bank	Loan for Xero...	Loan -Wells Fargo ...		Union Bank C...	-3,000.00	0.00
Check	9/20/2004	1007	Xerox Corporation	New Xerox M...	Union Bank Checking		Cost	-3,000.00	-3,000.00
Check	9/20/2004	1007	Xerox Corporation	New Xerox M...	Cost		Union Bank C...	3,000.00	0.00
Check	9/25/2004	1004	AICPA	50 Tax Guide...	Inventory Asset		Inventory Asset	-250.00	-250.00
Check	9/25/2004	1004	AICPA	Tax Guide	Inventory Asset		Union Bank C...	250.00	0.00
Sales Receipt	9/28/2004	3	Lompoc Hospital	Auditing	Union Bank Checking		Audit	7,500.00	7,500.00
Sales Receipt	9/28/2004	3	Lompoc Hospital		Audit		Union Bank C...	-7,500.00	0.00
Paycheck	9/30/2004	1005	Bob Humphrey		Union Bank Checking		-SPLIT-	-877.92	-877.92
Paycheck	9/30/2004	1005	Bob Humphrey		Payroll Expenses		Union Bank C...	960.00	82.08
Paycheck	9/30/2004	1005	Bob Humphrey		Payroll Liabilities		Union Bank C...	0.00	82.08
Paycheck	9/30/2004	1005	Bob Humphrey		Payroll Expenses		Union Bank C...	59.52	141.60
Paycheck	9/30/2004	1005	Bob Humphrey		Payroll Liabilities		Union Bank C...	-59.52	82.08
Paycheck	9/30/2004	1005	Bob Humphrey		Payroll Liabilities		Union Bank C...	-59.52	22.56
Paycheck	9/30/2004	1005	Bob Humphrey		Payroll Expenses		Union Bank C...	13.92	36.48
Paycheck	9/30/2004	1005	Bob Humphrey		Payroll Liabilities		Union Bank C...	-13.92	22.56
Paycheck	9/30/2004	1005	Bob Humphrey		Payroll Liabilities		Union Bank C...	-13.92	8.64
Paycheck	9/30/2004	1005	Bob Humphrey		Payroll Expenses		Union Bank C...	7.68	16.32
Paycheck	9/30/2004	1005	Bob Humphrey		Payroll Liabilities		Union Bank C...	-7.68	8.64
Paycheck	9/30/2004	1005	Bob Humphrey		Payroll Liabilities		Union Bank C...	-8.64	0.00
Paycheck	9/30/2004	1005	Bob Humphrey		Payroll Expenses		Union Bank C...	9.60	9.60
Paycheck	9/30/2004	1005	Bob Humphrey		Payroll Liabilities		Union Bank C...	-9.60	0.00
Paycheck	9/30/2004	1005	Bob Humphrey		Payroll Expenses		Union Bank C...	0.96	0.96
Paycheck	9/30/2004	1005	Bob Humphrey		Payroll Liabilities		Union Bank C...	-0.96	0.00
Paycheck	9/30/2004	1006	Sarah Duncan		Union Bank Checking		-SPLIT-	-2,543.50	-2,543.50
Paycheck	9/30/2004	1006	Sarah Duncan		Payroll Expenses		Union Bank C...	3,000.00	456.50
Paycheck	9/30/2004	1006	Sarah Duncan		Payroll Liabilities		Union Bank C...	-200.00	256.50
Paycheck	9/30/2004	1006	Sarah Duncan		Payroll Expenses		Union Bank C...	186.00	442.50
Paycheck	9/30/2004	1006	Sarah Duncan		Payroll Liabilities		Union Bank C...	256.50	256.50
Paycheck	9/30/2004	1006	Sarah Duncan		Payroll Expenses		Union Bank C...	-186.00	70.50
Paycheck	9/30/2004	1006	Sarah Duncan		Payroll Liabilities		Union Bank C...	114.00	114.00
Paycheck	9/30/2004	1006	Sarah Duncan		Payroll Expenses		Union Bank C...	70.50	70.50
Paycheck	9/30/2004	1006	Sarah Duncan		Payroll Liabilities		Union Bank C...	-43.50	70.50

Figure 3.11 Comprehensive Problem 1, Custom Transaction Detail Report, page 2

Sarah Duncan, CPA
Custom Transaction Detail Report
September 2004

Type	Date	Num	Name	Memo	Account	Clr	Split	Amount	Balance
Paycheck	9/30/2004	1006	Sarah Duncan		Payroll Liabilities		Union Bank C...	-43.50	27.00
Paycheck	9/30/2004	1006	Sarah Duncan		Payroll Expenses		Union Bank C...	24.00	51.00
Paycheck	9/30/2004	1006	Sarah Duncan		Payroll Liabilities		Union Bank C...	-24.00	27.00
Paycheck	9/30/2004	1006	Sarah Duncan		Payroll Liabilities		Union Bank C...	-27.00	0.00
Paycheck	9/30/2004	1006	Sarah Duncan		Payroll Expenses		Union Bank C...	30.00	30.00
Paycheck	9/30/2004	1006	Sarah Duncan		Payroll Liabilities		Union Bank C...	-30.00	0.00
Paycheck	9/30/2004	1006	Sarah Duncan		Payroll Expenses		Union Bank C...	3.00	3.00
Paycheck	9/30/2004	1006	Sarah Duncan		Payroll Liabilities		Union Bank C...	-3.00	0.00
Sep 04								0.00	0.00

Figure 3.12 Comprehensive Problem 1, Balance Sheet

Sarah Duncan, CPA
Balance Sheet
As of September 30, 2004

	Sep 30, 04	% of Column
ASSETS		
Current Assets		
Checking/Savings		
Union Bank Checking	47,328.58	66.1%
Total Checking/Savings	47,328.58	66.1%
Other Current Assets		
Inventory Asset	250.00	0.3%
Investment - Dean Witter	15,000.00	21.0%
Total Other Current Assets	15,250.00	21.3%
Total Current Assets	62,578.58	87.4%
Fixed Assets		
Furniture & Fixtures		
Cost	4,000.00	5.6%
Total Furniture & Fixtures	4,000.00	5.6%
Office Equipment		
Cost	3,000.00	4.2%
Total Office Equipment	3,000.00	4.2%
Total Fixed Assets	7,000.00	9.8%
Other Assets		
Prepaid Rent	1,000.00	1.4%
Security Deposit	1,000.00	1.4%
Total Other Assets	2,000.00	2.8%
TOTAL ASSETS	71,578.58	100.0%
LIABILITIES & EQUITY		
Liabilities		
Current Liabilities		
Other Current Liabilities		
Customer Deposits	5,000.00	7.0%
Payroll Liabilities	916.76	1.3%
Total Other Current Liabilities	5,916.76	8.3%
Total Current Liabilities	5,916.76	8.3%
Long Term Liabilities		
Loan -Wells Fargo Bank	3,000.00	4.2%
Total Long Term Liabilities	3,000.00	4.2%
Total Liabilities	8,916.76	12.5%
Equity		
Common Stock	50,000.00	69.9%
Net Income	12,661.82	17.7%
Total Equity	62,661.82	87.5%
TOTAL LIABILITIES & EQUITY	71,578.58	100.0%

Figure 3.13 Comprehensive Problem 1, Profit & Loss Statement

Sarah Duncan, CPA
Profit & Loss
September 2004

	Sep 04	% of Column
Ordinary Income/Expense		
Income		
Accounting Services		
Audit	13,500.00	106.6%
Total Accounting Services	13,500.00	106.6%
Tax Services		
Individual Taxes	4,500.00	35.5%
Total Tax Services	4,500.00	35.5%
Total Income	18,000.00	142.2%
Gross Profit	18,000.00	142.2%
Expense		
Payroll Expenses	4,338.18	34.3%
Rent	1,000.00	7.9%
Total Expense	5,338.18	42.2%
Net Ordinary Income	12,661.82	100.0%
Net Income	**12,661.82**	**100.0%**

Figure 3.14 Comprehensive Problem 1, Statement of Cash Flows

Sarah Duncan, CPA
Statement of Cash Flows
September 2004

	Sep 04
OPERATING ACTIVITIES	
Net Income	12,661.82
Adjustments to reconcile Net Income	
to net cash provided by operations:	
Inventory Asset	-250.00
Investment - Dean Witter	-15,000.00
Customer Deposits	5,000.00
Payroll Liabilities	916.76
Net cash provided by Operating Activities	3,328.58
INVESTING ACTIVITIES	
Furniture & Fixtures:Cost	-4,000.00
Office Equipment:Cost	-3,000.00
Prepaid Rent	-1,000.00
Security Deposit	-1,000.00
Net cash provided by Investing Activities	-9,000.00
FINANCING ACTIVITIES	
Loan - Wells Fargo Bank	3,000.00
Common Stock	50,000.00
Net cash provided by Financing Activities	53,000.00
Net cash increase for period	47,328.58
Cash at end of period	**47,328.58**

Figure 3.15

Chart of Accounts

Account	Type
Wells Fargo	Bank
Inventory Asset	Other Current Asset
Prepaid Rent	Other Current Asset
Short-Term Investments	Other Current Asset
Undeposited Funds	Other Current Asset
Equipment	Fixed Asset
Cost	Fixed Asset
Furniture/Fixtures	Fixed Asset
Cost	Fixed Asset
Payroll Liabilities	Other Current Liability
Notes Payable	Long Term Liability
Common Stock	Equity
Opening Bal Equity	Equity
Retained Earnings	Equity
Consulting Revenue	Income
Freight Income	Income
Reimbursed Expenses	Income
Resale Discounts	Income
Resale Income	Income
Sales	Income
Sales Discounts	Income
Cost of Goods Sold	Cost of Goods Sold
Automobile Expense	Expense
Bank Service Charge	Expense
Cash Discounts	Expense
Contributions	Expense
Depreciation Expense	Expense
Dues and Subscriptions	Expense
Equipment Rental	Expense
Filing Fees	Expense
Franchise Fees	Expense
Insurance	Expense
Disability Insurance	Expense
Liability Insurance	Expense
Interest Expense	Expense
Finance Charge	Expense
Loan Interest	Expense
Mortgage	Expense
Licenses and Permits	Expense
Miscellaneous	Expense
Payroll Expenses	Expense
Postage and Delivery	Expense

Figure 3.15 (Concluded)

Chart of Accounts

Account	**Type**
Printing and Reproduction	Expense
Professional Fees	Expense
Accounting	Expense
Legal Fees	Expense
Rent	Expense
Repairs	Expense
Building Repairs	Expense
Computer Repairs	Expense
Equipment Repairs	Expense
Storage	Expense
Supplies	Expense
Marketing	Expense
Office	Expense
Taxes	Expense
Federal	Expense
Local	Expense
Property	Expense
State	Expense
Telephone	Expense
Travel and Ent	Expense
Entertainment	Expense
Meals	Expense
Travel	Expense
Utilities	Expense
Gas and Electric	Expense
Water	Expense
Interest Income	Other Income
Other Income	Other Income
Other Expenses	Other Expense
Purchase Orders	Non-Posting

Figure 3.16

Customer Job List

Customer	Avalon Bistro		
Company	Avalon Bistro	**Phone**	707-555-0500
Bill To	Avalon Bistro	**Ship To**	Avalon Bistro
	1080 3rd St		1080 3rd St
	Arcata, CA 95521		Arcata, CA 95521
Balance		0.00	

Customer	Bon Jovi's		
Company	Bon Jovi's	**Phone**	707-555-5634
Bill To	Bon Jovi's	**Ship To**	Bon Jovi's
	4257 Petaluma Hill		4257 Petaluma Hill
	Santa Rosa, CA 95404		Santa Rosa, CA 95404
Balance		0.00	

Customer	Hole in the Wall		
Company	Hole in the Wall	**Phone**	707-555-7407
Bill To	Hole in the Wall	**Ship To**	Hole in the Wall
	590 G St		590 G St
	Arcata, CA 95521		Arcata, CA 95521
Balance		0.00	

Customer	Michael's Brew House		
Company	Michael's Brew House	**Phone**	415-555-9874
Bill To	Michael's Brew House	**Ship To**	Michael's Brew House
	2198 Union St		2198 Union St
	San Francisco, CA 94123		San Francisco, CA 94123
Balance		0.00	

Customer	Ocean Grove		
Company	Ocean Grove	**Phone**	707-555-5431
Bill To	Ocean Grove	**Ship To**	Ocean Grove
	570 Ewing St		570 Ewing St
	Trinidad, CA 95570		Trinidad, CA 95570
Balance		0.00	

Customer	River House		
Company	River House	**Phone**	707-555-0123
Bill To	River House	**Ship To**	River House
	222 Weller St		222 Weller St
	Petaluma, CA 95404		Petaluma, CA 95404
Balance		0.00	

Figure 3.17

Employee List

Employee	Emilio Duarte	**SS No.**	012-58-4654
Type	Regular		
Phone	707-555-6655		
Address	Emilio Duarte	**Hired**	02/07/2003
	23 Palm Dr. #23		
	Arcata, CA 95521		

Accrual	**Rate**	**Accrued**	**Limit**	**Used**	**By Year/Period**	**Reset Hrs**
Sick	0:00	0:00		0:00	Y	N
Vacation	0:00	0:00		0:00	Y	N

	FUTA:	**Soc. Sec.:**	**Medicare:**	**SDI:**	**SUI:**	**AEIC:**
Subject To	Y	Y	Y	Y	Y	N

Withholding	**Allowances**	**Extra**	**Status**	**State Lived**	**State Worked**
Federal	0	0.00	Single		
State	0	0.00	Single	CA	CA

Earnings

Name	**Hourly/Annual Rate**
Hourly Rate	11.00

Addition, Deduction, Commission, Company Contributions

Name	**Amount**	**Limit**

Employee	Michael Patrick	**SS No.**	655-85-1253
Type	Regular		
Phone	707-555-9847		
Address	Michael Patrick	Hired	01/01/2005
	333 Spring Rd.		
	Arcata, CA 95521		

Accrual	**Rate**	**Accrued**	**Limit**	**Used**	**By Year/Period**	**Reset Hrs**
Sick	0:00	0:00		0:00	Y	N
Vacation	0:00	0:00		0:00	Y	N

	FUTA	**Soc. Sec.:**	**Medicare:**	**SDI:**	**SUI:**	**AEIC:**
Subject To	Y	Y	Y	Y	Y	N

Withholding	**Allowances**	**Extra**	**Status**	**State Lived**	**State Worked**
Federal	0	0.00	Married		
State	0	0.00	Single	CA	CA

Earnings

Name	**Hourly/Annual Rate**
Salary	50,000.00

Addition, Deduction, Commission, Company Contributions

Name	**Amount**	**Limit**

Figure 3.17 (Concluded)

Employee List

Employee	Shawn Lopez			**SS No.**	702-54-8746
Type	Regular
Phone	707-555-1297
Address	Shawn Lopez			**Hired**	02/07/2003
	234 University Dr
	Arcata, CA 95521

Accrual	**Rate**	**Accrued**	**Limit**	**Used**	**By Year/Period**	**Reset Hrs**
Sick	0:00	0:00		0:00	Y	N
Vacation	0:00	0:00		0:00	Y	N

	FUTA	**Soc. Sec.:**	**Medicare:**	**SDI:**	**SUI:**	**AEIC:**
Subject To	Y	Y	Y	Y	Y	N

Withholding	**Allowances**	**Extra**	**Status**	**State Lived**	**State Worked**
Federal	0	0.00	Single		
State	0	0.00	Single	CA	CA

Earnings

Name	**Hourly/Annual Rate**
Hourly Rate	12.00

Addition, Deduction, Commission, Company Contributions

Name	**Amount**	**Limit**

Figure 3.18

Item List

Item Name/Nu...	100	Type	Service
Description	Consulting		
Price	85.00		
Account	Consulting Revenue		

Item Name/Nu...	302	Type	Inventory Part
Description	Mad River Pale Ale		
Price	6.00		
Inventory Asset	Inventory Asset	Unit Cost	5.00
Account	Sales	Avg. Cost	5.00
COGS Account	Cost of Goods Sold	Total Value	1,600.00
		Preferred Vendor	Mad River
Qty On Hand	320	On Purch Or... 0 On Sales Order	0

Item Name/Nu...	303	Type	Inventory Part
Description	Mad River Stout		
Price	7.00		
Inventory Asset	Inventory Asset	Unit Cost	6.00
Account	Sales	Avg. Cost	6.00
COGS Account	Cost of Goods Sold	Total Value	3,000.00
		Preferred Vendor	Mad River
Qty On Hand	500	On Purch Or... 0 On Sales Order	0

Item Name/Nu...	304	Type	Inventory Part
Description	Mad River Amber Ale		
Price	5.00		
Inventory Asset	Inventory Asset	Unit Cost	4.00
Account	Sales	Avg. Cost	4.00
COGS Account	Cost of Goods Sold	Total Value	1,880.00
		Preferred Vendor	Mad River
Qty On Hand	470	On Purch Or... 0 On Sales Order	0

Figure 3.18 (Continued)

Item List

Item Name/Nu...	305	Type	Inventory Part	
Description	Mad River Porter			
Price	6.50			
Inventory Asset	Inventory Asset	Unit Cost		5.50
Account	Sales	Avg. Cost		5.50
COGS Account	Cost of Goods Sold	Total Value		2,062.50
		Preferred Vendor	Mad River	
Qty On Hand	375	On Purch Or...	0	On Sales Order	0

Item Name/Nu...	402	Type	Inventory Part	
Description	Lost Coast Pale Ale			
Price	6.25			
Inventory Asset	Inventory Asset	Unit Cost		5.25
Account	Sales	Avg. Cost		5.25
COGS Account	Cost of Goods Sold	Total Value		0.00
		Preferred Vendor	Lost Coast	
Qty On Hand	0	On Purch Or...	300	On Sales Order	0

Item Name/Nu...	403	Type	Inventory Part	
Description	Lost Coast Stout			
Price	7.25			
Inventory Asset	Inventory Asset	Unit Cost		6.25
Account	Sales	Avg. Cost		6.25
COGS Account	Cost of Goods Sold	Total Value		0.00
		Preferred Vendor	Lost Coast	
Qty On Hand	0	On Purch Or...	300	On Sales Order	0

Item Name/Nu...	404	Type	Inventory Part	
Description	Lost Coast Amber Ale			
Price	5.25			
Inventory Asset	Inventory Asset	Unit Cost		4.25
Account	Sales	Avg. Cost		4.25
COGS Account	Cost of Goods Sold	Total Value		0.00
		Preferred Vendor	Lost Coast	
Qty On Hand	0	On Purch Or...	300	On Sales Order	0

Figure 3.18 (Concluded)

Item List

Item Name/Nu...	502	Type	Inventory Part	
Description	Humboldt Pale Ale			
Price	6.50			
Inventory Asset	Inventory Asset	Unit Cost		5.50
Account	Sales	Avg. Cost		5.50
COGS Account	Cost of Goods Sold	Total Value		1,925.00
		Preferred Vendor	Humboldt	
Qty On Hand	350	On Purch Or... 0	On Sales Order	0

Item Name/Nu...	506	Type	Inventory Part	
Description	Humboldt IPA			
Price	7.50			
Inventory Asset	Inventory Asset	Unit Cost		6.50
Account	Sales	Avg. Cost		6.50
COGS Account	Cost of Goods Sold	Total Value		1,527.50
		Preferred Vendor	Humboldt	
Qty On Hand	235	On Purch Or... 0	On Sales Order	0

Item Name/Nu...	507	Type	Inventory Part	
Description	Humboldt Red Nectar			
Price	8.00			
Inventory Asset	Inventory Asset	Unit Cost		7.00
Account	Sales	Avg. Cost		7.00
COGS Account	Cost of Goods Sold	Total Value		2.100.00
		Preferred Vendor	Humboldt	
Qty On Hand	300	On Purch Or... 0	On Sales Order	0

Figure 3.19

Vendor List

Vendor	EED	**Balance**	0.00

Vendor	Humboldt		
Company	Humboldt	**Phone**	707-555-2739
Address	Humboldt		
	856 10th St.		
	Arcata, CA 95521		
		Balance	0.00

Vendor	JD Salinger		
		Phone	707-555-6141
Address	JD Salinger		
	101 Market St.		
	San Francisco, CA 94102		
		Balance	0.00

Vendor	Lost Coast		
Company Name	Lost Coast	**Phone**	707-555-4484
Address	Lost Coast		
	123 West Third St.		
	Eureka, CA 95501		
		Balance	0.00

Vendor	Mad River		
Company Name	Mad River	**Phone**	707-555-4151
Address	Mad River		
	195 Taylor Way		
	Blue Lake, CA 95525		
		Balance	0.00

Vendor	United States Treasury		
		Balance	0.00

Vendor	Wells Fargo Bank		
Address	Wells Fargo Bank		
		Balance	0.00

Vendor	West Coast Computer Supply		
Address	West Coast Computer Supply		
		Balance	0.00

Figure 3.20

Pacific Brew, Inc.
Custom Transaction Detail Report
January 1-16, 2006

Type	Date	Num	Name	Memo	Account	Clr	Split	Amount	Balance
Jan 1-16, 06									
Deposit	1/3/2006		Shareholders	Deposit	Wells Fargo		Common Stock	50,000.00	50,000.00
Deposit	1/3/2006		Shareholders	Deposit	Common Stock		Wells Fargo	-50,000.00	0.00
Check	1/5/2006	101	JD Salinger		Wells Fargo		-SPLIT-	-5,000.00	-5,000.00
Check	1/5/2006	101	JD Salinger		Prepaid Rent		Wells Fargo	2,500.00	-2,500.00
Check	1/5/2006	101	JD Salinger		Rent		Wells Fargo	2,500.00	0.00
Check	1/6/2006	102	JD Salinger		Wells Fargo		-SPLIT-	-8,000.00	-8,000.00
Check	1/6/2006	102	JD Salinger		Cost		Wells Fargo	5,000.00	-3,000.00
Check	1/6/2006	102	JD Salinger		Cost		Wells Fargo	3,000.00	0.00
Check	1/9/2006	103	Schwab Investments		Wells Fargo		Short-Term In...	-30,000.00	-30,000.00
Check	1/9/2006	103	Schwab Investments		Short-Term Investm...		Wells Fargo	30,000.00	0.00
Deposit	1/10/2006		Wells Fargo Bank	Deposit	Wells Fargo		Notes Payable	40,000.00	40,000.00
Deposit	1/10/2006		Wells Fargo Bank	Deposit	Notes Payable		Wells Fargo	-40,000.00	0.00
Check	1/10/2006	104	West Coast Comput...		Wells Fargo		Cost	-10,200.00	-10,200.00
Check	1/10/2006	104	West Coast Comput...		Cost		Wells Fargo	10,200.00	0.00
Check	1/10/2006	105	Mad River		Wells Fargo		-SPLIT-	-10,250.00	-10,250.00
Check	1/10/2006	105	Mad River	Mad River Pa...	Inventory Asset		Wells Fargo	2,500.00	-7,750.00
Check	1/10/2006	105	Mad River	Mad River St...	Inventory Asset		Wells Fargo	3,000.00	-4,750.00
Check	1/10/2006	105	Mad River	Mad River A...	Inventory Asset		Wells Fargo	2,000.00	-2,750.00
Check	1/10/2006	105	Mad River	Mad River Po...	Inventory Asset		Wells Fargo	2,750.00	0.00
Check	1/11/2006	106	Humboldt		Wells Fargo		-SPLIT-	-7,600.00	-7,600.00
Check	1/11/2006	106	Humboldt	Humboldt Pal...	Inventory Asset		Wells Fargo	2,200.00	-5,400.00
Check	1/11/2006	106	Humboldt	Humboldt IPA	Inventory Asset		Wells Fargo	2,600.00	-2,800.00
Check	1/11/2006	106	Humboldt	Humboldt Re...	Inventory Asset		Wells Fargo	2,800.00	0.00
Sales Receipt	1/11/2006	5001	Michael's Brew Hou...		Wells Fargo		Consulting Re...	4,250.00	4,250.00
Sales Receipt	1/11/2006	5001	Michael's Brew Hou...	Consulting	Consulting Revenue		Wells Fargo	-4,250.00	0.00
Sales Receipt	1/13/2006	5002	Bon Jovi's		Wells Fargo		-SPLIT-	787.50	787.50
Sales Receipt	1/13/2006	5002	Bon Jovi's	Mad River Po...	Sales		Wells Fargo	-162.50	625.00
Sales Receipt	1/13/2006	5002	Bon Jovi's	Mad River Po...	Cost of Goods Sold		Wells Fargo	-137.50	487.50
Sales Receipt	1/13/2006	5002	Bon Jovi's	Mad River Po...	Sales		Wells Fargo	137.50	625.00
Sales Receipt	1/13/2006	5002	Bon Jovi's	Humboldt IPA	Inventory Asset		Wells Fargo	-225.00	400.00
Sales Receipt	1/13/2006	5002	Bon Jovi's	Humboldt IPA	Cost of Good Sold		Wells Fargo	-195.00	205.00
Sales Receipt	1/13/2006	5002	Bon Jovi's	Humboldt Re...	Sales		Wells Fargo	195.00	400.00
Sales Receipt	1/13/2006	5002	Bon Jovi's	Humboldt Re...	Cost of Goods Sold		Wells Fargo	-400.00	0.00
Sales Receipt	1/13/2006	5002	Bon Jovi's	Humboldt Re...	Sales		Wells Fargo	-350.00	-350.00
Sales Receipt	1/13/2006	5002	Bon Jovi's		Cost of Goods Sold		Wells Fargo	350.00	0.00
Sales Receipt	1/13/2006	5004	Ocean Grove		Wells Fargo		-SPLIT-	715.00	715.00
Sales Receipt	1/13/2006	5004	Ocean Grove	Mad River A...	Sales		Wells Fargo	-150.00	565.00
Sales Receipt	1/13/2005	5004	Ocean Grove	Mad River A...	Cost of Goods Sold		Wells Fargo	-120.00	445.00
Sales Receipt	1/13/2006	5004	Ocean Grove	Mad River A...	Sales		Wells Fargo	120.00	565.00
Sales Receipt	1/13/2006	5004	Ocean Grove	Mad River Pa...	Inventory Asset		Wells Fargo	-240.00	325.00
Sales Receipt	1/13/2006	5004	Ocean Grove	Mad River Pa...	Cost of Goods Sold		Wells Fargo	-200.00	125.00
Sales Receipt	1/13/2006	5004	Ocean Grove	Humboldt Pal...	Sales		Wells Fargo	200.00	325.00
Sales Receipt	1/13/2006	5004	Ocean Grove	Humboldt Pal...	Inventory Asset		Wells Fargo	-325.00	0.00
Sales Receipt	1/13/2006	5004	Ocean Grove	Humboldt Pal...	Cost of Goods Sold		Wells Fargo	-275.00	-275.00
Sales Receipt	1/13/2006	5004	Ocean Grove		Sales		Wells Fargo	275.00	0.00
Sales Receipt	1/13/2006	5003	River House	Consulting	Wells Fargo		Consulting Re...	5,100.00	5,100.00
Sales Receipt	1/13/2006	5003	River House		Consulting Revenue		Wells Fargo	-5,100.00	0.00
Sales Receipt	1/16/2006	5005	Avalon Bistro		Wells Fargo		-SPLIT-	902.50	902.50

Figure 3.20 (Continued)

Type	Date	Num	Name	Memo	Account	Clr	Split	Amount	Balance
Sales Receipt	1/16/2006	5005	Avalon Bistro	Mad River Pa...	Sales		Wells Fargo	-240.00	662.50
Sales Receipt	1/16/2006	5005	Avalon Bistro	Mad River Pa...	Inventory Asset		Wells Fargo	-200.00	462.50
Sales Receipt	1/16/2006	5005	Avalon Bistro	Mad River Pa...	Cost of Goods Sold		Wells Fargo	200.00	662.50
Sales Receipt	1/16/2006	5005	Avalon Bistro	Humboldt Re...	Sales		Wells Fargo	-400.00	262.50
Sales Receipt	1/16/2006	5005	Avalon Bistro	Humboldt Re...	Inventory Asset		Wells Fargo	-350.00	-87.50
Sales Receipt	1/16/2006	5005	Avalon Bistro	Humboldt Re...	Cost of Goods Sold		Wells Fargo	350.00	262.50
Sales Receipt	1/16/2006	5005	Avalon Bistro	Humboldt IPA	Sales		Wells Fargo	-262.50	0.00
Sales Receipt	1/16/2006	5005	Avalon Bistro	Humboldt IPA	Inventory Asset		Wells Fargo	-227.50	-227.50
Sales Receipt	1/16/2006	5005	Avalon Bistro	Humboldt IPA	Cost of Goods Sold		Wells Fargo	227.50	0.00
Paycheck	1/16/2006	107	Emilio Duarte		Wells Fargo		-SPLIT-	-639.32	-639.32
Paycheck	1/16/2006	107	Emilio Duarte		Payroll Expenses		Wells Fargo	880.00	240.68
Paycheck	1/16/2006	107	Emilio Duarte		Payroll Expenses		Wells Fargo	0.88	241.56
Paycheck	1/16/2006	107	Emilio Duarte		Payroll Liabilities		Wells Fargo	-0.88	240.68
Paycheck	1/16/2006	107	Emilio Duarte		Payroll Liabilities		Wells Fargo	-120.56	120.12
Paycheck	1/16/2006	107	Emilio Duarte		Payroll Expenses		Wells Fargo	54.56	174.68
Paycheck	1/16/2006	107	Emilio Duarte		Payroll Liabilities		Wells Fargo	-54.56	120.12
Paycheck	1/16/2006	107	Emilio Duarte		Payroll Expenses		Wells Fargo	-54.56	65.56
Paycheck	1/16/2006	107	Emilio Duarte		Payroll Liabilities		Wells Fargo	12.76	78.32
Paycheck	1/16/2006	107	Emilio Duarte		Payroll Expenses		Wells Fargo	-12.76	65.56
Paycheck	1/16/2006	107	Emilio Duarte		Payroll Liabilities		Wells Fargo	-12.76	52.80
Paycheck	1/16/2006	107	Emilio Duarte		Payroll Expenses		Wells Fargo	7.04	59.84
Paycheck	1/16/2006	107	Emilio Duarte		Payroll Liabilities		Wells Fargo	-7.04	52.80
Paycheck	1/16/2006	107	Emilio Duarte		Payroll Liabilities		Wells Fargo	-48.40	4.40
Paycheck	1/16/2006	107	Emilio Duarte		Payroll Liabilities		Wells Fargo	-4.40	0.00
Paycheck	1/16/2006	107	Emilio Duarte		Payroll Expenses		Wells Fargo	26.40	26.40
Paycheck	1/16/2006	107	Emilio Duarte		Payroll Liabilities		Wells Fargo	-26.40	0.00
Paycheck	1/16/2006	108	Michael Patrick		Wells Fargo		-SPLIT-	-1,513.53	-1,513.53
Paycheck	1/16/2006	108	Michael Patrick		Payroll Expenses		Wells Fargo	2,083.33	569.80
Paycheck	1/16/2006	108	Michael Patrick		Payroll Expenses		Wells Fargo	2.08	571.88
Paycheck	1/16/2006	108	Michael Patrick		Payroll Liabilities		Wells Fargo	-2.08	569.80
Paycheck	1/16/2006	108	Michael Patrick		Payroll Expenses		Wells Fargo	-285.42	284.38
Paycheck	1/16/2006	108	Michael Patrick		Payroll Expenses		Wells Fargo	129.17	413.55
Paycheck	1/16/2006	108	Michael Patrick		Payroll Liabilities		Wells Fargo	-129.17	284.38
Paycheck	1/16/2006	108	Michael Patrick		Payroll Liabilities		Wells Fargo	-129.17	155.21
Paycheck	1/16/2006	108	Michael Patrick		Payroll Expenses		Wells Fargo	30.21	185.42
Paycheck	1/16/2006	108	Michael Patrick		Payroll Liabilities		Wells Fargo	-30.21	155.21
Paycheck	1/16/2006	108	Michael Patrick		Payroll Liabilities		Wells Fargo	-30.21	125.00
Paycheck	1/16/2006	108	Michael Patrick		Payroll Liabilities		Wells Fargo	16.67	141.67
Paycheck	1/16/2006	108	Michael Patrick		Payroll Expense		Wells Fargo	-16.67	125.00
Paycheck	1/16/2006	108	Michael Patrick		Payroll Liabilities		Wells Fargo	-114.58	10.42
Paycheck	1/16/2006	108	Michael Patrick		Payroll Liabilities		Wells Fargo	-10.42	0.00
Paycheck	1/16/2006	108	Michael Patrick		Payroll Expenses		Wells Fargo	62.50	62.50
Paycheck	1/16/2006	108	Michael Patrick		Payroll Liabilities		Wells Fargo	-62.50	0.00
Paycheck	1/16/2006	109	Shawn Lopez		Wells Fargo		-SPLIT-	-653.85	-653.85
Paycheck	1/16/2006	109	Shawn Lopez		Payroll Expenses		Wells Fargo	900.00	246.15
Paycheck	1/16/2006	109	Shawn Lopez		Payroll Expenses		Wells Fargo	0.90	247.05
Paycheck	1/16/2006	109	Shawn Lopez		Payroll Liabilities		Wells Fargo	-0.90	246.15
Paycheck	1/16/2006	109	Shawn Lopez		Payroll Liabilities		Wells Fargo	-123.30	122.85
Paycheck	1/16/2006	109	Shawn Lopez		Payroll Expenses		Wells Fargo	55.80	178.65
Paycheck	1/16/2006	109	Shawn Lopez		Payroll Liabilities		Wells Fargo	-55.80	122.85
Paycheck	1/16/2006	109	Shawn Lopez		Payroll Expenses		Wells Fargo	-55.80	67.05
Paycheck	1/16/2006	109	Shawn Lopez		Payroll Liabilities		Wells Fargo	13.05	80.10
Paycheck	1/16/2006	109	Shawn Lopez		Payroll Expenses		Wells Fargo	-13.05	67.05
Paycheck	1/16/2006	109	Shawn Lopez		Payroll Liabilities		Wells Fargo	-13.05	54.00
Paycheck	1/16/2006	109	Shawn Lopez		Payroll Expenses		Wells Fargo	7.20	61.20

Figure 3.20 (Concluded)

Type	Date	Num	Name	Memo	Account	Clr	Split	Amount	Balance
Paycheck	1/16/2006	109	Shawn Lopez		Payroll Liabilities		Wells Fargo	-7.20	54.00
Paycheck	1/16/2006	109	Shawn Lopez		Payroll Liabilities		Wells Fargo	-49.50	4.50
Paycheck	1/16/2006	109	Shawn Lopez		Payroll Liabilities		Wells Fargo	-4.50	0.00
Paycheck	1/16/2006	109	Shawn Lopez		Payroll Expenses		Wells Fargo	27.00	27.00
Paycheck	1/16/2002	109	Shawn Lopez		Payroll Liabilities		Wells Fargo	-27.00	0.00
Sales Receipt	1/16/2006	5006	Michael's Brew Hou...		Wells Fargo		-SPLIT-	2,000.00	2,000.00
Sales Receipt	1/16/2006	5006	Michael's Brew Hou...	Mad River Pa...	Sales		Wells Fargo	-600.00	1,400.00
Sales Receipt	1/16/2006	5006	Michael's Brew Hou...	Mad River Pa...	Inventory Asset		Wells Fargo	-500.00	900.00
Sales Receipt	1/16/2006	5006	Michael's Brew Hou...	Mad River Pa...	Cost of Goods Sold		Wells Fargo	500.00	1,400.00
Sales Receipt	1/16/2006	5006	Michael's Brew Hou...	Mad River Po...	Sales		Wells Fargo	-650.00	750.00
Sales Receipt	1/16/2006	5006	Michael's Brew Hou...	Mad River Po...	Inventory Asset		Wells Fargo	-550.00	200.00
Sales Receipt	1/16/2006	5006	Michael's Brew Hou...	Mad River Po...	Cost of Goods Sold		Wells Fargo	550.00	750.00
Sales Receipt	1/16/2006	5006	Michael's Brew Hou...	Humboldt IPA	Sales		Wells Fargo	-750.00	0.00
Sales Receipt	1/16/2006	5006	Michael's Brew Hou...	Humboldt IPA	Inventory Asset		Wells Fargo	-650.00	-650.00
Sales Receipt	1/16/2006	5006	Michael's Brew Hou...	Humboldt IPA	Cost of Goods Sold		Wells Fargo	650.00	0.00
Jan 1-16, 06								**0.00**	**0.00**

Figure 3.21

Pacific Brew, Inc.
Balance Sheet
As of January 16, 2006

	Jan 16, 06
ASSETS	
Current Assets	
Checking/Savings	
Wells Fargo	29,898.30
Total Checking/Savings	29,898.30
Other Current Assets	
Inventory Asset	14,095.00
Prepaid Rent	2,500.00
Short-Term Investments	30,000.00
Total Other Current Assets	46,595.00
Total Current Assets	76,493.30
Fixed Assets	
Equipment	
Cost	13,200.00
Total Equipment	13,200.00
Furniture Fixtures	
Cost	5,000.00
Total Furniture Fixtures Cost	5,000.00
Total Fixed Assets	18,200.00
TOTAL ASSETS	**94,693.30**
LIABILITIES AND EQUITY	
Liabilities	
Current Liabilities	
Other Current Liabilities	
Payroll Liabilities	1,502.85
Total Other Current Liabilities	1,502.85
Total Current Liabilities	1,502.85
Long Term Liabilities	
Notes Payable	40,000.00
Total Long Term Liabilities	40,000.00
Total Liabilities	41,502.85
Equity	
Common Stock	50,000
Net Income	3,190.45
Total Equity	53,190.45
TOTAL LIABILITIES & EQUITY	**94,693.30**

Figure 3.22

Pacific Brew, Inc.
Profit & Loss
January 1-16, 2006

	Jan 1-16, 06	% of Income
Ordinary Income Expense		
Income		
Consulting Revenue	9,350.00	68.0%
Sales	4,405.00	32.0%
Total Income	13,755.00	100.0%
Cost of Goods Sold		
Cost of Goods Sold	3,755.00	27.3%
Total COGS	3,755.00	27.3%
Gross Profit	10,000.00	72.7%
Expense		
Payroll Expenses	4,309.55	31.3%
Rent	2,500.00	18.2%
Total Expense	6.809.55	49.5%
Net Ordinary Income	3,190.45	23.2%
Net Income	3,190.45	23.2%

Figure 3.23

Pacific Brew, Inc.
Statement of Cash Flows
January 1-16, 2006

	Jan 1-16, 06
OPERATING ACTIVITIES	
Net Income	3,190.45
Adjustments to reconcile Net Income	
to net cash provided by operations:	
Inventory Asset	-14,095.00
Prepaid Rent	-2,500.00
Short Term Investments	-30,000.00
Payroll Liabilities	1,502.85
Net cash provided by Operating Activities	-41,901.70
INVESTING ACTIVITIES	
Equipment: Cost	-13,200.00
Furniture/Fixtures: Cost	-5,000.00
Net cash provided by Investing Activities	-18,200.00
FINANCING ACTIVITIES	
Notes Payable	40,000.00
Common Stock	50,000.00
Net cash provided by Financing Activities	90,000.00
Net cash increase for period	29,898.30
Cash at end of period	29,898.30

Figure 3.24

Chart of Accounts

Account	Type
Checking	Bank
Accounts Receivable	Accounts Receivable
Inventory Asset	Other Current Asset
Short-term investments	Other Current Asset
Undeposited Funds	Other Current Asset
Equipment	Fixed Asset
Cost	Fixed Asset
Furniture/Fixtures	Fixed Asset
Cost	Fixed Asset
Prepaid Rent	Other Asset
Accounts Payable	Accounts Payable
Payroll Liabilities	Other Current Liability
Sales Tax Payable	Other Current Liability
Note Payable	Long Term Liability
Common Stock	Equity
Opening Bal Equity	Equity
Retained Earnings	Equity
Cash Discrepancies	Income
Overages	Income
Shortages	Income
Sales	Income
Consignment Sales	Income
Discounts Given	Income
Merchandise	Income
Service	Income
Shipping and Handling	Income
Cost of Goods Sold	Cost of Goods Sold
Purchase Discounts	Cost of Goods Sold
Purchases	Cost of Goods Sold
Automobile Expense	Expense
Bad Debt Expense	Expense
Bank Service Charges	Expense
Charitable Contributions	Expense
Depreciation Expense	Expense
Dues and Subscriptions	Expense

Figure 3.24 (Concluded)

Chart of Accounts

Account	**Type**
Equipment Rental	Expense
Franchise Fees	Expense
Insurance	Expense
Health Insurance	Expense
Liability Insurance	Expense
Interest Expense	Expense
Licenses and Permits	Expense
Marketing & Advertising	Expense
Merchant Fees	Expense
Miscellaneous	Expense
Office Expenses	Expense
Office Supplies	Expense
Postage and Delivery	Expense
Printing and Reproduction	Expense
Payroll Expenses	Expense
Professional Fees	Expense
Accounting	Expense
Legal Fees	Expense
Rent	Expense
Repairs	Expense
Building Repairs	Expense
Computer Repairs	Expense
Equipment Repairs	Expense
Taxes	Expense
Telephone	Expense
Travel & Ent	Expense
Entertainment	Expense
Meals	Expense
Travel	Expense
Utilities	Expense
Interest Income	Other Income
Other Income	Other Income
Other Expenses	Other Expense
Purchase Orders	Non-Posting

Figure 3.25

Customer Job List

Customer	J's Landscaping		
Company	J's Landscaping	**Phone**	858-555-1348
Bill To	J's Landscaping	**Ship To**	J's Landscaping
	12 Bones Way		12 Bones Way
	San Diego, CA 92345		San Diego, CA 92345
Balance	0.00		
		Pmt Terms	Due on receipt
		Sales Tax Code	Tax

Customer	Marriott Hotels		
Company	Marriott Hotels	**Phone**	858-555-7407
Bill To	Marriott Hotels	**Ship To**	Marriott Hotels
	97444 Miramar		97444 Miramar
	San Diego, CA 92145		San Diego, CA 92145
Balance	−5,000.00		
		Pmt Terms	Due on receipt
		Sales Tax Code	Tax

Customer	Pam's Designs		
Company	Pam's Designs	**Phone**	707-555-5748
Bill To	Pam's Designs	**Ship To**	Pam's Designs
	5144 Union		5144 Union
	San Diego, CA 92129		San Diego, CA 92129
Balance	0.00		
		Pmt Terms	Due on receipt
		Sales Tax Code	Tax

Figure 3.26

Item List

Item Name/Nu...	100	**Type**	Service
Description	Installation		
Price	75.00		
Account	Service		

Item Name/Nu...	101	**Type**	Service
Description	Consulting services		
Price	80.00	Taxable	
Account	Service		

Item Name/Nu...	201	**Type**	Inventory Part
Description	Maxus		
Price	7,000.00	Taxable	
Inventory Asset	Inventory Asset	**Unit Cost**	5,000.00
Account	Merchandise	**Avg. Cost**	5,000.00
COGS Account	Cost of Goods Sold	**Total Value**	35,000.00
		Preferred Vendor	Sundance Spas
Qty On Hand	7	**On Purch Ord...** 0	**On Sales Order** 0

Item Name/Nu...	202	**Type**	Inventory Part
Description	Optima		
Price	8,000.00	Taxable	
Inventory Asset	Inventory Asset	**Unit Cost**	6,000.00
Account	Merchandise	**Avg. Cost**	6,000.00
COGS Account	Cost of Goods Sold	**Total Value**	54,000.00
		Preferred Vendor	Sundance Spas
Qty On Hand	9	**On Purch Ord...** 0	**On Sales Order** 0

Item Name/Nu...	203	**Type**	Inventory Part
Description	Cameo		
Price	9,000.00	Taxable	
Inventory Asset	Inventory Asset	**Unit Cost**	7,000.00
Account	Merchandise	**Avg. Cost**	7,000.00
COGS Account	Cost of Goods Sold	**Total Value**	56,000.00
		Preferred Vendor	Sundance Spas
Qty On Hand	8	**On Purch Ord...** 0	**On Sales Order** 0

Figure 3.26 (Concluded)

Item List

Item Name/Nu...	301	**Type**	Inventory Part
Description	Galaxy		
Price	6,500.00	Taxable	
Inventory Asset	Inventory Asset	**Unit Cost**	4,500.00
Account	Merchandise	**Avg. Cost**	4,500.00
COGS Account	Cost of Goods Sold	**Total Value**	9,000.00
		Preferred Vendor	Cal Spas
Qty On Hand	2	**On Purch Ord...** 0	**On Sales Order** 0

Item Name/Nu...	302	**Type**	Inventory Part
Description	Ultimate		
Price	7,500.00	Taxable	
Inventory Asset	Inventory Asset	**Unit Cost**	5,500.00
Account	Merchandise	**Avg. Cost**	5,500.00
COGS Account	Cost of Goods Sold	**Total Value**	27,500.00
		Preferred Vendor	Cal Spas
Qty On Hand	5	**On Purch Ord...** 0	**On Sales Order** 0

Item Name/Nu...	303	**Type**	Inventory Part
Description	Aqua		
Price	9,500.00	Taxable	
Inventory Asset	Inventory Asset	**Unit Cost**	7,500.00
Account	Merchandise	**Avg. Cost**	7,500.00
COGS Account	Cost of Goods	**Sold Total Value**	30,000.00
		Preferred Vendor	Cal Spas
Qty On Hand	4	**On Purch Ord...** 0	**On Sales Order** 0

Item Name/Nu...	Sales Tax	**Type**	Sales Tax Item
Description	Sales Tax		
Price	7.75%		
Account	Sales Tax Payable		

Figure 3.27

Vendor List

Vendor	Cal Spas		
Company Name	Cal Spas	**Phone**	909-623-8781
Address	Cal Spas		
	1462 East Ninth St.		
	Pomona, CA 91766		
		Balance	0.00
Vendor	Coast Computer Supply		
Address	Coast Computer Supply		
		Balance	0.00
Vendor	EDD		
		Balance	0.00
Vendor	K Realty		
Address	K Realty		
		Balance	0.00
Vendor	Office Max		
Address	Office Max		
		Balance	0.00
Vendor	State Board of Equalization		
Address	State Board of Equalization		
		Balance	6,001.60
Vendor	Sundance Spas		
Company Name	Sunance Spas	**Phone**	909-614-0679
Address	Sunance Spas		
	14525 Monte Vista Ave.		
	Chino, CA 91710		
		Balance	0.00
Vendor	United States Treasury		
		Balance	0.00

Figure 3.28

Employee List

| **Employee** | Bryan Christopher | | **SS No.** | 556-95-4789 | |

Type	Regular
Phone	858-555-1264
Address	Bryan Christopher
	12 Mesa Way
	Del Mar, CA 92014

Hired 01/01/2007

Salary 60,000.00

Accrual	**Rate**	**Accrued**	**Limit**	**Used**	**By Year/Period**	**Reset Hrs**
Sick	0:00	0:00		0:00	Y	N
Vacation	0:00	0:00		0:00	Y	N

	FUTA:	**Soc. Sec.:**	**Medicare:**	**SDI:**	**SUI:**	**AEIC:**
Subject To	Y	Y	Y	Y	Y	N

Withholding	**Allowances**	**Extra**	**Status**	**State Lived**	**State Worked**
Federal	0	0.00	Married		
State	0	0.00	Married (one income)	CA	CA

Earnings

Name	**Hourly/Annual Rate**
Salary	60.000.00

Addition, Deduction, Commission, Company Contributions

Name	**Amount**	**Limit**

| **Employee** | Loriel Sanchez | | **SS No.** | 475-54-8746 | |

Type	Regular
Phone	858-555-3365
Address	Loriel Sanchez
	2342 Court
	Del Mar, CA 92014

Hired 09/15/2004

Accrual	**Rate**	**Accrued**	**Limit**	**Used**	**By Year/Period**	**Reset Hrs**
Sick	0:00	0:00		0:00	Y	N
Vacation	0:00	0:00		0:00	Y	N

	FUTA:	**Soc. Sec.:**	**Medicare:**	**SDI:**	**SUI:**	**AEIC:**
Subject To	Y	Y	Y	Y	Y	N

Withholding	**Allowances**	**Extra**	**Status**	**State Lived**	**State Worked**
Federal	0	0.00	Married		
State	0	0.00	Married (one income)	CA	CA

Earnings

Name	**Hourly/Annual Rate**
Hourly Rate	13.00

Addition, Deduction, Commission, Company Contributions

Name	**Amount**	**Limit**

Figure 3.28 (Concluded)

Employee	Sharon Lee			**SS No.**		125-58-8452	
Type	Regular						
Phone	858-555-3365						
Address	Sharon Lee			**Hired**		09/15/2004	
	323 Ridgefield Pl.						
	Del Mar, CA 92014						

Accrual	**Rate**	**Accrued**	**Limit**		**Used**	**By Year/Period**	**Reset Hrs**
Sick	0:00	0:00			0:00	Y	N
Vacation	0:00	0:00			0:00	Y	N

	FUTA:	**Soc. Sec.:**	**Medicare:**	**SDI:**	**SUI:**	**AEIC:**
Subject To	Y	Y	Y	Y	Y	N

Withholding	**Allowances**	**Extra**	**Status**	**State Lived**	**State Worked**
Federal	0	0.00	Single		
State	0	0.00	Single	CA	CA

Earnings

Name	**Hourly/Annual Rate**
Hourly Rate	12.00

Addition, Deduction, Commission, Company Contributions

Name	**Amount**	**Limit**

Figure 3.29

Sunset Spas
Custom Transaction Detail Report
January 1-16, 2007

Type	Date	Num	Name	Memo	Cir	Account	Split	Amount	Balance
Jan 1-16, 07									
Deposit	1/3/2007			Deposit		Checking	Common	100,000.00	100,000.00
Deposit	1/3/2007		Shareholders	Deposit		Common Stock	Checking	-100,000.00	0.00
Deposit	1/4/2007			Deposit		Checking	Note Payable	200,000.00	200,000.00
Deposit	1/5/2007		Hacienda Bank	Deposit		Checking	Checking	-200,000.00	0.00
Check	1/5/2007	101	K Realty			Checking	-SPLIT-	-6,000.00	-6,000.00
Check	1/5/2007	101	K Realty			Prepaid Rent	Checking	3,000.00	-3,000.00
Check	1/5/2007	101	K Realty			Rent	Checking	3,000.00	0.00
Check	1/8/2007	102	Office Max			Checking	-SPLIT-	-8,000.00	-8,000.00
Check	1/8/2007	102	Office Max			Cost	Checking	4,500.00	-3,500.00
Check	1/8/2007	102	Office Max			Cost	Checking	3,500.00	0.00
Check	1/9/2007	103	Poole Investments			Checking	Short-term inv...	-30,000.00	-30,000.00
Check	1/9/2007	103	Poole Investments			Short-term inv...	Checking	30,000.00	0.00
Check	1/10/2007	104	Coast Computer Su...			Checking	Cost	-8,900.00	-8,900.00
Check	1/10/2007	104	Coast Computer Su...			Cost	Checking	8,900.00	0.00
Check	1/11/2007	105	Sundance Spas			Checking	-SPLIT-	-180,000.00	-180,000.00
Check	1/11/2007	105	Sundance Spas	Maxus		Inventory Asset	Checking	50,000.00	-130,000.00
Check	1/11/2007	105	Sundance Spas	Optima		Inventory Asset	Checking	60,000.00	-70,000.00
Check	1/11/2007	105	Sundance Spas	Cameo		Inventory Asset	Checking	70,000.00	0.00
Sales Receipt	1/11/2007	7001	J's Landscaping			Checking	-SPLIT-	862.00	862.00
Sales Receipt	1/11/2007	7001	J's Landscaping	Consulting se...		Service	Checking	-800.00	62.00
Sales Receipt	1/11/2007	7001	State Board of Equa...	Sales Tax		Sales Tax Payable	Checking	-62.00	0.00
Check	1/12/2007	106	Cal Spas			Checking	-SPLIT-	-87,500.00	-87,500.00
Check	1/12/2007	106	Cal Spas	Galaxy		Inventory Asset	Checking	22,500.00	-65,000.00
Check	1/12/2007	106	Cal Spas	Ultimate		Inventory Asset	Checking	27,500.00	-37,500.00
Check	1/12/2007	106	Cal Spas	Aqua		Inventory Asset	Checking	37,500.00	0.00
Sales Receipt	1/15/2007	7002	Pam's Designs			Checking	-SPLIT-	39,867.50	39,867.50
Sales Receipt	1/15/2007	7002	Pam's Designs	Galaxy		Merchandise	Checking	-19,500.00	20,367.50
Sales Receipt	1/15/2007	7002	Pam's Designs	Galaxy		Inventory Asset	Checking	-13,500.00	6,867.50
Sales Receipt	1/15/2007	7002	Pam's Designs	Galaxy		Cost of Goods Sold	Checking	13,500.00	20,367.50
Sales Receipt	1/15/2007	7002	Pam's Designs	Optima		Merchandise	Checking	-8,000.00	12,367.50
Sales Receipt	1/15/2007	7002	Pam's Designs	Optima		Inventory Asset	Checking	-6,000.00	6,367.50
Sales Receipt	1/15/2007	7002	Pam's Designs	Optima		Cost of Goods Sold	Checking	6,000.00	12,367.50
Sales Receipt	1/15/2007	7002	Pam's Designs	Aqua		Merchandise	Checking	-9,500.00	2,867.50
Sales Receipt	1/15/2007	7002	Pam's Designs	Aqua		Inventory Asset	Checking	-7,500.00	-4,632.50
Sales Receipt	1/15/2007	7002	Pam's Designs	Aqua		Cost of Goods Sold	Checking	7,500.00	2,867.50
Sales Receipt	1/15/2007	7002	State Board of Equa...	Sales Tax		Sales Tax Payable	Checking	-2,867.50	0.00
Sales Receipt	1/15/2007	7003	Marriott Hotels			Checking	-SPLIT-	689.60	689.60
Sales Receipt	1/15/2007	7003	Marriott Hotels	Consulting se...		Service	Checking	-640.00	49.60
Sales Receipt	1/15/2007	7003	State Board of Equa...	Sales Tax		Sales Tax Payable	Checking	-49.60	0.00
Sales Receipt	1/16/2007	7004	J's Landscaping			Checking	-SPLIT-	42,022.50	42,022.50
Sales Receipt	1/16/2007	7004	J's Landscaping	Maxus		Merchandise	Checking	-21,000.00	21,022.50
Sales Receipt	1/16/2007	7004	J's Landscaping	Maxus		Inventory Asset	Checking	-15,000.00	6,022.50
Sales Receipt	1/16/2007	7004	J's Landscaping	Maxus		Cost of Goods Sold	Checking	15,000.00	21,022.50
Sales Receipt	1/16/2007	7004	J's Landscaping	Cameo		Merchandise	Checking	-18,000.00	3,022.50
Sales Receipt	1/16/2007	7004	J's Landscaping	Cameo		Inventory Asset	Checking	-14,000.00	-10,977.50
Sales Receipt	1/16/2007	7004	J's Landscaping	Cameo		Cost of Goods Sold	Checking	14,000.00	3,022.50
Sales Receipt	1/16/2007	7004	State Board of Equa...	Sales Tax		Sales Tax Payable	Checking	-3,022.50	0.00
Payment	1/16/2007	7004	Marriott Hotels			Checking	Accounts Rec...	5,000.00	5,000.00

Figure 3.29 (Continued)

Sunset Spas
Custom Transaction Detail Report
January 1-16, 2007

Type	Date	Num	Name	Memo	Cir	Account	Split	Amount	Balance
Payment	1/16/2007		Marriott Hotels			Accounts Receivable	Checking	-5,000.00	0.00
Paycheck	1/16/2007	107	Bryan Christopher				-SPLIT-	-1,816.25	-1816.25
Paycheck	1/16/2007	107	Bryan Christopher			Payroll Expenses	Checking	2,500.00	683.75
Paycheck	1/16/2007	107	Bryan Christopher			Payroll Expenses	Checking	-2.50	686.25
Paycheck	1/16/2007	107	Bryan Christopher			Payroll Liabilities	Checking	-342.50	683.75
Paycheck	1/16/2007	107	Bryan Christopher			Payroll Expenses	Checking	155.00	341.25
Paycheck	1/16/2007	107	Bryan Christopher			Payroll Expenses	Checking	155.00	496.25
Paycheck	1/16/2007	107	Bryan Christopher			Payroll Liabilities	Checking	-155.00	341.25
Paycheck	1/16/2007	107	Bryan Christopher			Payroll Liabilities	Checking	-155.00	186.25
Paycheck	1/16/2007	107	Bryan Christopher			Payroll Expenses	Checking	36.25	222.50
Paycheck	1/16/2007	107	Bryan Christopher			Payroll Liabilities	Checking	-36.25	186.25
Paycheck	1/16/2007	107	Bryan Christopher			Payroll Liabilities	Checking	-36.25	150.00
Paycheck	1/16/2007	107	Bryan Christopher			Payroll Expenses	Checking	20.00	170.00
Paycheck	1/16/2007	107	Bryan Christopher			Payroll Liabilities	Checking	-20.00	150.00
Paycheck	1/16/2007	107	Bryan Christopher			Payroll Liabilities	Checking	-137.50	12.50
Paycheck	1/16/2007	107	Bryan Christopher			Payroll Liabilities	Checking	-12.50	0.00
Paycheck	1/16/2007	107	Bryan Christopher			Payroll Expenses	Checking	6.25	6.25
Paycheck	1/16/2007	107	Bryan Christopher			Payroll Liabilities	Checking	-6.25	0.00
Paycheck	1/16/2007	108	Loriel Sanchez			Checking	-SPLIT-	-708.32	-708.32
Paycheck	1/16/2007	108	Loriel Sanchez			Payroll Expenses	Checking	975.00	266.68
Paycheck	1/16/2007	108	Loriel Sanchez			Payroll Expenses	Checking	0.98	267.66
Paycheck	1/16/2007	108	Loriel Sanchez			Payroll Liabilities	Checking	-0.98	266.66
Paycheck	1/16/2007	108	Loriel Sanchez			Payroll Liabilities	Checking	-133.58	133.10
Paycheck	1/16/2007	108	Loriel Sanchez			Payroll Expenses	Checking	60.45	193.55
Paycheck	1/16/2007	108	Loriel Sanchez			Payroll Liabilities	Checking	-60.45	133.10
Paycheck	1/16/2007	108	Loriel Sanchez			Payroll Liabilities	Checking	-60.45	72.65
Paycheck	1/16/2007	108	Loriel Sanchez			Payroll Expenses	Checking	14.14	86.79
Paycheck	1/16/2007	108	Loriel Sanchez			Payroll Liabilities	Checking	-14.14	72.65
Paycheck	1/16/2007	108	Loriel Sanchez			Payroll Liabilities	Checking	-14.14	58.51
Paycheck	1/16/2007	108	Loriel Sanchez			Payroll Expenses	Checking	7.80	66.31
Paycheck	1/16/2007	108	Loriel Sanchez			Payroll Liabilities	Checking	-7.80	58.51
Paycheck	1/16/2007	108	Loriel Sanchez			Payroll Liabilities	Checking	-53.63	4.88
Paycheck	1/16/2007	108	Loriel Sanchez			Payroll Liabilities	Checking	-4.88	0.00
Paycheck	1/16/2007	108	Loriel Sanchez			Payroll Expenses	Checking	2.44	2.44
Paycheck	1/16/2007	108	Loriel Sanchez			Payroll Liabilities	Checking	-2.44	0.00
Paycheck	1/16/2007	109	Sharon Lee			Checking	-SPLIT-	-723.60	-723.60
Paycheck	1/16/2007	109	Sharon Lee			Payroll Expenses	Checking	996.00	272.40
Paycheck	1/16/2007	109	Sharon Lee			Payroll Expenses	Checking	1.00	273.40
Paycheck	1/16/2007	109	Sharon Lee			Payroll Liabilities	Checking	-1.00	272.40
Paycheck	1/16/2007	109	Sharon Lee			Payroll Liabilities	Checking	-136.45	135.95
Paycheck	1/16/2007	109	Sharon Lee			Payroll Expenses	Checking	61.75	197.70
Paycheck	1/16/2007	109	Sharon Lee			Payroll Liabilities	Checking	-61.75	135.95
Paycheck	1/16/2007	109	Sharon Lee			Payroll Liabilities	Checking	-61.75	74.20
Paycheck	1/16/2007	109	Sharon Lee			Payroll Expenses	Checking	14.44	88.64
Paycheck	1/16/2007	109	Sharon Lee			Payroll Liabilities	Checking	-14.44	74.20
Paycheck	1/16/2007	109	Sharon Lee			Payroll Liabilities	Checking	-14.44	59.76
Paycheck	1/16/2007	109	Sharon Lee			Payroll Expenses	Checking	7.97	67.73
Paycheck	1/16/2007	109	Sharon Lee			Payroll Liabilities	Checking	-7.97	59.76
Paycheck	1/16/2007	109	Sharon Lee			Payroll Liabilities	Checking	-54.78	4.98

Figure 3.29 (Contcluded)

Sunset Spas
Custom Transaction Detail Report
January 1-16, 2007

Type	Date	Num	Name	Memo	Account	Clr	Split	Amount	Balance
Paycheck	1/16/2007	109	Sharon Lee		Payroll Liabilities		Checking	-4.98	0.00
Paycheck	1/16/2007	109	Sharon Lee		Payroll Expenses		Checking	2.49	2.49
Paycheck	1/16/2007	109	Sharon Lee		Payroll Liabilities		Checking	-2.49	0.00
Jan 1–16, 07								**0.00**	**0.00**

Page 3

Figure 3.30

Sunset Spas

Inventory Valuation Summary
As of January 16, 2007

Item Description	On Hand	Avg Cost	Asset Value	% of Tot As...	Sales Price	Retail Value	% of Tot Re...
Inventory							
201 Maxus	7	5,000.00	35,000.00	16.5%	7,000.00	49,000.00	17.4%
202 Optima	9	6,000.00	54,000.00	25.5%	8,000.00	72,000.00	25.6%
203 Cameo	8	7,000.00	56,000.00	26.5%	9,000.00	72,000.00	25.6%
301 Galaxy	2	4,500.00	9,000.00	4.3%	6,500.00	13,000.00	4.6%
302 Ultimate	5	5,500.00	27,500.00	13%	7,500.00	37,500.00	13.3%
303 Aqua	4	7,500.00	30,000.00	14.2%	9,500.00	38,000.00	13.5%
Total Inventory	35		211,500.00	100.00%		281,500.00	100.00%
TOTAL	35		211,500.00	100.00%		281,500.00	100.00%

Figure 3.31

Sunset Spas
Balance Sheet
As of January 16, 2007

	Jan 16, 07	% of Column
ASSETS		
Current Assets		
Checking/Savings		
Checking	64,793.43	20.2%
Total Checking/Savings	64,793.43	20.2%
Accounts Receivable		
Accounts Receivable	−5,000.00	−1.6%
Total Accounts Receivable	−5,000.00	−1.6%
Other Current Assets		
Inventory Asset	211,500.00	65.8%
Short-term investments	30,000.00	9.3%
Total Other Current Assets	241,500.00	75.2%
Total Current Assets	301,293.43	93.8%
Fixed Assets		
Equipment		
Cost	12,400.00	3.9%
Total Equipment	12,400.00	3.9%
Furniture/Fixtures		
Cost	4,500.00	1.4%
Total Furniture/Fixtures	4,500.00	1.4%
Total Fixed Assets	16,900.00	5.3%
Other Assets		
Prepaid Rent	3,000.00	0.9%
Total Other Assets	3,000.00	0.9%
TOTAL ASSETS	321,193.43	100.0%
LIABILITIES & EQUITY		
Liabilities		
Current Liabilities		
Other Current Liabilities		
Payroll Liabilities	1,616.29	0.5%
Sales Tax Payable	6,001.60	1.9%
Total Other Current Liabilities	7,617.89	2.4%
Total Current Liabilities	7,617.89	2.4%
Long Term Liabilities		
Note Payable	200,000.00	62.3%
Total Long Term Liabilities	200,000.00	62.3%
Total Liabilities	207,617.89	64.6%
Equity		
Common Stock	100,000.00	31.1%
Net Income	13,575.54	4.2%
Total Equity	113,575.54	35.4%
TOTAL LIABILITIES & EQUITY	321,193.43	100.0%

Figure 3.32

Sunset Spas
Profit & Loss
January 1-16, 2007

	Jan 1-16, 07	% of Income
Ordinary Income Expense		
Income		
Sales		
Merchandise	76,000.00	98.1%
Service	1,440.00	1.9%
Total Sales	77,440.00	100.0%
Total Income	77,440.00	100.0%
Cost of Goods Sold		
Cost of Goods Sold	56,000.00	72.3%
Total COGS	56,000.00	72.3%
Gross Profit	21,440.00	27.7%
Expense		
Payroll Expenses	4,864.46	6.3%
Rent	3,000.00	3.9%
Total Expense	7,864.46	10.2%
Net Ordinary Income	13,575.54	15.5%
Net Income	**13,575.54**	**17.5%**

Figure 3.33

Sunset Spas
Statement of Cash Flows
January 1-16, 2007

	Jan 1-16, 07
OPERATING ACTIVITIES	
Net Income	13,575.54
Adjustments to reconcile Net Income to net cash provided by operations:	
Accounts Receivable	5,000.00
Inventory Asset	-211,500.00
Short Term Investments	-30,000.00
Payroll Liabilities	1,616.29
Sales Tax Payable	6,001.60
Net cash provided by Operating Activities	-215,306.57
INVESTING ACTIVITIES	
Equipment:Cost	-12,400.00
Furniture/Fixtures:Cost	-4,500.00
Prepaid Rent	-3,000.00
Net cash provided by Investing Activities	-19,900.00
FINANCING ACTIVITIES	
Notes Payable	200,000.00
Common Stock	100,000.00
Net cash provided by Financing Activities	300,000.00
Net cash increase for period	64,793.43
Cash at end of period	**64,793.43**

Additional Business Activities

In Chapter 4 students learn to record additional operating, investing, and financing activities—including both cash and non-cash transactions. This includes sales and purchases on account, borrowing and investing transactions, as well as non-cash debt for asset exchanges.

Chapter 4 Questions

1. You can create purchase orders either by selecting the Purchase Orders button in the QuickBooks Navigator or selecting Create Purchase Orders from the Vendors menu.

2. To record the receipt of inventory and related bills in QuickBooks:

    a. Select Vendors, then Receive Items and Enter Bills.

    b. Select a vendor from the drop-down list.

    c. Enter the date, amount, terms, item, and quantity (enter this information after clicking the Item tab).

    d. Click Save & Close or Save & New to enter the bill and inventory receipt.

3. Vendor names are available in the Enter Bills window using the drop-down list next to the Vendor title.

4. In most cases the standard payment terms are available when entering bills. These include 1% 10 net 30, 2% 10 net 30, due on receipt, net 15, net 30, and net 60.

5. QuickBooks defaults to the accrual basis of accounting in which revenue is recognized when a product is delivered or a service performed.

6. The Receive Payments item on the Customers menu is used to record payments received on account.

7. Ideally, payments should be deposited immediately. However, from a practical standpoint they are not. When you do not make deposits immediately, QuickBooks provides you with a method to group payments received for later deposit. An account called Undeposited Funds is used to record those receipts which will be deposited at a later date.

8. Whenever you enter a bill with a vendor name that is not part of the vendor list, QuickBooks prompts you with a Vendor Not Found window. In this window, you can either quickly add this vendor or go through the regular set-up process to add the vendor and all related information.

9. Non-cash investing and financing activities are standard investing and financing activities such as receiving a capital contribution, purchasing a long-term asset, borrowing, and repayment of borrowing with no cash inflow or outflow. These types of transactions are usually recorded in the QuickBooks accounting system using registers or special journal entry transactions.

10. To print checks in QuickBooks:

    a. Select Print Forms from the File menu.

    b. Choose Checks from the submenu.

    c. Select a bank account from the drop-down list.

    d. Select checks to print.

    e. Click OK.

Chapter 4 Assignments

1. Adding More Information to Phoenix Systems, Inc.

    a. The completed Balance Sheet is shown in Figure 4.1.

    b. The completed Income Statement is shown in Figure 4.2.

2. Adding more information to Central Coast Cellular.

    Items a.–e. have no output required.

    f. Item *f* requires three outputs.
        *   The completed Profit and Loss statement is shown in Figure 4.3.
        *   The completed Balance Sheet is shown in Figure 4.4.
        *   The completed Transaction Report is shown in Figure 4.5.

3. Internet assignments and related solutions are found at *http://owen.swlearning.com.*

Chapter 4   Case Problems

1. Ocean View Flowers

    a.   The completed Balance Sheet is shown in Figure 4.6.

    b.   The completed Profit & Loss statement is shown in Figure 4.7.

    c.   The completed Transactions Report is shown in Figure 4.8.

2. Jennings & Associates—Cash-Oriented Activities

    a.   The completed Balance Sheet is shown in Figure 4.9.

    b.   The completed Profit & Loss statement is shown in Figure 4.10.

Solution Figures for Chapter 4

Figure 4.1

Phoenix Software 04cp
Balance Sheet
As of March 31, 2003

	Mar 31, 03
ASSETS	
Current Assets	
Checking/Savings	
Bank of Cupertino	103,898.55
Short-term Investments	13,000.00
Total Checking/Savings	116,898.55
Accounts Receivable	
Accounts Receivable	27,234.51
Total Accounts Receivable	27,234.51
Other Current Assets	
Inventory Asset	22,979.40
Investments	12,000.00
Prepaid Insurance	1,384.67
Prepaid Rent	1,600.00
Undeposited Funds	10,000.00
Total Other Current Assets	47,964.07
Total Current Assets	192,097.13
Fixed Assets	
Computer Equipment	
Cost	28,750.00
Total Computer Equipment	28,750.00
Furniture	
Cost	3,756.44
Total Furniture	3,756.44
Total Fixed Assets	32,506.44
TOTAL ASSETS	**224,603.57**
LIABILITIES & EQUITY	
Liabilities	
Current Liabilities	
Accounts Payable	
Accounts Payable	24,699.50
Total Accounts Payable	24,699.50
Other Current Liabilities	
Payroll Liabilities	7,992.81
Sales Tax Payable	7,202.63
Short-Term Debt	5,000.00
Total Other Current Liabilities	20,195.44
Total Current Liabilities	44,894.94
Long Term Liabilities	
Long-Term Debt	86,500.00
Total Long Term Liabilities	86,500.00
Total Liabilities	131,394.94
Equity	
Capital Stock	75,000.00
Net Income	18,208.63
Total Equity	93,208.63
TOTAL LIABILITIES & EQUITY	**224,603.57**

Figure 4.2

Phoenix Software 04cp
Profit & Loss
January through March 2003

	Jan - Mar 03
Ordinary Income/Expense	
Income	
Computer Add-ons	2,000.00
Computer Sales	75,550.00
Consulting Income	7,800.00
Maintenance & Repairs	10,535.00
Parts income	149.85
Total Income	96,034.85
Cost of Goods Sold	
Cost of Goods Sold	53,769.85
Total COGS	53,769.85
Gross Profit	42,265.00
Expense	
Office Supplies	650.16
Payroll Expenses	22,859.05
Rent	1,600.00
Telephone	328.16
Utilities	
Gas and Electric	619.00
Total Utilities	619.00
Total Expense	26,056.37
Net Ordinary Income	16,208.63
Other Income/Expense	
Other Income	
Investment Income	3,000.00
Other Income	-1,000.00
Total Other Income	2,000.00
Net Other Income	2,000.00
Net Income	**18,208.63**

Figure 4.3

Central Coast Cellular
Profit and Loss
January 2003

	Jan 03
Ordinary Income/Expense	
Income	
Commissions	1,750.00
Consulting	7,600.00
Phone Sales	10,375.00
Total Income	19,725.00
Cost of Goods Sold	
Cost of Goods Sold	6,875.00
Total COGS	6,875.00
Gross Profit	12,850.00
Expense	
Payroll Expenses	9,812.44
Rent	3,000.00
Total Expense	12,812.44
Net Ordinary Income	37.56
Net Income	**37.56**

Figure 4.4

Central Coast Cellular
Balance Sheet
As of January 31, 2003

	Jan 31, 03
ASSETS	
Current Assets	
Checking/Savings	
Checking	130,472.87
Total Checking/Savings	130,472.87
Accounts Receivable	
Accounts Receivable	3,878.00
Total Accounts Receivable	3,878.00
Other Current Assets	
Store Supplies	3,000.00
Inventory Asset	14,750.00
Short-term Investments	75,000.00
Total Other Current Assets	92,750.00
Total Current Assets	227,100.87
Fixed Assets	
Equipment	
Cost	95,000.00
Total Equipment	95,000.00
Office Furniture	
Cost	20,000.00
Total Furniture	20,000.00
Total Fixed Assets	115,000.00
Other Assets	
Security Deposit	3,000.00
Total Other Assets	3,000.00
TOTAL ASSETS	**345,100.87**
LIABILITIES & EQUITY	
Liabilities	
Current Liabilities	
Accounts Payable	
Accounts Payable	15,125.00
Total Accounts Payable	15,125.00
Other Current Liabilities	
Payroll Liabilities	3,360.31
Sales Tax Payable	1,578.00
Total Other Current Liabilities	4,938.31
Total Current Liabilities	20,063.31
Long Term Liabilities	
Notes Payable	125,000.00
Total Long Term Liabilities	125,000.00
Total Liabilities	145,063.31
Equity	
Common Stock	200,000.00
Net Income	37.56
Total Equity	200,037.56
TOTAL LIABILITIES & EQUITY	**345,100.87**

Figure 4.5

Central Coast Cellular
Custom Transaction Detail Report
January 20-31, 2003

Type	Date	Num	Name	Memo	Account	Cir	Split	Amount	Balance
Jan 20 – 31,03									
Bill	1/20/2003		Nokia Mobile Phones		Accounts Payable		-SPLIT-	-15,125.00	-15,125.00
Bill	1/20/2003		Nokia Mobile Phones	Nokia 3285	Inventory Asset		Accounts Pay...	5,000.00	-10,125.00
Bill	1/20/2003		Nokia Mobile Phones	Nokia 8290	Inventory Asset		Accounts Pay...	7,500.00	-2,625.00
Bill	1/20/2003		Nokia Mobile Phones	Nokia 8890	Inventory Asset		Accounts Pay...	2,625.00	0.00
Invoice	1/21/2003	10001	City of San Luis Obi...		Accounts Receivable		-SPLIT-	13,878.00	13,878.00
Invoice	1/21/2003	10001	City of San Luis Obi...	Nokia 8290	Phone Sales		Accounts Rec...	-4,500.00	9,378.00
Invoice	1/21/2003	10001	City of San Luis Obi...	Nokia 8290	Inventory Asset		Accounts Rec...	-3,000.00	6,378.00
Invoice	1/21/2003	10001	City of San Luis Obi...	Nokia 8290	Cost of Goods Sold		Accounts Rec...	3,000.00	9,378.00
Invoice	1/21/2003	10001	City of San Luis Obi...	Nokia 8890	Phone Sales		Accounts Rec...	-3,750.00	5,628.00
Invoice	1/21/2003	10001	City of San Luis Obi...	Nokia 8890	Inventory Asset		Accounts Rec...	-2,625.00	3,003.00
Invoice	1/21/2003	10001	City of San Luis Obi...	Nokia 8890	Cost of Goods Sold		Accounts Rec...	2,625.00	5,628.00
Invoice	1/21/2003	10001	City of San Luis Obi...	Consulting	Consulting		Accounts Rec...	-2,850.00	2,778.00
Invoice	1/21/2003	10001	City of San Luis Obi...	Commissions	Commissions		Accounts Rec...	-1,750.00	1,028.00
Invoice	1/21/2003	10001	State Board of Equ...	Sales Tax	Sales Tax Payable		Accounts Rec...	-1,028.00	0.00
Check	1/22/2003		Kyle Equipment, Inc.		Checking		Cost	-95,000.00	-95,000.00
Check	1/24/2003		Kyle Equipment, Inc.		Cost		Checking	95,000.00	0.00
Check	1/24/2003		Ericsson, Inc.		Checking		Accounts Pay...	-6,500.00	-6,500.00
Check	1/24/2003		Ericsson, Inc.		Accounts Payable		Checking	6,500.00	0.00
Paycheck	1/31/2003		Alex Rodriguez		Checking		-SPLIT-	-1,437.00	-1,437.00
Paycheck	1/31/2003		Alex Rodriguez		Payroll Expenses		Checking	2,000.00	563.00
Paycheck	1/31/2003		Alex Rodriguez		Payroll Liabilities		Checking	-300.00	263.00
Paycheck	1/31/2003		Alex Rodriguez		Payroll Expenses		Checking	124.00	387.00
Paycheck	1/31/2003		Alex Rodriguez		Payroll Liabilities		Checking	-124.00	263.00
Paycheck	1/31/2003		Alex Rodriguez		Payroll Liabilities		Checking	-124.00	139.00
Paycheck	1/31/2003		Alex Rodriguez		Payroll Expenses		Checking	29.00	168.00
Paycheck	1/31/2003		Alex Rodriguez		Payroll Liabilities		Checking	-29.00	139.00
Paycheck	1/31/2003		Alex Rodriguez		Payroll Liabilities		Checking	-29.00	110.00
Paycheck	1/31/2003		Alex Rodriguez		Payroll Expenses		Checking	6.40	116.40
Paycheck	1/31/2003		Alex Rodriguez		Payroll Liabilities		Checking	-6.40	110.00
Paycheck	1/31/2003		Alex Rodriguez		Payroll Liabilities		Checking	-100.00	10.00
Paycheck	1/31/2003		Alex Rodriguez		Payroll Liabilities		Checking	-10.00	0.00
Paycheck	1/31/2003		Alex Rodriguez		Payroll Expenses		Checking	24.00	24.00
Paycheck	1/31/2003		Alex Rodriguez		Payroll Liabilities		Checking	-24.00	0.00
Paycheck	1/31/2003		Alex Rodriguez		Payroll Expenses		Checking	2.00	2.00
Paycheck	1/31/2003		Alex Rodriguez		Payroll Liabilities		Checking	-2.00	0.00
Paycheck	1/31/2003		Jay Bruner		Checking		-SPLIT-	-1,077.75	-1,077.75
Paycheck	1/31/2003		Jay Bruner		Payroll Expenses		Checking	1,500.00	422.25
Paycheck	1/31/2003		Jay Bruner		Payroll Liabilities		Checking	-225.00	197.25
Paycheck	1/31/2003		Jay Bruner		Payroll Expenses		Checking	93.00	290.25
Paycheck	1/31/2003		Jay Bruner		Payroll Liabilities		Checking	-93.00	197.25
Paycheck	1/31/2003		Jay Bruner		Payroll Liabilities		Checking	-93.00	104.25
Paycheck	1/31/2003		Jay Bruner		Payroll Expenses		Checking	21.75	126.00
Paycheck	1/31/2003		Jay Bruner		Payroll Liabilities		Checking	-21.75	104.25
Paycheck	1/31/2003		Jay Bruner		Payroll Liabilities		Checking	-21.75	82.50
Paycheck	1/31/2003		Jay Bruner		Payroll Expenses		Checking	4.80	87.30
Paycheck	1/31/2003		Jay Bruner		Payroll Liabilities		Checking	-4.80	82.50
Paycheck	1/31/2003		Jay Bruner		Payroll Liabilities		Checking	-75.00	7.50
Paycheck	1/31/2003		Jay Bruner		Payroll Liabilities		Checking	-7.50	0.00

Figure 4.5 (Concluded)

Type	Date	Num	Name	Memo	Account	Clr	Split	Amount	Balance
Paycheck	1/31/2003		Jay Bruner		Payroll Expenses		Checking	18.00	18.00
Paycheck	1/31/2003		Jay Bruner		Payroll Liabilities		Checking	-18.00	0.00
Paycheck	1/31/2003		Jay Bruner		Payroll Expenses		Checking	1.50	1.50
Paycheck	1/31/2003		Jay Bruner		Payroll Liabilities		Checking	-1.50	0.00
Paycheck	1/31/2003		Megan Paulson		Checking		-SPLIT-	-732.87	-732.87
Paycheck	1/31/2003		Megan Paulson		Payroll Expenses		Checking	1,020.00	287.13
Paycheck	1/31/2003		Megan Paulson		Payroll Liabilities		Checking	-153.00	134.13
Paycheck	1/31/2003		Megan Paulson		Payroll Expenses		Checking	63.24	197.37
Paycheck	1/31/2003		Megan Paulson		Payroll Liabilities		Checking	-63.24	134.13
Paycheck	1/31/2003		Megan Paulson		Payroll Liabilities		Checking	-63.24	70.89
Paycheck	1/31/2003		Megan Paulson		Payroll Expenses		Checking	14.79	85.68
Paycheck	1/31/2003		Megan Paulson		Payroll Liabilities		Checking	-14.79	70.89
Paycheck	1/31/2003		Megan Paulson		Payroll Expenses		Checking	-14.79	56.10
Paycheck	1/31/2003		Megan Paulson		Payroll Liabilities		Checking	3.26	59.36
Paycheck	1/31/2003		Megan Paulson		Payroll Expenses		Checking	-3.26	56.10
Paycheck	1/31/2003		Megan Paulson		Payroll Liabilities		Checking	-51.00	5.10
Paycheck	1/31/2003		Megan Paulson		Payroll Liabilities		Checking	-5.10	0.00
Paycheck	1/31/2003		Megan Paulson		Payroll Expenses		Checking	12.24	12.24
Paycheck	1/31/2003		Megan Paulson		Payroll Liabilities		Checking	-12.24	0.00
Paycheck	1/31/2003		Megan Paulson		Payroll Expenses		Checking	1.02	1.02
Paycheck	1/31/2003		Megan Paulson		Payroll Liabilities		Checking	-1.02	0.00
Jan 20 – 31, 03								0.00	0.00

Figure 4.6

Ocean View Flowers Ch #4
Balance Sheet
As of February 29, 2004

	Feb 29, '04
ASSETS	
Current Assets	
Checking/Savings	
Union Checking	29,367.06
Total Checking/Savings	29,367.06
Accounts Receivable	
Accounts Receivable	30,500.00
Total Accounts Receivable	30,500.00
Other Current Assets	
Short-term investments	20,000.00
Prepaid Insurance	2,500.00
Undeposited Funds	9,000.00
Office Supplies	1,500.00
Inventory Asset	43,900.00
Total Other Current Assets	76,900.00
Total Current Assets	136,767.06
Fixed Assets	
Land	50,000.00
Building	
Cost	250,000.00
Total Building	250,000.00
Computer Equipment	
Cost	15,000.00
Total Computer Equipment	15,000.00
Office Equipment	
Cost	20,000.00
Total Office Equipment	20,000.00
Total Fixed Assets	335,000.00
TOTAL ASSETS	**471,767.06**
LIABILITIES & EQUITY	
Liabilities	
Current Liabilities	
Accounts Payable	
Accounts Payable	47,860.00
Total Accounts Payable	47,860.00
Other Current Liabilities	
Payroll Liabilities	14,086.68
Total Other Current Liabilities	14,086.68
Total Current Liabilities	61,946.68
Long Term Liabilities	
Long Term Note Payable	319,000.00
Total Long Term Liabilities	319,000.00
Total Liabilities	380,946.68
Equity	
Capital Stock	100,000.00
Net Income	-9,179.62
Total Equity	90,820.38
TOTAL LIABILITIES & EQUITY	**471,767.06**

Figure 4.7

Ocean View Flowers
Profit & Loss
February 2004

	Feb 04
Ordinary Income/Expense	
Income	
Sales	
Anthuriums	35,500.00
Daylilies	9,000.00
Total Sales	44,500.00
Total Income	44,500.00
Cost of Goods Sold	
Cost of Goods Sold	24,000.00
Total COGS	24,000.00
Gross Profit	20,500.00
Expense	
Payroll Expenses	19,553.72
Subscriptions	60.00
Telephone	250.00
Utilities	
Gas and Electric	300.00
Total Expense	20,163.72
Net Ordinary Income	336.28
Other Income/Expense	
Other Income	
Interest Revenue	200.00
Total Other Income	200.00
Net Other Income	200.00
Net Income	**536.28**

Figure 4.8

Ocean View Flowers
Transactions by Date
February 2004

Type	Date	Num	Name	Memo	Account	Clr	Split	Amount
Feb '04								
Check	2/1/2004	119	Santa Barbara Ban...		Union Checking		Long-Term No....	-1,000.00
Check	2/3/2004	120	State Farm Insurance		Union Checking		Prepaid Insurance	-2,500.00
Deposit	2/9/2004			Deposit	Union Checking		-SPLIT-	5,200.00
Bill	2/12/2004		GTE		Accounts Payable		Telephone	-250.00
Bill	2/12/2004		Edison Inc.		Accounts Payable		Utilities	-300.00
Bill	2/12/2004		FlowerMart		Accounts Payable		Subscriptions	-60.00
Paycheck	2/15/2004	121	Edward Thomas		Union Checking		-SPLIT-	-1,819.66
Paycheck	2/15/2004	122	Kelly Gusland		Union Checking		-SPLIT-	-710.28
Paycheck	2/15/2004	123	Margie Coe		Union Checking		-SPLIT-	-671.98
Paycheck	2/15/2004	124	Marie McAninch		Union Checking		-SPLIT-	-1,740.70
Paycheck	2/15/2004	125	Stan Comstock		Union Checking		-SPLIT-	-1,565.68
Bill	2/18/2004		Vordale Farms		Accounts Payable		-SPLIT-	-47,800.00
Invoice	2/22/2004	10001	Latin Ladies		Accounts Receivable		Anthuriums	9,000.00
Invoice	2/22/2004	10002	California Beauties		Accounts Receivable		Anthuriums	25,000.00
Invoice	2/22/2004	10003	FTD		Accounts Receivable		Anthuriums	10,500.00
Bill Pmt -Check	2/24/2004	126	Edison Inc.		Union Checking		Accounts Payable	-300.00
Bill Pmt -Check	2/24/2004	127	GTE		Union Checking		Accounts Payable	-250.00
Payment	2/25/2004		Latin Ladies		Undeposited Funds		Accounts Receivable	9,000.00
Check	2/26/2004	128	Hawaiian Farms		Union Checking		-SPLIT-	-30,000.00
Paycheck	2/26/2004	129	Edward Thomas		Union Checking		-SPLIT-	-1,819.67
Paycheck	2/26/2004	130	Kelly Gusland		Union Checking		-SPLIT-	-579.55
Paycheck	2/26/2004	131	Margie Coe		Union Checking		-SPLIT-	-431.99
Paycheck	2/26/2004	132	Marie McAninch		Union Checking		-SPLIT-	-1,740.70
Paycheck	2/26/2004	133	Stan Comstock		Union Checking		-SPLIT-	-1,565.67
Feb '04								

Figure 4.9

Jennings & Associates (KJ04cp)
Balance Sheet
As of March 31, 2004

	Mar 31, 04
ASSETS	
Current Assets	
Checking/Savings	
First Valley Savings & Loan	56,793.50
Union Bank Checking	9,052.99
Total Checking/Savings	65,846.49
Accounts Receivable	
Accounts Receivable	13,175.00
Total Accounts Receivable	13,175.00
Other Current Assets	
Interest Receivable	41.17
Inventory Asset	1,760.29
Prepaid Insurance	2,200.00
Short-term investments	2,000.00
Total Other Current Assets	6,001.46
Total Current Assets	85,022.95
Fixed Assets	
Computer Equipment	
Accumulated Depreciation	-1,083.33
Cost	14,000.00
Total Computer Equipment	12,916.67
Furniture	
Accumulated Depreciation	-541.67
Cost	2,500.00
Total Furniture	1,958.33
Vehicles	
Cost	18,500.00
Total Vehicles	18,500.00
Total Fixed Assets	33,375.00
TOTAL ASSETS	**118,397.95**
LIABILITIES & EQUITY	
Liabilities	
Current Liabilities	
Accounts Payable	
Accounts Payable	8,640.00
Total Accounts Payable	8,640.00
Other Current Liabilities	
Payroll Liabilities	6,694.08
Short-term Note Payable	8,000.00
Total Other Current Liabilities	14,694.08
Total Current Liabilities	23,334.08
Long Term Liabilities	
Vehicle Loan	18,500.00
Total Long Term Liabilities	18,500.00
Total Liabilities	41,834.08
Equity	
Capital Stock	70,000.00
Opening Bal Equity	3,590.00
Retained Earnings	2,250.00
Net Income	723.87
Total Equity	76,563.87
TOTAL LIABILITIES & EQUITY	**118,397.95**

Figure 4.10

Jennings & Associates (KJ04cp)
Profit & Loss
March 2004

	Mar 04
Ordinary Income/Expense	
Income	
Fee Income	
Film	75.00
Magazine	500.00
Press Release	250.00
Television	5,625.00
Total Fee Income	6,450.00
Total Income	6,450.00
Gross Profit	6,450.00
Expense	
Film expenses	45.00
Professional Fees	
Legal Fees	375.00
Total Professional Fees	375.00
Rent	700.00
TV Commercial Spots	7,500.00
Utilities	
Gas and Electric	65.00
Total Utilities	65.00
Total Expense	8,685.00
Net Ordinary Income	-2,235.00
Other Income/Expense	
Other Income	
Other Income	500.00
Total Other Income	500.00
Net Other Income	500.00
Net Income	**-1,735.00**

Adjusting Entries

In Chapter 5 students learn essential accrual accounting concepts. This includes the concepts of accruing revenues and expenses—emphasizing the revenue recognition, matching, and expense recognition. This chapter also includes the amortization and recognition of deferred asset cost and unearned revenue—again emphasizing the concepts of revenue recognition, matching, and expense recognition. Journal entries are not used in this chapter. Instead QuickBooks's register format is used. See the Appendix of the textbook for how you can use QuickBooks with debits and credits.

Chapter 5   Questions

1. This method requires you to debit one account and credit another.

2. Interest revenue is the accrued revenue example used in the text. Another example might be accrued fee revenue for services performed but not invoiced. To accrue this revenue at period end you would debit Accrued Fees Receivable and credit Fee Revenue.

3. Interest expense was the accrued expense example used in the text. Another example might be accrued rent expense for space used but not billed. To accrue this expense at period end, you would credit Accrued Liability and debit Rent Expense.

4. Prepaid Insurance and Depreciation are the two examples of adjusted assets used in the text. Another example might be an adjustment for office supplies used. Assuming office supplies are originally recorded as an asset, an adjustment is required at the end of the month to record the use of supplies. To account for this use at period end you would credit Office Supplies and debit Supplies Expense.

5. Advance payments from customers is the unearned revenue example used in the text. The initial payment received from the customer is recorded as a reduction in that customer's accounts receivable account. At period end, if you have credited an invoice to bill the customer, that portion billed needs to be offset against the prepayment. To do so, you must first apply the advance to the invoice by modifying the Receive Payment previously recorded. Using the Auto Apply button, you apply the advance payment to all open invoices. Secondly, you must reclassify any remaining credit balance in the customer's account to a liability account called Unearned Revenue. You accomplish this by crediting Unearned Revenue and debiting the accounts receivable account specific to that customer. (Sometimes, you must create an unearned revenue account.)

6. Click the Company menu, then click Make General Journal Entries.

7. The Reconcile item on the Banking menu is used to start a bank reconciliation.

8. Bank service charges are typically charged to a bank service charge expense account.

9. The difference between the ending balance and the cleared balance at the completion of a bank reconciliation, should be 0.

10. Included in the Reconciliation Summary report is

    a. the previous bank balance.

    b. cleared checks and payments.

    c. cleared deposits and other credits.

    d. the ending bank balance.

    e. uncleared checks and payments.

    f. uncleared deposits and other credits.

    g. the checking account balance as of the end of the period.

Chapter 5   Assignments

1. Adding more information to Phoenix Systems Consulting, Inc.

    a. n/a

    b. The completed bank Reconciliation Summary report is shown in Figure 5.1.

    c. The completed Balance Sheet is shown in Figure 5.2. The completed Income Statement is shown in Figure 5.3.

2. Adding more information: Central Coast Cellular.

   Items *a.–d.* have no output required

   e. Item *e* requires four outputs.
      - The completed Profit & Loss statement is shown in Figure 5.4.

      - The completed Balance Sheet is shown in Figure 5.5.

      - The completed Transaction Report is in Figure 5.6.

      - The completed bank Reconciliation Report is shown in Figure 5.7.

3. Internet assignments and related solutions are found at *http://owen.swlearning.com.*

Chapter 5 Case Problems

1. Ocean View Flowers

   a. The completed bank Reconciliation Summaries are shown in Figures 5.8 and 5.9.

   b. The completed Balance Sheet is shown in Figure 5.10.

   c. The completed Profit & Loss statement is shown in Figure 5.11.

   d. The completed Transactions Report is shown in Figure 5.12.

2. Jennings & Associates—Adjustments

   a. n/a

   b. The completed summary bank Reconciliation Report is shown in Figure 5.13.

   c. The completed standard Balance Sheet is shown in Figure 5.14.

   d. Completed standard Income Statement is shown in Figure 5.15.

Solution Figures for Chapter 5

Figure 5.1

Phoenix Software 05cp
Reconciliation Summary
Bank of Cupertino, Period Ending 03/31/03

	Mar 31, 03
Beginning Balance	85,086.27
Cleared Transactions	
Checks and Payments – 12 Items	-65,122.72
Deposits and Credits – 4 Items	28,334.25
Total Cleared Transactions	-36,788.47
Cleared Balance	**48,297.80**
Uncleared Transactions	
Checks and Payments – 3 Items	-7,502.29
Deposits and Other Credits – 1 Item	40,000.00
Total Uncleared Transactions	32,497.71
Register Balance as of 03/31/03	**80,795.51**
Ending Balance	80,795.51

Figure 5.2

Phoenix Software 05cp
Balance Sheet
As of March 31, 2003

	Mar 31 03
ASSETS	
Current Assets	
Checking/Savings	
Bank of Cupertino	80,795.51
Short-term Investments	13,225.00
Total Checking/Savings	94,020.51
Accounts Receivable	
Accounts Receivable	31,397.01
Total Accounts Receivable	31,397.01
Other Current Assets	
Inventory Asset	17,579.40
Investments	12,500.00
Prepaid Insurance	1,038.50
Prepaid Rent	800.00
Undeposited Funds	10,000.00
Total Other Current Assets	41,917.90
Total Current Assets	167,335.42
Fixed Assets	
Computer Equipment	
Cost	28,750.00
Accumulated Depreciation	-375.00
Total Computer Equipment	28,375.00
Furniture	
Cost	3,756.44
Accumulated Depreciation	-313.04
Total Furniture	3,443.40
Total Fixed Assets	31,818.40
TOTAL ASSETS	**199,153.82**
LIABILITIES & EQUITY	
Liabilities	
Current Liabilities	
Accounts Payable	
Accounts Payable	2,199.50
Total Accounts Payable	2,199.50
Other Current Liabilities	
Payroll Liabilities	11,754.36
Sales Tax Payable	7,696.88
Short-term Debt	5,250.00
Unearned Revenue	4,162.50
Total Other Current Liabilities	28,863.74
Total Current Liabilities	31,063.24
Long Term Liabilities	
Long-Term Debt	86,775.00
Total Long Term Liabilities	86,775.00
Total Liabilities	117,838.24
Equity	
Capital Stock	75,000.00
Net Income	6,315.58
Total Equity	81,315.58
TOTAL LIABILITIES & EQUITY	**199,153.82**

Figure 5.3

Phoenix Software 05cp
Profit & Loss
January through March 2003

	Jan – Mar 03
Ordinary Income/Expense	
Income	
Computer Add-ons	3,100.00
Computer Sales	80,950.00
Consulting Income	7,800.00
Maintenance & Repairs	10,625.00
Parts income	149.85
Total Income	102,624.85
Cost of Goods Sold	
Cost of Goods Sold	59,169.85
Total COGS	59,169.85
Gross Profit	43,455.00
Expense	
Bank Service Charges	185.00
Depreciation Expense	688.04
Insurance	
Liability Insurance	346.17
Total Insurance	346.17
Interest Expense	
Loan Interest	525.00
Total Interest Expense	525.00
Office Supplies	650.16
Payroll Expenses	34,122.89
Rent	2,400.00
Telephone	328.16
Utilities	
Gas and Electric	619.00
Total Utilities	619.00
Total Expense	39,864.42
Net Ordinary Income	3,590.58
Other Income/Expense	
Other Income	
Investment Income	2,000.00
Interest Revenue	725.00
Total Other Income	2,725.00
Net Other Income	2,725.00
Net Income	**6,315.58**

Figure 5.4

Central Coast Cellular
Profit & Loss
January 2003

	Jan 03
Ordinary Income/Expense	
Income	
Commissions	1,750.00
Consulting	7,600.00
Phone Sales	10,375.00
Total Income	19,725.00
Cost of Goods Sold	
Cost of Goods Sold	6,875.00
Total COGS	6,875.00
Gross Profit	12,850.00
Expense	
Bank Service Charges	80.00
Depreciation Expense	1,500.00
Interest Expense	
Loan Interest	950.00
Total Interest Expense	950.00
Payroll Expenses	9,812.44
Rent	3,000.00
Total Expense	15,342.44
Net Ordinary Income	-2,492.44
Net Income	**-2,492.44**

Figure 5.5

Central Coast Cellular
Balance Sheet
As of January 31, 2003

	Jan 31, 03
ASSETS	
Current Assets	
Checking/Savings	
Checking	130,392.87
Total Checking/Savings	130,392.87
Accounts Receivable	
Accounts Receivable	13,878.00
Total Accounts Receivable	13,878.00
Other Current Assets	
Store Supplies	3,000.00
Inventory Asset	14,750.00
Short-term Investments	75,000.00
Total Other Current Assets	92,750.00
Total Current Assets	237,020.87
Fixed Assets	
Equipment	
Cost	95,000.00
Accumulated Depreciation	-1,000.00
Total Equipment	94,000.00
Office Furniture	
Cost	20,000.00
Accumulated Depreciation	-500.00
Total Office Furniture	19,500.00
Total Fixed Assets	113,500.00
Other Assets	
Security Deposit	3,000.00
Total Other Assets	3,000.00
TOTAL ASSETS	**353,520.87**
LIABILITIES & EQUITY	
Liabilities	
Current Liabilities	
Accounts Payable	
Accounts Payable	15,125.00
Total Accounts Payable	15,125.00
Other Current Liabilities	
Interest Payable	950.00
Unearned Revenue	10,000.00
Payroll Liabilities	3,360.31
Sales Tax Payable	1,578.00
Total Other Current Liabilities	15,888.31
Total Current Liabilities	31,013.31
Long Term Liabilities	
Notes Payable	125,000.00
Total Long Term Liabilities	125,000.00
Total Liabilities	156,013.31
Equity	
Common Stock	200,000.00
Net Income	-2,492.44
Total Equity	197,507.56
TOTAL LIABILITIES & EQUITY	**353,520.87**

Figure 5.6

Central Coast Cellular
Custom Transaction Detail Report
January 31, 2003

Type	Date	Num	Name	Memo	Account	Clr	Split	Amount	Balance
Jan 31,03									
General Journal	1/31/2003	1			Depreciation Expense		-SPLIT-	1,500.00	1,500.00
General Journal	1/31/2003	1			Accumulated Depre...		Depreciation E...	-1,000.00	500.00
General Journal	1/31/2003	1			Accumulated Depre...		Depreciation E...	-500.00	0.00
General Journal	1/31/2003	2			Interest Expense		Interest Payable	950.00	950.00
General Journal	1/31/2003	2			Interest Payable		Interest Expen...	-950.00	0.00
Paycheck	1/31/2003	3010	Alex Rodriguez		Checking		-SPLIT-	-1,437.00	-1,437.00
Paycheck	1/31/2003	3010	Alex Rodriguez		Payroll Expenses		Checking	2,000.00	563.00
Paycheck	1/31/2003	3010	Alex Rodriguez		Payroll Expenses		Checking	-300.00	263.00
Paycheck	1/31/2003	3010	Alex Rodriguez		Payroll Liabilities		Checking	124.00	387.00
Paycheck	1/31/2003	3010	Alex Rodriguez		Payroll Liabilities		Checking	-124.00	263.00
Paycheck	1/31/2003	3010	Alex Rodriguez		Payroll Expenses		Checking	-124.00	139.00
Paycheck	1/31/2003	3010	Alex Rodriguez		Payroll Liabilities		Checking	29.00	168.00
Paycheck	1/31/2003	3010	Alex Rodriguez		Payroll Liabilities		Checking	-29.00	139.00
Paycheck	1/31/2003	3010	Alex Rodriguez		Payroll Expenses		Checking	-29.00	110.00
Paycheck	1/31/2003	3010	Alex Rodriguez		Payroll Expenses		Checking	6.40	116.40
Paycheck	1/31/2003	3010	Alex Rodriguez		Payroll Liabilities		Checking	-6.40	110.00
Paycheck	1/31/2003	3010	Alex Rodriguez		Payroll Liabilities		Checking	-100.00	10.00
Paycheck	1/31/2003	3010	Alex Rodriguez		Payroll Liabilities		Checking	-10.00	0.00
Paycheck	1/31/2003	3010	Alex Rodriguez		Payroll Expenses		Checking	24.00	24.00
Paycheck	1/31/2003	3010	Alex Rodriguez		Payroll Liabilities		Checking	-24.00	0.00
Paycheck	1/31/2003	3010	Alex Rodriguez		Payroll Expenses		Checking	2.00	2.00
Paycheck	1/31/2003	3010	Alex Rodriguez		Payroll Liabilities		Checking	-2.00	0.00
Paycheck	1/31/2003	3011	Jay Bruner		Checking		-SPLIT-	-1,077.75	-1,077.75
Paycheck	1/31/2003	3011	Jay Bruner		Payroll Expenses		Checking	1,500.00	422.25
Paycheck	1/31/2003	3011	Jay Bruner		Payroll Expenses		Checking	-225.00	197.25
Paycheck	1/31/2003	3011	Jay Bruner		Payroll Liabilities		Checking	93.00	290.25
Paycheck	1/31/2003	3011	Jay Bruner		Payroll Liabilities		Checking	-93.00	197.25
Paycheck	1/31/2003	3011	Jay Bruner		Payroll Expenses		Checking	-93.00	104.25
Paycheck	1/31/2003	3011	Jay Bruner		Payroll Liabilities		Checking	21.75	126.00
Paycheck	1/31/2003	3011	Jay Bruner		Payroll Liabilities		Checking	-21.75	104.25
Paycheck	1/31/2003	3011	Jay Bruner		Payroll Expenses		Checking	-21.75	82.50
Paycheck	1/31/2003	3011	Jay Bruner		Payroll Expenses		Checking	4.80	87.30
Paycheck	1/31/2003	3011	Jay Bruner		Payroll Liabilities		Checking	-4.80	82.50
Paycheck	1/31/2003	3011	Jay Bruner		Payroll Liabilities		Checking	-75.00	7.50
Paycheck	1/31/2003	3011	Jay Bruner		Payroll Liabilities		Checking	-7.50	0.00
Paycheck	1/31/2003	3011	Jay Bruner		Payroll Expenses		Checking	18.00	18.00
Paycheck	1/31/2003	3011	Jay Bruner		Payroll Liabilities		Checking	-18.00	0.00
Paycheck	1/31/2003	3011	Jay Bruner		Payroll Expenses		Checking	1.50	1.50
Paycheck	1/31/2003	3011	Jay Bruner		Payroll Liabilities		Checking	-1.50	0.00
Paycheck	1/31/2003	3012	Megan Paulson		Checking		-SPLIT-	-732.87	-732.87
Paycheck	1/31/2003	3012	Megan Paulson		Payroll Expenses		Checking	1,020.00	287.13
Paycheck	1/31/2003	3012	Megan Paulson		Payroll Expenses		Checking	-153.00	134.13
Paycheck	1/31/2003	3012	Megan Paulson		Payroll Liabilities		Checking	63.24	197.37
Paycheck	1/31/2003	3012	Megan Paulson		Payroll Liabilities		Checking	-63.24	134.13
Paycheck	1/31/2003	3012	Megan Paulson		Payroll Expenses		Checking	-63.24	70.89
Paycheck	1/31/2003	3012	Megan Paulson		Payroll Liabilities		Checking	14.79	85.68
Paycheck	1/31/2003	3012	Megan Paulson		Payroll Liabilities		Checking	-14.79	70.89
Paycheck	1/31/2003	3012	Megan Paulson		Payroll Expenses		Checking	-14.79	56.10
Paycheck	1/31/2003	3012	Megan Paulson		Payroll Expenses		Checking	3.26	59.36
Paycheck	1/31/2003	3012	Megan Paulson		Payroll Liabilities		Checking	-3.26	56.10
Paycheck	1/31/2003	3012	Megan Paulson		Payroll Liabilities		Checking	-51.00	5.10
Paycheck	1/31/2003	3012	Megan Paulson		Payroll Liabilities		Checking	-5.10	0.00
Paycheck	1/31/2003	3012	Megan Paulson		Payroll Expenses		Checking	12.24	12.24
Paycheck	1/31/2003	3012	Megan Paulson		Payroll Liabilities		Checking	-12.24	0.00
Paycheck	1/31/2003	3012	Megan Paulson		Payroll Expenses		Checking	1.02	1.02
Paycheck	1/31/2003	3012	Megan Paulson		Payroll Liabilities		Checking	-1.02	0.00
General Journal	1/31/2003	3	City of San Luis Obi...		Accounts Receivable		Unearned Rev...	10,000.00	10,000.00
General Journal	1/31/2003	3	City of San Luis Obi...		Unearned Revenue		Accounts Rec...	-10,000.00	0.00
Check	1/31/2003	3		Service Charge	Checking		Bank Service	-80.00	-80.00
Check	1/31/2003			Service Charge	Bank Service Charge...	X	Checking	80.00	0.00
Jan 31,03								**0.00**	**0.00**

Figure 5.7

Central Coast Cellular
Reconciliation Report
Checking, Period Ending 01/31/03

	Jan 31, 03
Beginning Balance	0.00
Cleared Transactions	
Cleared Checks and Payments – 10 Items	-208,784.51
Cleared Deposits and Credits – 4 Items	342,425.00
Total Cleared Transactions	133,640.49
Cleared Balance	**133,640.49**
Uncleared Transactions	
Checks and Payments – 3 Items	-3,247.62
Total Uncleared Transactions	-3,247.62
Register Balance as of 01/31/03	**130,392.87**
Ending Balance	130,392.87

Figure 5.8

Ocean View Flowers
Reconciliation Summary
Union Checking, Period Ending 01/31/04

	Jan 31, 04
Beginning Balance	0.00
Cleared Transactions	
Checks and Payments – 11 Items	-102,559.70
Deposits and Credits – 5 Items	178,900.00
Total Cleared Transactions	76,340.30
Cleared Balance	**76,340.30**
Uncleared Transactions	
Checks and Payments – 8 Items	-10,422.36
Deposits and Credits – 1 Items	5,000.00
Total Uncleared Transactions	-5,422.36
Register Balance as of 01/31/04	**70,917.94**
New Transactions	
Checks and Payments – 15 Items	-46,695.88
Deposits and Credits – 1 Items	5,200.00
Total New Transactions	-41,495.88
Ending Balance	**29,422.06**

Figure 5.9

Ocean View Flowers
Reconciliation Summary
Union Checking, Period Ending 02/29/04

	Feb 29, 04
Beginning Balance	76,340.30
Cleared Transactions	
Checks and Payments – 18 Items	-21,035.66
Deposits and Credits – 3 Items	10,275.00
Total Cleared Transactions	-10,760.66
Cleared Balance	**65,579.64**
Uncleared Transactions	
Checks and Payments – 6 Items	-36,137.58
Total Uncleared Transactions	-36,137.58
Register Balance as of 02/29/04	**29,442.06**
Ending Balance	29,442.06

Figure 5.10

Ocean View Flowers
Balance Sheet
As of February 29, 2004

	Feb 29, '04
ASSETS	
Current Assets	
Checking/Savings	
Union Checking	29,442.06
Total Checking/Savings	29,442.06
Accounts Receivable	
Accounts Receivable	30,500.00
Total Accounts Receivable	30,500.00
Other Current Assets	
Short-term investments	20,800.00
Prepaid Insurance	2,300.00
Undeposited Funds	9,000.00
Office Supplies	1,500.00
Inventory Asset	43,900.00
Total Other Current Assets	77,500.00
Total Current Assets	137,442.06
Fixed Assets	
Land	50,000.00
Building	
Cost	250,000.00
Accumulated Depreciation	-2,000.00
Total Building	248,000.00
Computer Equipment	
Cost	15,000.00
Accumulated Depreciation	-600.00
Total Computer Equipment	14,400.00
Office Equipment	
Cost	20,000.00
Accumulated Depreciation	-500.00
Total Office Equipment	19,500.00
Total Fixed Assets	331,900.00
TOTAL ASSETS	**469,342.06**
LIABILITIES & EQUITY	
Liabilities	
Current Liabilities	
Accounts Payable	
Accounts Payable	47,860.00
Total Accounts Payable	47,860.00
Other Current Liabilities	
Legal Fees Payable	2,500.00
Payroll Liabilities	14,086.68
Total Other Current Liabilities	16,586.68
Total Current Liabilities	64,446.68
Long Term Liabilities	
Long-term Note Payable	319,000.00
Total Long Term Liabilities	319,000.00
Total Liabilities	383,446.68

Figure 5.10 (Concluded)

Ocean View Flowers
Balance Sheet
As of February 29, 2004

	Feb 29, '04
Equity	
Common Stock	100,000.00
Net Income	-14,104.62
Total Equity	85,895.38
TOTAL LIABILITIES & EQUITY	469,342.06

Figure 5.11

Ocean View Flowers
Profit & Loss
January through February 2004

	Jan - Feb 04
Ordinary Income/Expense	
Income	
Sales	
Anthuriums	35,500.00
Daylilies	37,800.00
Total Sales	73,300.00
Total Income	73,300.00
Cost of Goods Sold	
Cost of Goods Sold	38,400.00
Total COGS	38,400.00
Gross Profit	34,900.00
Expense	
Bank Service Charges	100.00
Depreciation Expense	3,100.00
Insurance	
Liability Insurance	200.00
Total Insurance	200.00
Payroll Expenses	39,769.62
Professional Fees	
Legal Fees	2,500.00
Total Professional Fees	2,500.00
Rent	3,000.00
Subscriptions	60.00
Telephone	650.00
Utilities	
Gas & Electric	800.00
Total Utilities	800.00
Total Expense	50,179.62
Net Ordinary Income	-15,279.62
Other Income/Expense	
Other Income	
Interest Revenue	1,175.00
Total Other Income	1,175.00
Net Other Income	1,175.00
Net Income	-14,104.62

Figure 5.12

Ocean View Flowers Ch #5
Transactions by Date
January through February 2004

Jan - Feb 04

Type	Date	Num	Name	Memo	Account	Cir	Split	Amount
Deposit	1/4/2004			Deposit	Union Checking	X	Common Stock	100,000.00
Deposit	1/6/2004			Deposit	Union Checking	X	Long-Term No...	50,000.00
Check	1/8/2004	101	Prudent Investments		Union Checking	X	Short-term inv....	-25,000.00
Check	1/11/2004	102	Stateside Office Su...		Union Checking	X	Cost	-20,000.00
Check	1/12/2004	103	Gateway Computers		Union Checking	X	Cost	-15,000.00
Paycheck	1/15/2004	104	Edward Thomas		Union Checking	X	-SPLIT-	-1,819.67
Paycheck	1/15/2004	105	Kelly Gusland		Union Checking	X	-SPLIT-	-689.33
Paycheck	1/15/2004	106	Margie Coe		Union Checking	X	-SPLIT-	-689.33
Paycheck	1/15/2004	107	Marie McAninch		Union Checking	X	-SPLIT-	-1,740.70
Paycheck	1/15/2004	108	Stan Comstock		Union Checking	X	-SPLIT-	-1,565.67
Check	1/18/2004	109	Brophy Bros. Farms		Union Checking	X	-SPLIT-	-34,500.00
Check	1/18/2004	110	Stateside Office Su...		Union Checking	X	Office Supplies	-1,500.00
Sales Receipt	1/22/2004	1	Valley Florists		Union Checking	X	-SPLIT-	6,600.00
Sales Receipt	1/25/2004	2	Eastern Scents		Union Checking	X	-SPLIT-	22,200.00
Payment	1/28/2004		FTD		Union Checking	X	Accounts Rec...	5,000.00
Check	1/29/2004	111	Hawaiian Farms		Union Checking	X	Rent	-3,000.00
Check	1/29/2004	112	Edison Inc.		Union Checking	X	Utilities	-500.00
Check	1/29/2004	113	GTE		Union Checking	X	Telephone	-400.00
Paycheck	1/29/2004	114	Edward Thomas		Union Checking	X	-SPLIT-	-1,819.65
Paycheck	1/29/2004	115	Kelly Gusland		Union Checking	X	-SPLIT-	-741.90
Paycheck	1/29/2004	116	Margie Coe		Union Checking	X	-SPLIT-	-654.42
Paycheck	1/29/2004	117	Marie McAninch		Union Checking	X	-SPLIT-	-1,740.70
Paycheck	1/29/2004	118	Stan Comstock		Union Checking	X	-SPLIT-	-1,565.69
Check	1/31/2004		Santa Barbara Ban...	Service Charge	Union Checking	X	Bank Service ...	-45.00
Deposit	1/31/2004			Interest	Union Checking	X	Interest Reven...	100.00
Check	2/1/2004	119	Santa Barbara Ban...		Union Checking	X	Long-Term No...	-1,000.00
Check	2/3/2004	120	State Farm Insurance		Union Checking	X	Prepaid Insura...	-2,500.00
Deposit	2/9/2004			Deposit	Union Checking	X	-SPLIT-	5,000.00
Bill	2/12/2004		GTE		Accounts Payable		Telephone	-250.00
Bill	2/12/2004		Edison Inc.		Accounts Payable		Utilities	-300.00
Bill	2/12/2004		FlowerMart		Accounts Payable		Subscriptions	-60.00
Paycheck	2/15/2004	121	Edward Thomas		Union Checking	X	-SPLIT-	-1,819.66
Paycheck	2/15/2004	122	Kelly Gusland		Union Checking	X	-SPLIT-	-710.28
Paycheck	2/15/2004	123	Margie Coe		Union Checking	X	-SPLIT-	-671.98
Paycheck	2/15/2004	124	Marie McAninch		Union Checking	X	-SPLIT-	-1,740.70
Paycheck	2/15/2004	125	Stan Comstock		Union Checking	X	-SPLIT-	-1,565.68
Bill	2/18/2004		Vordale Farms		Accounts Payable		-SPLIT-	-47,800.00
Invoice	2/22/2004	10001	Latin Ladies		Accounts Receivable		Anthuriums	9,000.00
Invoice	2/22/2004	10002	California Beauties		Accounts Receivable		Anthuriums	25,000.00
Invoice	2/22/2004	10003	FTD		Accounts Receivable		Anthuriums	10,500.00
Bill Pmt -Check	2/24/2004	126	Edison Inc.		Union Checking	X	Accounts Pay...	-300.00
Bill Pmt -Check	2/24/2004	127	GTE		Union Checking	X	Accounts Pay...	-250.00
Payment	2/25/2004		Latin Ladies		Undeposited Funds		Accounts Rec...	9,000.00
Check	2/26/2004	128	Hawaiian Farms		Union Checking		-SPLIT-	-30,000.00
Paycheck	2/26/2004	129	Edward Thomas		Union Checking		-SPLIT-	-1,819.67
Paycheck	2/26/2004	130	Kelly Gusland		Union Checking		-SPLIT-	-579.55
Paycheck	2/26/2004	131	Margie Coe		Union Checking		-SPLIT-	-431.99
Paycheck	2/26/2004	132	Marie McAninch		Union Checking		-SPLIT-	-1,740.70
Paycheck	2/26/2004	133	Stan Comstock		Union Checking		-SPLIT-	-1,565.67
Check	2/28/2004			Service Charge	Union Checking	X	Bank Service ...	-55.00
Deposit	2/28/2004			Interest	Union Checking	X	Interest Reven...	75.00
Deposit	2/28/2004				Short-term investm...		Interest Reven...	800.00
General Journal	2/28/2004				Prepaid Insurance		Liability Insura...	-200.00
General Journal	2/28/2004				Accumulated Depre...		Depreciation E...	-2,000.00
General Journal	2/28/2004				Accumulated Depre...		Depreciation E...	-600.00
General Journal	2/28/2004				Accumulated Depre...		Depreciation E...	-500.00
General Journal	2/28/2004		Bear and Bull, Attor...		Legal fees payable		Legal Fees	-2,500.00

Jan - Feb 04

Figure 5.13

Jennings & Associates (KJ05cp)
Reconciliation Report
First Valley Savings & Loan, Period Ending 03/31/04

	Mar 31, 04
Beginning Balance	63,185.00
Cleared Transactions	
Checks and Payments – 14 Items	-18,914.50
Deposits and Other Credits – 5 Items	12,675.00
Total Cleared Transactions	-6,239.50
Cleared Balance	**56,945.50**
Uncleared Transactions	
Checks and Payments – 3 Items	-287.00
Total Uncleared Transactions	-287.00
Register Balance as of 03/31/04	**56,658.50**
Ending Balance	56,658.50

Figure 5.14

Jennings & Associates (KJ05cp)
Balance Sheet
As of March 31, 2004

	Mar 31, 04
ASSETS	
Current Assets	
Checking/Savings	
First Valley Savings & Loan	56,658.50
Union Bank Checking	2,518.47
Total Checking/Savings	59,176.97
Accounts Receivable	
Accounts Receivable	14,600.00
Total Accounts Receivable	14,600.00
Other Current Assets	
Interest Receivable	41.17
Inventory Asset	1,760.29
Prepaid Insurance	1,800.00
Short-term investments	2,459.00
Total Other Current Assets	6,060.46
Total Current Assets	79,837.43
Fixed Assets	
Computer Equipment	
Accumulated Depreciation	-1,518.33
Cost	14,000.00
Total Computer Equipment	12,481.67
Furniture	
Accumulated Depreciation	-625.01
Cost	2,500.00
Total Furniture	1,874.99
Vehicles	
Accumulated Depreciation	-300.00
Cost	18,500.00
Total Vehicles	18,200.00
Total Fixed Assets	32,556.66
TOTAL ASSETS	**112,394.09**
LIABILITIES & EQUITY	
Liabilities	
Current Liabilities	
Accounts Payable	
Accounts Payable	8,640.00
Total Accounts Payable	8,640.00
Other Current Liabilities	
Payroll Liabilities	9,941.80
Short-term Note Payable	8,000.00
Unearned Revenue	1,425.00
Total Other Current Liabilities	19,366.80
Total Current Liabilities	28,006.80
Long Term Liabilities	
Vehicle loan	18,580.00
Total Long Term Liabilities	18,580.00
Total Liabilities	46,586.80

Figure 5.14 (Concluded)

Jennings & Associates (KJ05cp)
Balance Sheet
As of March 31, 2004

	Mar 31, 04
Equity	
Capital Stock	70,000.00
Opening Bal Equity	3,590.00
Retained Earnings	2,250.00
Net Income	-10,032.71
Total Equity	65,807.29
TOTAL LIABILITIES & EQUITY	**112,394.09**

Figure 5.15

Jennings & Associates (KJ05cp)
Profit & Loss
January through March 2004

	Jan – Mar '04
Ordinary Income/Expense	
Income	
Fee Income	
Film	965.00
Magazine	8,600.00
Press Release	475.00
Promotion	7,600.00
Radio	2,177.50
Television	13,675.00
Total Fee Income	33,492.50
Total Income	33,492.50
Gross Profit	33,492.50
Expense	
Bank Service Charges	270.00
Depreciation Expense	943.34
Equipment Rental	75.00
Film Expenses	632.21
Insurance	
Liability Insurance	775.00
Total Insurance	775.00
Interest Expense	
Loan Interest	80.00
Total Interest Expense	80.00
Office Supplies	101.00
Payroll Expenses	29,023.83
Postage and Delivery	109.00
Practice Development	35.00
Printing and Reproduction	25.00
Professional Fees	
Legal Fees	650.00
Total Professional Fees	650.00
Radio Spots	0.00
Rent	1,400.00
Repairs	
Computer Repairs	95.00
Total Repairs	95.00
Telephone	89.00
TV Commercial Spots	10,000.00
Utilities	
Gas and Electric	165.00
Water	57.00
Total Utilities	222.00
Total Expense	44,525.38
Net Ordinary Income	-11,032.88
Other Income/Expense	
Other Income	
Net Income	**-10,032.71**

6

Budgeting

In Chapter 6 students learn the essentials of budgeting with QuickBooks. The importance of planning and control is emphasized in the overall purpose of accounting. Further reporting on the control aspects of an accounting information system is covered in Chapter 7, where budgets are compared to actual results.

Chapter 6   Questions

1. QuickBooks allows you to set up budgets for specific accounts within financial statements or for all specific financial statements.

2. Multiple yearly budgets are not allowed in QuickBooks. Each fiscal year can have a different budget but only one budget is allowed for each year.

3. The Fill Down feature of QuickBooks's budgeting process allows you to enter one amount for January and fill that amount down for each month thereafter. You can choose to keep the same values or increment or decrement each month by some amount or percentage.

4. As mentioned above, the amount by which QuickBooks can increment or decrement the previous month's balance can be either a dollar amount or a percentage.

5. Cost of goods sold is usually a fairly constant percentage of sales. Thus, when entering the budget for cost of goods sold you can use the calculator feature of QuickBooks's budget system and multiply sales by a constant percentage.

6. Budgets for revenues and expenses are made based on expected results for each month. Budgets for assets, liabilities, and equities are based on expected month-end balances. In many cases there is a relationship between each. For instance, budgets for accounts receivable are dependent on sales, while budgets for inventory and accounts payable are dependent on cost of sales and projected sales.

7. Budgeted accumulated depreciation accounts are increased by monthly depreciation expenses.

8. The Budget menu item in the Reports menu is used to access budget reports in QuickBooks.

9. You can access QuickBooks's calculator feature for budgeting by typing a formula into the monthly budget cell. For instance, when you type the formula 500 * 10% into the budget cell, QuickBooks will calculate the result ($50) for you.

10. Retained earnings at the end of each month is calculated as beginning of the month Retained Earnings plus Net Income less Dividends. Thus, when budgeting Retained Earnings, be sure to adjust the balance by the amount of Net Income budgeted less the amount of Dividends budgeted.

Chapter 6   Assignments

1. Modifying Budgets for Phoenix Systems, Inc.

    a. The Profit & Loss Budget Overview report for the period 1/1/03 through 3/31/03 is shown in Figure 6.1.

    b. The Balance Sheet Budget Overview report for the period 1/1/03 through 3/31/03 is shown in Figure 6.2.

2. Adding more information: Central Coast Cellular

    Items *a.–d.* have no output required.

    e. Item *e* requires two outputs. (Remember: This assignment requires student budget amounts, and thus the solutions below will not be what the student provides unless he or she copied my answers!)

    • The Profit & Loss Budget Overview report is shown in Figure 6.3.
    • The Balance Sheet Budget Overview report is shown in Figure 6.4.

3. Internet assignments and related solutions are found at *http://owen.swlearning.com.*

Chapter 6   Case Problems

1. Ocean View Flowers

    a. The Profit & Loss Budget Overview report is shown in Figure 6.5.

    b. The Balance Sheet Budget Overview report is shown in Figure 6.6.

2. Jennings & Associates—Budgets

    a. The Profit & Loss Budget Overview report for the period 1/1/04 through 3/31/04 is shown in Figure 6.7.

    b. The Balance Sheet Budget Overview report for the period 1/1/04 through 3/31/04 is shown in Figure 6.8.

Solution Figures for Chapter 6

Figure 6.1

Phoenix Software 06cp
Profit & Loss Budget Overview
January through March 2003

	Jan 03	Feb 03	Mar 03	TOTAL Jan - Mar 03
Ordinary Income/Expense				
Income				
Computer Add-ons	1,000.00	1,000.00	1,000.00	3,000.00
Computer Sales	13,000.00	19,000.00	25,000.00	57,000.00
Consulting Income	3,000.00	3,000.00	3,000.00	9,000.00
Maintenance & Repairs	3,000.00	3,300.00	3,630.00	9,930.00
Parts Income	0.00	0.00	0.00	0.00
Total Income	20,000.00	26,300.00	32,630.00	78,930.00
Cost of Goods Sold				
Cost of Goods Sold	11,200.00	14,700.00	18,200.00	44,100.00
Total COGS	11,200.00	14,700.00	18,200.00	44,100.00
Gross Profit	8,800.00	11,600.00	14,430.00	34,830.00
Expense				
Depreciation Expense			700.00	700.00
Payroll Expenses	12,000.00	12,000.00	12,000.00	36,000.00
Total Expense	12,000.00	12,000.00	12,700.00	36,700.00
Net Ordinary Income	-3,200.00	-400.00	1,730.00	-1,870.00
Net Income	**-3,200.00**	**-400.00**	**1,730.00**	**-1,870.00**

Figure 6.2

Phoenix Software 06cp
Balance Sheet Budget Overview
As of March 31, 2003

	Jan 31, 03	Feb 28, 03	Mar 31, 03
ASSETS			
Current Assets			
Checking/Savings			
Bank of Cupertino	24,300.00	22,900.00	23,330.00
Short-term Investments	25,000.00	34,000.00	50,000.00
Total Checking/Savings	49,300.00	56,900.00	73,330.00
Accounts Receivable			
Accounts Receivable	15,000.00	20,000.00	25,000.00
Total Accounts Receivable	15,000.00	20,000.00	25,000.00
Other Current Assets			
Inventory Asset	20,000.00	30,000.00	40,000.00
Total Other Current Assets,	20,000.00	30,000.00	40,000.00
Total Current Assets	84,300.00	106,900.00	138,330.00
Fixed Assets			
Computer Equipment			
Cost	0.00	7,000.00	30,000.00
Accumulated Depreciation			-400.00
Total Computer Equipment	0.00	7,000.00	29,600.00
Furniture			
Cost	3,500.00	3,500.00	3,500.00
Accumulated Depreciation			-300.00
Total Furniture	3,500.00	3,500.00	3,200.00
Total Fixed Assets	3,500.00	10,500.00	32,800.00
TOTAL ASSETS	87,800.00	117,400.00	171,130.00
LIABILITIES & EQUITY			
Liabilities			
Current Liabilities			
Accounts Payable			
Accounts Payable	10,000.00	13,000.00	13,000.00
Total Accounts Payable	10,000.00	13,000.00	13,000.00
Other Current Liabilities			
Payroll Liabilities	4,000.00	8,000.00	12,000.00
Sales Tax Payable	2,000.00	5,000.00	8,000.00
Short-Term Debt		10,000.00	10,000.00
Total Other Current Liabilities	6,000.00	23,000.00	30,000.00
Total Current Liabilities	16,000.00	36,000.00	43,000.00
Long Term Liabilities			
Long-Term Debt	0.00	10,000.00	55,000.00
Total Long Term Liabilities	0.00	10,000.00	55,000.00
Total Liabilities	16,000.00	46,000.00	98,000.00
Equity			
Capital Stock	75,000.00	75,000.00	75,000.00
Retained Earnings	-3,200.00	-3,600.00	-1,870.00
Total Equity	71,800.00	71,400.00	73,130.00
TOTAL LIABILITIES & EQUITY	87,800.00	117,400.00	171,130.00

Figure 6.3

Central Coast Cellular
Profit & Loss Budget Overview
January through March 2003

	Jan 03	Feb 03	Mar 03	TOTAL Jan - Mar 03
Ordinary Income/Expense				
Income				
Commissions	2,000.00	2,000.00	2,000.00	2,000.00
Consulting	8,000.00	8,800.00	9,680.00	26,480.00
Phone Sales	15,000.00	20,000.00	30,000.00	65,000.00
Total Income	25,000.00	30,800.00	41,680.00	97,480.00
Cost of Goods Sold				
Cost of Goods Sold	8,000.00	10,000.00	15,000.00	33,000.00
Total COGS	8,000.00	10,000.00	15,000.00	33,000.00
Gross Profit	17,000.00	20,800.00	26,680.00	64,480.00
Expense				
Bank Service Charges	80.00	80.00	80.00	240.00
Depreciation Expense	1,500.00	1,500.00	1,500.00	4,500.00
Interest Expense				
Loan Interest	1,000.00	1,000.00	1,000.00	3,000.00
Total Interest Expense	1,000.00	1,000.00	1,000.00	3,000.00
Payroll Expenses	10,000.00	12,000.00	14,000.00	36,000.00
Rent	3,000.00	3,000.00	3,000.00	9,000.00
Telephone	500.00	600.00	700.00	1,800.00
Utilities				
Gas and Electric	300.00	315.00	330.75	945.75
Total Utilities	300.00	315.00	330.75	945.75
Total Expense	16,380.00	18,495.00	20,610.75	55,485.75
Net Ordinary Income	620.00	2,305.00	6,069.25	8,994.25
Net Income	**620.00**	**2,305.00**	**6,069.25**	**8,994.25**

Figure 6.4

Central Coast Cellular
Balance Sheet Budget Overview
As of March 31, 2003

	Jan 31, 03	Feb 28, 03	Mar 31, 03
ASSETS			
Current Assets			
Checking/Savings			
Checking	125,500.00	113,300.00	95,000.00
Total Checking/Savings	125,500.00	113,300.00	95,000.00
Accounts Receivable			
Accounts Receivable	15,000.00	20,000.00	30,000.00
Total Accounts Receivable	15,000.00	20,000.00	30,000.00
Other Current Assets			
Store Supplies	3,000.00	1,700.00	1,500.00
Inventory Asset	15,000.00	20,000.00	30,000.00
Short-term Investments	75,000.00	70,000.00	65,000.00
Total Other Current Assets	93,000.00	91,700.00	96,500.00
Total Current Assets	233,500.00	225,000.00	221,500.00
Fixed Assets			
Equipment			
Cost	95,000.00	95,000.00	95,000.00
Accumulated Depreciation	-1,000.00	-2,000.00	-3,000.00
Total Equipment	94,000.00	93,000.00	92,000.00
Office Furniture			
Cost	20,000.00	20,000.00	20,000.00
Accumulated Depreciation	-500.00	-1,000.00	-1,500.00
Total Office Furniture	19,500.00	19,000.00	18,500.00
Total Fixed Assets	113,500.00	112,000.00	110,500.00
Other Assets			
Security Deposit	3,000.00	3,000.00	3,000.00
Total Other Assets	3,000.00	3,000.00	3,000.00
TOTAL ASSETS	350,000.00	340,000.00	335,000.00
LIABILITIES & EQUITY			
Liabilities			
Current Liabilities			
Accounts Payable			
Accounts Payable	18,380.00	4,575.00	23,005.75
Total Accounts Payable	18,380.00	4,575.00	23,005.75
Other Current Liabilities			
Interest Payable	1,000.00	2,000.00	3,000.00
Payroll Liabilities	3,500.00	3,500.00	
Sales Tax Payable	1,500.00	2,000.00	
Total Other Current Liabilities	6,000.00	7,500.00	3,000.00
Total Current Liabilities	24,380.00	12,075.00	26,005.75
Long Term Liabilities			
Notes Payable	125,000.00	125,000.00	100,000.00
Total Long Term Liabilities	125,000.00	125,000.00	100,000.00
Total Liabilities	149,380.00	137,075.00	126,005.75
Equity			
Common Stock	200,000.00	200,000.00	200,000.00
Retained Earnings	620.00	2,925.00	8,994.25
Total Equity	200,620.00	202,925.00	208,994.25
TOTAL LIABILITIES & EQUITY	350,000.00	340,000.00	335,000.00

Figure 6.5

Ocean View Flowers
Profit & Loss Budget Overview
January through March 2004

	Jan 04	Feb 04	Mar 04	TOTAL Jan - Mar 04
Ordinary Income/Expense				
Income				
Sales				
Anthuriums		30,000.00	30,000.00	60,000.00
Daylilies	35,000.00	10,000.00	35,000.00	80,000.00
Total Sales	35,000.00	40,000.00	65,000.00	140,000.00
Total Income	35,000.00	40,000.00	65,000.00	140,000.00
Cost of Goods Sold				
Cost of Goods Sold	15,000.00	25,000.00	30,000.00	70,000.00
Total COGS	15,000.00	25,000.00	30,000.00	70,000.00
Gross Profit	20,000.00	15,000.00	35,000.00	70,000.00
Expense				
Payroll Expenses	20,000.00	20,000.00	20,000.00	60,000.00
Professional Fees				
Legal Fees	500.00	500.00	500.00	1,500.00
Total Professional Fees	500.00	500.00	500.00	1,500.00
Rent	3,000.00	3,000.00	3,000.00	9,000.00
Telephone	400.00	400.00	400.00	1,200.00
Utilities	300.00	300.00	300.00	900.00
Total Expenses	24,200.00	24,200.00	24,200.00	72,600.00
Net Ordinary Income	-4,200.00	-9,200.00	10,800.00	-2,600.00
Net Income	**-4,200.00**	**-9,200.00**	**10,800.00**	**-2,600.00**

Figure 6.6

Ocean View Flowers
Balance Sheet Budget Overview
As of March 31, 2004

	Jan 31, 04	Feb 28, 04	Mar 31, 04
ASSETS			
Current Assets			
Checking/Savings			
Union Checking	83,300.00	46,300.00	58,900.00
Short-term investments	25,000.00	25,000.00	25,000.00
Total Checking/Savings	108,300.00	71,300.00	83,900.00
Accounts Receivable			
Accounts Receivable	10,000.00	15,000.00	20,000.00
Total Accounts Receivable	10,000.00	15,000.00	20,000.00
Other Current Assets			
Prepaid Insurance	1,000.00	1,000.00	1,000.00
Office Supplies	1,500.00	1,500.00	1,500.00
Inventory Asset	25,000.00	30,000.00	35,000.00
Total Other Current Assets	27,500.00	32,500.00	37,500.00
Total Current Assets	145,800.00	118,800.00	141,400.00
Fixed Assets			
Land		50,000.00	50,000.00
Building			
Cost		250,000.00	250,000.00
Total Building		250,000.00	250,000.00
Computer Equipment			
Cost	16,000.00	16,000.00	16,000.00
Total Computer Equipment	16,000.00	16,000.00	16,000.00
Office Equipment			
Cost	21,000.00	21,000.00	21,000.00
Total Office Equipment	21,000.00	21,000.00	21,000.00
Total Fixed Assets	37,000.00	337,000.00	337,000.00
TOTAL ASSETS	**182,800.00**	**455,800.00**	**478,400.00**
LIABILITIES & EQUITY			
Liabilities			
Current Liabilities			
Accounts Payable			
Accounts Payable	30,000.00	35,000.00	40,000.00
Total Accounts Payable	30,000.00	35,000.00	40,000.00
Other Current Liabilities			
Payroll Liabilities	7,000.00	14,000.00	21,000.00
Total Other Current Liabilities	7,000.00	14,000.00	21,000.00
Total Current Liabilities	37,000.00	49,000.00	61,000.00
Long Term Liabilities			
Long-Term Note Payable	50,000.00	320,000.00	320,000.00
Total Long Term Liabilities	50,000.00	320,000.00	320,000.00
Total Liabilities	87,000.00	369,000.00	381,000.00
Equity			
Common Stock	100,000.00	100,000.00	100,000.00
Retained Earnings	-4,200.00	-13,200.00	-2,600.00
Total Equity	95,800.00	86,800.00	97,400.00
TOTAL LIABILITIES & EQUITY	**182,800.00**	**455,800.00**	**478,400.00**

Figure 6.7

Jennings & Associates (KJ06cp)
Profit & Loss Budget Overview
January through March 2004

	Jan 04	Feb 04	Mar 04	TOTAL Jan - Mar 04
Ordinary Income/Expense				
Income				
Fee Income	14,000.00	15,400.00	16,940.00	46,340.00
Total Income	14,000.00	15,400.00	16,940.00	46,340.00
Gross Profit	14,000.00	15,400.00	16,940.00	46,340.00
Expense				
Depreciation Expense	200.00	200.00	200.00	600.00
Payroll Expenses	10,000.00	14,000.00	14,000.00	38,000.00
Rent	700.00	700.00	700.00	2,100.00
Total Expense	10,900.00	14,900.00	14,900.00	40,700.00
Net Ordinary Income	3,100.00	500.00	2,040.00	5,640.00
Net Income	3,100.00	500.00	2,040.00	5,640.00

Figure 6.8

Jennings & Associates (KJ06cp)
Balance Sheet Budget Overview
As of March 31, 2004

	Jan 31, 04	Feb 29, 04	Mar 31, 04
ASSETS			
Current Assets			
Checking/Savings			
First Valley Savings & Loan	2,000.00	50,000.00	45,000.00
Union Bank Checking	3,840.00	26,600.00	29,227.20
Total Checking/Savings	5,840.00	76,600.00	74,227.20
Accounts Receivable			
Accounts Receivable	12,000.00	13,440.00	15,052.80
Total Accounts Receivable	12,000.00	13,440.00	15,052.80
Other Current Assets			
Inventory Asset	2,500.00	2,500.00	2,500.00
Total Other Current Assets	2,500.00	2,500.00	2,500.00
Total Current Assets	20,340.00	92,540.00	91,780.00
Fixed Assets			
Computer Equipment			
Cost	4,000.00	8,000.00	14,000.00
Accumulated Depreciation	-1,000.00	-1,175.00	-1,350.00
Total Computer Equipment	3,000.00	6,825.00	12,650.00
Furniture			
Cost	2,500.00	2,500.00	2,500.00
Accumulated Depreciation	-500.00	-525.00	-550.00
Total Furniture	2,000.00	1,975.00	1,950.00
Total Fixed Assets	5,000.00	8,800.00	14,600.00
TOTAL ASSETS	**25,340.00**	**101,340.00**	**106,380.00**
LIABILITIES & EQUITY			
Liabilities			
Current Liabilities			
Accounts Payable			
Accounts Payable	8,000.00	9,000.00	10,000.00
Total Accounts Payable	8,000.00	9,000.00	10,000.00
Other Current Liabilities			
Payroll Liabilities	3,500.00	8.000.00	10,000.00
Total Other Current Liabilities	3,500.00	8,000.00	10,000.00
Total Current Liabilities	11,500.00	17,000.00	20,000.00
Long Term Liabilities			
Bank of San Martin	5,000.00	5,000.00	5,000.00
Total Long Term Liabilities	5,000.00	5,000.00	5,000.00
Total Liabilities	16,500.00	22,000.00	25,000.00
Equity			
Capital Stock	3,590.00	73,590.00	73,590.00
Retained Earnings	5,250.00	5,750.00	7,790.00
Total Equity	8,840.00	79,340.00	81,380.00
TOTAL LIABILITIES & EQUITY	**25,340.00**	**101,340.00**	**106,380.00**

Reporting Business Activities

In Chapter 7 students learn the essentials of reporting business activities with QuickBooks. The basic reporting concepts in accounting are reinforced, especially the providing of comparative and extensive information to both internal and external users of financial statements.

Chapter 7 Questions

1. QuickBooks allows you to modify each report by adding percentages, hiding cents, changing report titles, and changing the page layout. You can also compare the current period's results with the budget information, prior periods, etc. In addition, QuickBooks enables you to create reports for any period you desire. It also lets you create separate columns for a time segment—such as day, week, four weeks, month, quarter, and so on—within each period.

2. When you create a balance sheet in QuickBooks, the Modify Report window gives you the following columns options: Total only, day, week, two week, four week, half month, month, quarter, and year.

3. QuickBooks allows you to report other column time periods in a balance sheet, namely the previous period and/or previous year.

4. Options available in the Fonts and Numbers tab for a balance sheet include how to show negative numbers, how to show numbers in general, and what font you can use for labels, report data, etc.

5. To resize a report that would normally print on two pages to one page, check the Fit Report To 1 Page(s) Wide checkbox located in the Print Report window activated when you print any report, and enter the number 1.

6. When you click the Collapse button, QuickBooks hides subaccounts, jobs, or subprojects in the report and summarizes their amounts under the main heading. This button affects both the onscreen and the printed report. After you choose the Collapse button, the button name changes to Expand. You can click Expand to display the subgroups that were previously hidden.

7. QuickBooks provides six different graph options: Income and Expenses, Sales, Accounts Receivable, Accounts Payable, Net Worth, and Budget vs. Actual.

8. Percentage changes identified in the budgeted vs. actual reports need to be interpreted carefully since often the percentages by themselves can be misleading. For instance, a large percentage change on small dollar differences can be discounted, while a small percentage change involving large dollar amounts might be cause for concern. In other words, percentages and dollar changes need to be examined together.

9. The accounts receivable and accounts payable aging reports provide information to support the balance sheet. The aging concept refers to the tracking of outstanding invoices and unpaid bills. For both A/R (accounts receivable) and A/P (accounts payable), QuickBooks offers preset aging reports that show how much is currently due, and how much is overdue. For example, an A/R aging summary report breaks down what your customers owe so that you can see how much is currently due, 1 to 30 days overdue, 31 to 60 days overdue, 61 to 90 days overdue, and over 90 days overdue.

10. The inventory stocks status by item report shows an item description, preferred vendor, reorder point, on hand, on order, next delivery, order, and sales/week.

Chapter 7   Assignments

1. Creating Financial Reports and Supporting Schedules for Phoenix Systems, Inc.

    a. The Profit & Loss statement for the month ended January 31, 2003 is shown in Figure 7.1.

    b. The exported Excel spreadsheet is shown in Figure 7.2.

    c. The Balance Sheet as of January 31, 2003 is shown in Figure 7.3.

    d. The exported Excel spreadsheet is shown in Figure 7.4.

    e. The budgeted Income Statement vs. Actual Income Statement for the month ended January 31, 2003 is shown in Figure 7.5.

    f. The budgeted Balance Sheet vs. Actual Balance Sheet as of January 31, 2003 is shown in Figure 7.6.

g. The Sales by Customer Summary for the month ended January 31, 2003 is shown in Figure 7.7.

h. The Sales by Item Summary for the month ended January 31, 2003 is shown in Figure 7.8.

i. The Accounts Receivable Aging report as of January 31, 2003 is shown in Figure 7.9.

j. The Accounts Payable Aging report as of January 31, 2003 is shown in Figure 7.10.

k. The Inventory Valuation Summary as of January 31, 2003 is shown in Figure 7.11.

2. Creating Graphs for Phoenix Systems, Inc.

a. A graph illustrating sales for the month ended January 31, 2003 is shown in Figure 7.12.

b. A graph illustrating revenue (income) and expense for the month ended January 31, 2003 is shown in Figure 7.13.

c. A graph illustrating the accounts receivable aging as of January 31, 2003 is shown in Figure 7.14.

d. A graph illustrating the accounts payable aging as of January 31, 2003 is shown in Figure 7.15.

3. Adding More Information: Central Coast Cellular

a. The Profit & Loss standard report is shown in Figure 7.16.

b. The Excel Profit & Loss printout is shown in Figure 7.17.

c. The Balance Sheet standard report is shown in Figure 7.18.

d. The Excel Balance Sheet printout is shown in Figure 7.19.

e. The Profit & Loss Budget vs. Actual report is shown in Figure 7.20

f. A Balance Sheet Budget vs. Actual report is shown in Figure 7.21.

g. An Inventory Valuation Summary report is shown in Figure 7.22.

4. Internet assignments and related solutions are found at *http://owen.swlearning.com*.

Chapter 7 Case Problems

1. Ocean View Flowers

Reports:

a. The completed Budget vs. Actual report is shown is shown in Figure 7.23.

b. The completed Balance Sheet Budget comparison report is shown in Figure 7.24.

c. The exported spreadsheet is shown in Figure 7.25.

d. The Sales by Customer Summary is shown in Figure 7.26.

e. The Inventory Stock Status by Item report is shown in Figure 7.27.

Graphs:

a. The graph of income and expenses is shown in Figure 7.28.

b. The graph of sales is shown in Figure 7.29.

2. Jennings & Associates—Financial Reports and Graphs

Reports:

a. The Income Statement for the quarter ended March 31, 2004 is shown in Figure 7.30.

b. The Balance Sheet as of March 31, 2004 is shown in Figure 7.31.

c. The Balance Sheet showing Budgeted vs. Actual as of March 31, 2004 is shown in Figure 7.32.

d. The Income Statement showing Budgeted vs. Actual for the quarter ended March 31, 2004 is shown in Figure 7.33.

e. The exported spreadsheet is shown in Figure 7.34.

f. The Sales by Customer Summary for the quarter ended March 31, 2004 is shown in Figure 7.35.

g. The Sales by Item Summary for the quarter ended March 31, 2004 is shown in Figure 7.36.

h. The Accounts Receivable Aging Summary report as of March 31, 2004 is shown in Figure 7.37.

i. The Accounts Payable Aging Summary report as of March 31, 2004 is shown in Figure 7.38.

j. The Inventory Valuation Summary as of March 31, 2004 is shown in Figure 7.39.

Graphs:

a. A graph showing sales for the quarter ended March 31, 2004 is shown in Figure 7.40.

b. A graph showing revenue (income) and expense for the quarter ended March 31, 2004 is shown in Figure 7.41.

c. A graph showing an accounts receivable aging period as of March 31, 2004 is shown in Figure 7.42.

d. A graph showing an accounts payable aging period as of March 31, 2004 is shown in Figure 7.43.

Chapter 7 Comprehensive Problem 1—Sports City

1. n/a

2. n/a

3. Lists/Reports

    a.   The Custom Transaction Detail Report is shown in Figure 7.44.

    b.   The standard Balance Sheet is shown in Figure 7.45.

    c.   The standard Profit & Loss statement is shown in Figure 7.46.

    d.   The Statement of Cash Flows is shown in Figure 7.47.

    e.   The Profit & Loss Budget vs. Actual report is shown in Figure 7.48.

    f.   The Profit & Loss Budget Overview is shown in Figure 7.49.

    g.   The Bank Reconciliation Summary is shown in Figure 7.50.

    h.   The Balance Sheet in Excel is shown in Figure 7.51.

Chapter 7 Comprehensive Problem 2—Pacific Brew

1. n/a

2. n/a

3. Lists/Reports

    a.   The Custom Transaction Detail Report is shown in Figure 7.52

    b.   The standard Balance Sheet is shown in Figure 7.53

    c.   The standard Profit & Loss statement is shown in Figure 7.54

    d.   The Statement of Cash Flows is shown in Figure 7.55.

    e.   The Profit & Loss Budget vs. Actual report is shown in Figure 7.56.

    f.   The Profit & Loss Budget Overview report is shown in Figure 7.57.

    g.   The Reconciliation Summary is shown in Figure 7.58.

    h.   The Excel Profit & Loss report is shown in Figure 7.59.

    i.   The Sales by Customer Summary is shown in Figure 7.60.

    j.   The Sales by Item Summary is shown in Figure 7.61.

    k.   The Sales by Month graph is shown in Figure 7.62.

    l.   The Inventory Stock Status by Item report is shown in Figure 7.63.

Chapter 7 Comprehensive Problem 3—Sunset Spas

1. n/a

2. n/a

3. Lists/Reports

    a.   The Chart of Accounts is shown in Figure 7.64.

    b.   The Employee List is shown in Figure 7.65.

    c.   The Customer:Job List is shown in Figure 7.66.

    d.   The Custom Transaction Detail report is shown in Figure 7.67.

    e.   The Balance Sheet is shown in Figure 7.68.

    f.   The Profit & Loss is shown in Figure 7.69.

    g.   The Statement of Cash Flows is shown in Figure 7.70.

    h.   The Profit & Loss Budget Overview report is shown in Figure 7.71.

    i.   The Profit & Loss Budget Overview report is shown in Figure 7.72.

    j.   The Summary Bank Reconciliation report is shown in Figure 7.73.

    k.   The Excel Profit & Loss is shown in Figure 7.74.

    l.   The Sales by Customer Detail report is shown in Figure 7.75.

    m.   The Sales by Item report is shown in Figure 7.76.

    n.   The Sales Graph is shown in Figure 7.77.

    o.   The Inventory Stock Status report by item is shown in Figure 7.78.

Solution Figures for Chapter 7

Figure 7.1

Phoenix Software 07
Profit & Loss
January 2003

	Jan 03
Ordinary Income/Expense	
Income	
Computer Add-ons	550.00
Computer Sales	13,750.00
Consulting Income	5,250.00
Maintenance & Repairs	5,090.00
Total Income	24,640.00
Cost of Goods Sold	
Cost of Goods Sold	9,450.00
Total COGS	9,450.00
Gross Profit	15,190.00
Expense	
Bank Service Charges	45.00
Office Supplies	560.00
Payroll Expenses	11,553.65
Telephone	159.65
Utilities	
Gas and Electric	230.00
Total Utilities	230.00
Total Expense	12,548.30
Net Ordinary Income	2,641.70
Other Income/Expense	
Other Income	
Investment Income	3,000.00
Total Other Income	3,000.00
Net Other Income	3,000.00
Net Income	**5,641.70**

Figure 7.2

Phoenix Software 07
Profit & Loss
January 2003

	A	B	C	D	E	F	G
1							**Jan 03**
2		Ordinary Income/Expense					
3				Income			
4						Computer Add-ons	550.00
5						Computer Sales	13,750.00
6						Consulting Income	5,250.00
7						Maintenance & Repairs	5,090.00
8				Total Income			24,640.00
9				Cost of Goods Sold			
10					Cost of Goods Sold		9,450.00
11				Total COGS			9,450.00
12			Gross Profit				15,190.00
13				Expense			
14						Bank Service Charges	45.00
15						Office Supplies	560.00
16						Payroll Expenses	11,553.65
17					Telephone		159.65
18					Utilities		
19						Gas and Electric	230.00
20					Total Utilities		230.00
21				Total Expense			12,548.30
22		Net Ordinary Income					2,641.70
23		Other Income/Expense					
24			Other Income				
25					Investment Income		3,000.00
26			Total Other Income				3,000.00
27		Net Other Income					3,000.00
28	Net Income						**5,641.70**

Figure 7.3

Phoenix Software 07
Balance Sheet
As of January 31, 2003

	Jan 31, 03
ASSETS	
Current Assets	
Checking/Savings	
Bank of Cupertino	59,255.80
Short-term Investments	6,000.00
Total Checking/Savings	65,255.80
Accounts Receivable	
Accounts Receivable	17,284.38
Total Accounts Receivable	17,284.38
Other Current Assets	
Inventory Asset	16,999.75
Investments	8,000.00
Prepaid Insurance	1,384.67
Prepaid Rent	1,600.00
Total Other Current Assets	27,984.42
Total Current Assets	110,524.60
Fixed Assets	
Furniture	
Cost	3,756.44
Total Furniture	3,756.44
Total Fixed Assets	3,756.44
TOTAL ASSETS	**114,281.04**
LIABILITIES & EQUITY	
Liabilities	
Current Liabilities	
Accounts Payable	
Accounts Payable	15,199.75
Total Accounts Payable	15,199.75
Other Current Liabilities	
Payroll Liabilities	4,091.58
Sales Tax Payable	1,848.01
Short-Term Debt	12,500.00
Total Other Current Liabilities	18,439.59
Total Current Liabilities	33,639.34
Total Liabilities	33,639.34
Equity	
Capital Stock	75,000.00
Net Income	5,641.70
Total Equity	80,641.70
TOTAL LIABILITIES & EQUITY	**114,281.04**

Figure 7.4

Phoenix Software 07
Balance Sheet
As of January 31, 2003

	A	B	C	D	E	F
1						**Jan 31, 03**
2	ASSETS					
3		Current Assets				
4			Checking/Savings			
5					Bank of Cupertino	59,255.80
6					Short-term Investments	6,000.00
7				Total Checking/Savings		65,255.80
8			Accounts Receivable			
9					Accounts Receivable	17,284.38
10				Total Accounts Receivable		17,284.38
11			Other Current Assets			
12					Inventory Asset	16,999.75
13					Investments	8,000.00
14					Prepaid Insurance	1,384.67
15					Prepaid Rent	1,600.00
16				Total Other Current Assets		27,984.42
17			Total Current Assets			110,524.60
18			Fixed Assets			
19				Furniture		
20					Cost	3,756.44
21				Total Furniture		3,756.44
22			Total Fixed Assets			3,756.44
23	TOTAL ASSETS					**114,281.04**
24	LIABILITIES & EQUITY					
25		Liabilities				
26			Current Liabilities			
27				Accounts Payable		
28					Accounts Payable	15,199.75
29				Total Accounts Payable		15,199.75
30				Other Current Liabilities		
31					Payroll Liabilities	4,091.58

Figure 7.4 (Concluded)

Phoenix Software 07
Balance Sheet
As of January 31, 2003

	A	B	C	D	E	F
1						**Jan 31, 03**
32					**Sales Tax Payable**	1,848.01
33					**Short-Term Debt**	12,500.00
34					**Total Other Current Liabilities**	18,439.59
35				**Total Current Liabilities**		33,639.34
36		**Total Liabilities**				33,639.34
37		**Equity**				
38			**Capital Stock**			75,000.00
39			**Net Income**			5,641.70
40		**Total Equity**				80,641.70
41	**TOTAL LIABILITIES & EQUITY**					114,281.04

Figure 7.5

Phoenix Software 07
Profit & Loss Budget vs. Actual
January 2003

	Jan 03	Budget	$ Over Budget	% of Budget
Ordinary Income/Expense				
Income				
Computer Add-ons	550.00	1,000.00	-450.00	55.0%
Computer Sales	13,750.00	13,000.00	750.00	105.8%
Consulting Income	5,250.00	3,000.00	2,250.00	175.0%
Maintenance & Repairs	5,090.00	3,000.00	2,090.00	169.7%
Total Income	24,640.00	20,000.00	4,640.00	123.2%
Cost of Goods Sold				
Cost of Goods Sold	9,450.00	11,200.00	-1,750.00	84.4%
Total COGS	9,450.00	11,200.00	-1,750.00	84.4%
Gross Profit	15,190.00	8,800.00	6,390.00	172.6%
Expense				
Bank Service Charges	45.00			
Office Supplies	560.00			
Payroll Expenses	11,553.65	12,000.00	-446.35	96.3%
Telephone	159.65			
Utilities				
Gas and Electric	230.00			
Total Utilities	230.00			
Total Expense	12,548.30	12,000.00	548.30	104.6%
Net Ordinary Income	2,641.70	-3,200.00	5,841.70	-82.6%
Other Income/Expense				
Other Income				
Investment Income	3,000.00			
Total Other Income	3,000.00			
Net Other Income	3,000.00			
Net Income	5,641.70	-3,200.00	8,841.70	-176.3%

Figure 7.6

Phoenix Software 07
Balance Sheet Budget vs. Actual
As of January 31, 2003

	Jan 31, 03	Budget	$ Over Budget	% of Budget
ASSETS				
Current Assets				
Checking/Savings				
Bank of Cupertino	59,255.80	24,300.00	34,955.80	243.9%
Short-term Investments	6,000.00	25,000.00	-19,000.00	24.0%
Total Checking/Savings	65,255.80	49,300.00	15,955.80	132.4%
Accounts Receivable				
Accounts Receivable	17,284.38	15,000.00	2,284.38	115.2%
Total Accounts Receivable	17,284.38	15,000.00	2,284.38	115.2%
Other Current Assets				
Inventory Asset	16,999.75	20,000.00	-3,000.25	85.0%
Investments	8,000.00			
Prepaid Insurance	1,384.67			
Prepaid Rent	1,600.00			
Total Other Current Assets	27,984.42	20,000.00	7,984.42	139.9%
Total Current Assets	110,524.60	84,300.00	26,224.60	131.1%
Fixed Assets				
Furniture				
Cost	3,756.44	3,500.00	256.44	107.3%
Total Furniture	3,756.44	3,500.00	256.44	107.3%
Total Fixed Assets	3,756.44	3,500.00	256.44	107.3%
TOTAL ASSETS	**114,281.04**	**87,800.00**	**26,481.04**	**130.2%**
LIABILITIES & EQUITY				
Liabilities				
Current Liabilities				
Accounts Payable				
Accounts Payable	15,199.75	10,000.00	5,199.75	152.0%
Total Accounts Payable	15,199.75	10,000.00	5,199.75	152.0%
Other Current Liabilities				
Payroll Liabilities	4,091.58	4,000.00	91.58	102.3%
Sales Tax Payable	1,848.01	2,000.00	-151.99	92.4%
Short-Term Debt	12,500.00	0.00	12,500.00	100.0%
Total Other Current Liabilities	18,439.59	6,000.00	12,439.59	307.3%
Total Current Liabilities	33,639.34	16,000.00	17,639.34	210.2%
Total Liabilities	33,639.34	16,000.00	17,639.34	210.2%
Equity				
Capital Stock	75,000.00	75,000.00	0.00	100.0%
Retained Earnings	0.00	-3,200.00	3,200.00	0.0%
Net Income	5,641.70	0.00	5,641.70	100.0%
Total Equity	80,641.70	71,800.00	8,841.70	112.3%
TOTAL LIABILITIES & EQUITY	**114,281.04**	**87,800.00**	**26,481.04**	**130.2%**

Figure 7.7

Phoenix Software 07
Sales by Customer Summary
January 2003

	Jan 03
Jdesign	640.00
Los Gatos School District	17,125.00
St. Johns Hospital	6,875.00
TOTAL	**24,640.00**

Figure 7.8

Phoenix Software 07
Sales by Item Summary
January 2003

				Jan 03				
	Qty	Amount	% of Sa...	Avg Price	COGS	Avg CO...	Gross Ma...	Gross Ma...
Inventory								
1 gig HD	1	550.00	2.2%	550.00	450.00	450.00	100.00	18.2%
Power Mac 100	5	13,750.00	55.8%	2,750.00	9,000.00	1,800.00	4,750.00	34.5%
Total inventory		14,300.00	58.0%		9,450.00		4,850.00	33.9%
Service								
Consulting	70	5,250.00	21.3%	75.00				
Installation	2	90.00	0.4%	45.00				
Maintenance	100	5,000.00	20.3%	50.00				
Total Service		10,340.00	42.0%					
TOTAL		**24,640.00**	**100.0**					

Figure 7.9

Phoenix Software 07
A/R Aging Summary
As of January 31, 2003

	Current	1 - 30	31 - 60	61 - 90	> 90	TOTAL
Los Gatos School District	18,409.38	0.00	0.00	0.00	0.00	18,409.38
Netscape	0.00	-6,500.00	0.00	0.00	0.00	-6,500.00
St. Johns Hospital	5,375.00	0.00	0.00	0.00	0.00	5,375.00
TOTAL	**23,784.38**	**-6,500.00**	**0.00**	**0.00**	**0.00**	**17,284.38**

Figure 7.10

Phoenix Software 07
A/P Aging Summary
As of January 31, 2003

	Current	1 - 30	31 - 60	61 - 90	> 90	TOTAL
Computer Wholesale Inc.	15,199.75	0.00	0.00	0.00	0.00	15,199.75
TOTAL	**15,199.76**	**0.00**	**0.00**	**0.00**	**0.00**	**15,199.75**

Figure 7.11

Phoenix Software 07
Inventory Valuation Summary
As of January 31, 2003

	Item Description	On Hand	Avg Cost	Asset Value	% of Tot Asset	Sales Price	Retail Value	% of Tot Retail
1 gig HD	1,000mb Bengal Hard Disk	4	450.00	1,800.00	10.6%	550.00	2,200.00	10.8%
1 mb memory	Memory modules	5	39.95	199.75	1.2%	49.95	249.75	1.2%
586-100	Phoenix Pentium Computer…	10	1,500.00	15,000.00	88.2%	1,800.00	18,000.00	88%
586-160	Phoenix 586 160 Megahertz	0	2,300.00	0.00	0%	3,900.00	0.00	0%
800 mb HD	800mb Bengal Hard Disk	0	250.00	0.00	0%	300.00	0.00	0%
IBM Pentium P	IBM Pentium Plus Compute…	0	7,500.00	0.00	0%	10,500.00	0.00	0%
Power Mac 100	Apple Power Mac 100	0	1,800.00	0.00	0%	2,750.00	0.00	0%
TOTAL		19		16,999.75	100.00%		20,449.75	100.00%

Figure 7.12

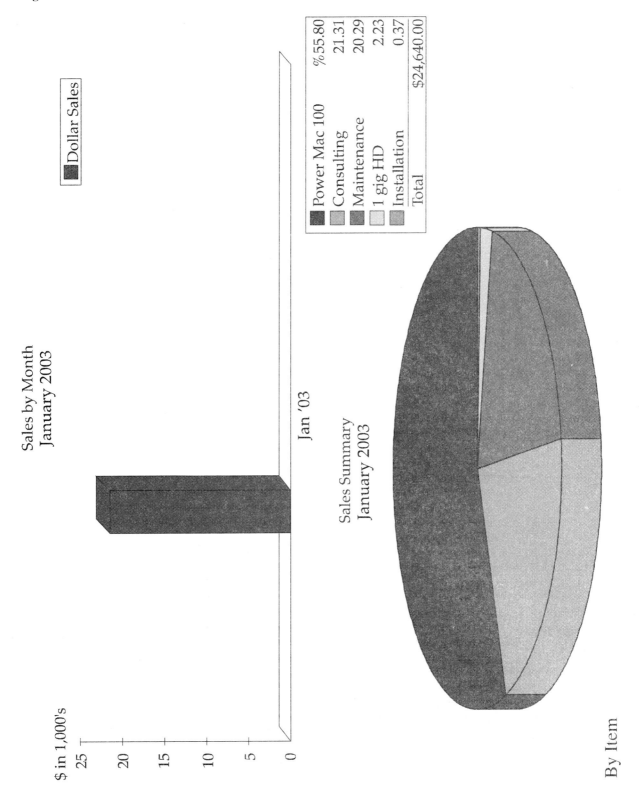

Figure 7.13

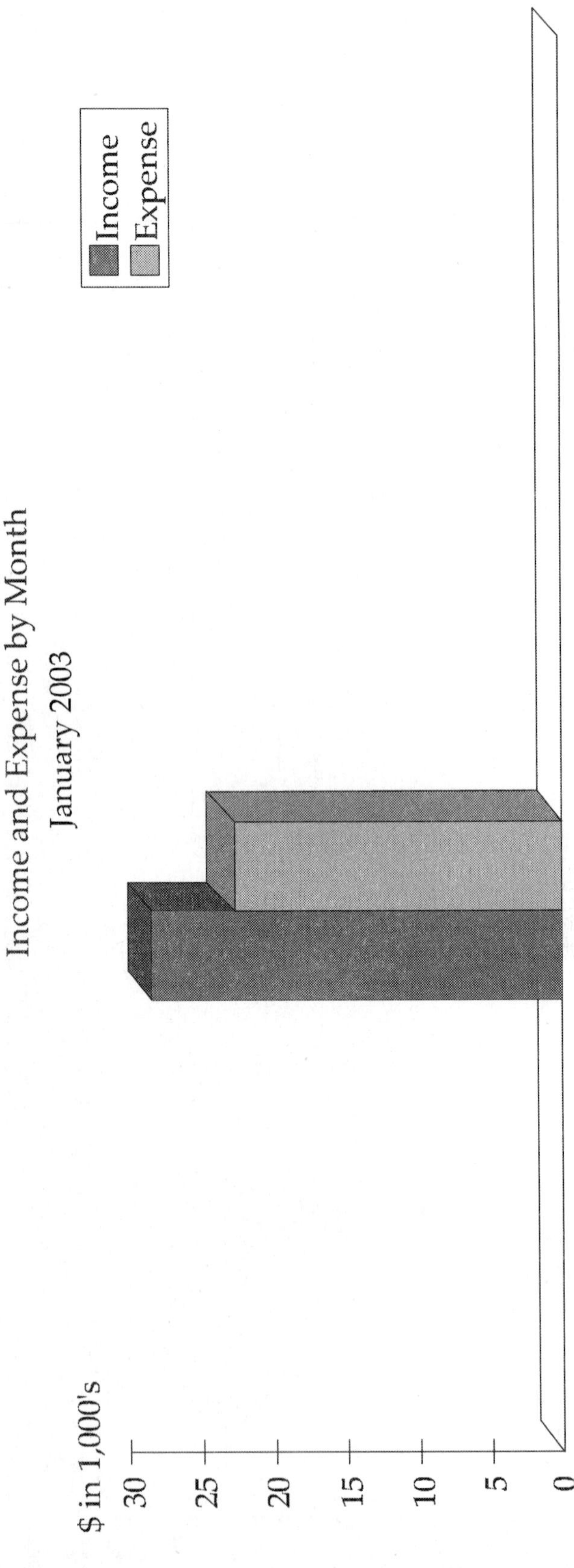

Income and Expense by Month
January 2003

$ in 1,000's

| Income |
| Expense |

30

25

20

15

10

5

0

Jan'03

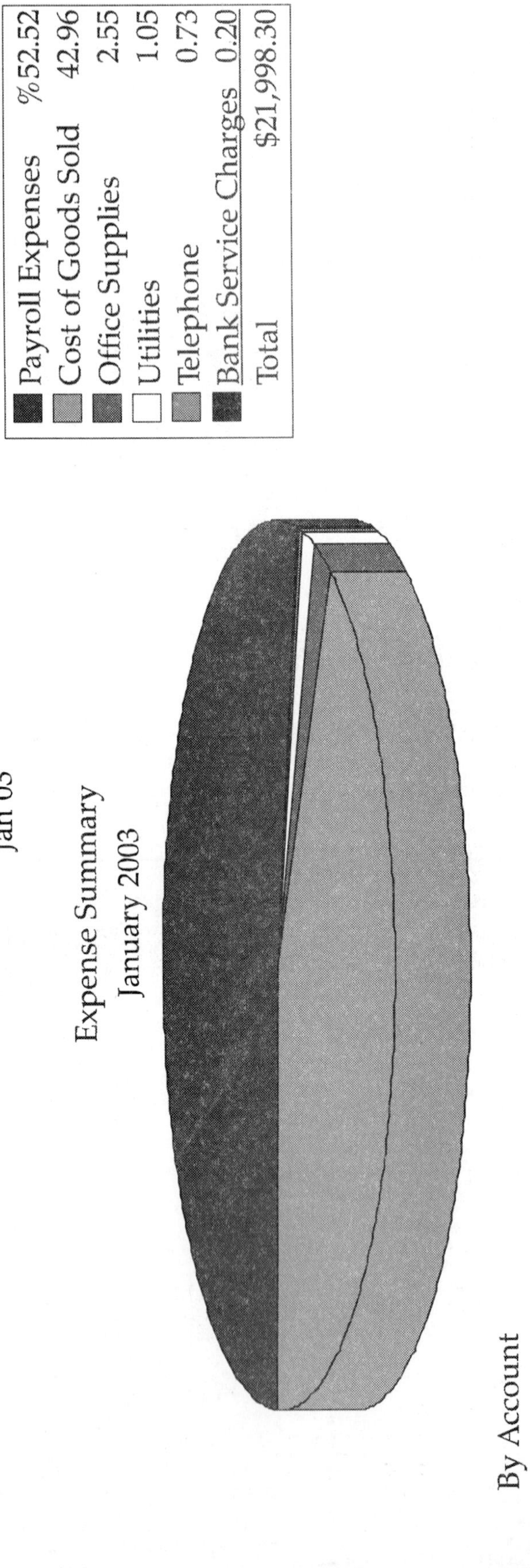

Expense Summary
January 2003

	Payroll Expenses	% 52.52
	Cost of Goods Sold	42.96
	Office Supplies	2.55
	Utilities	1.05
	Telephone	0.73
	Bank Service Charges	0.20
	Total	$21,998.30

By Account

Figure 7.14

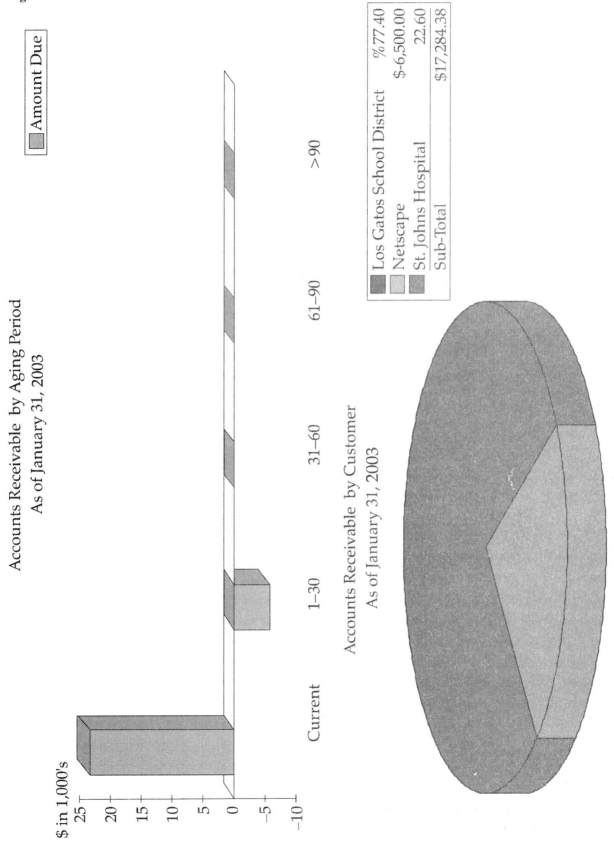

Accounts Receivable by Aging Period
As of January 31, 2003

Accounts Receivable by Customer
As of January 31, 2003

		%	
Los Gatos School District		77.40	
Netscape		$-6,500.00	
St. Johns Hospital		22.60	
Sub-Total			$17,284.38

Figure 7.15

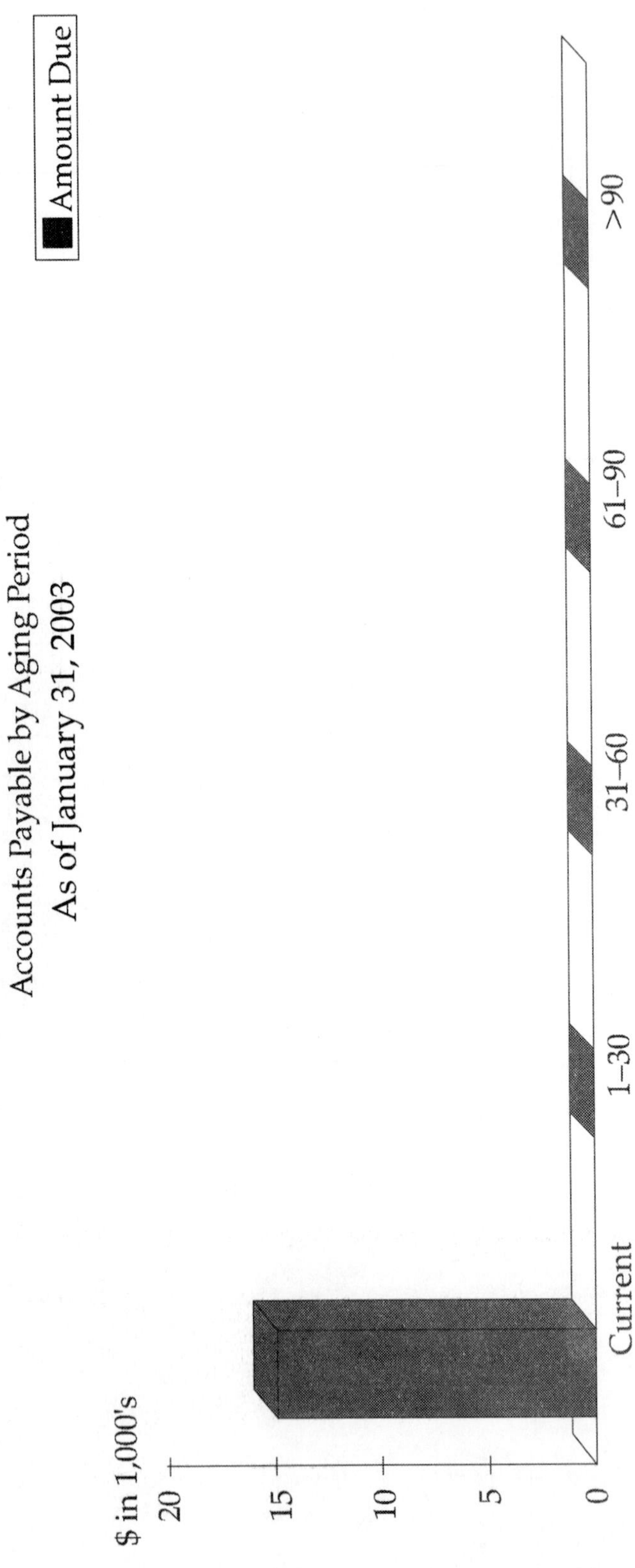
Accounts Payable by Aging Period
As of January 31, 2003
Amount Due
$ in 1,000's
20
15
10
5
0
Current
1–30
31–60
61–90
>90

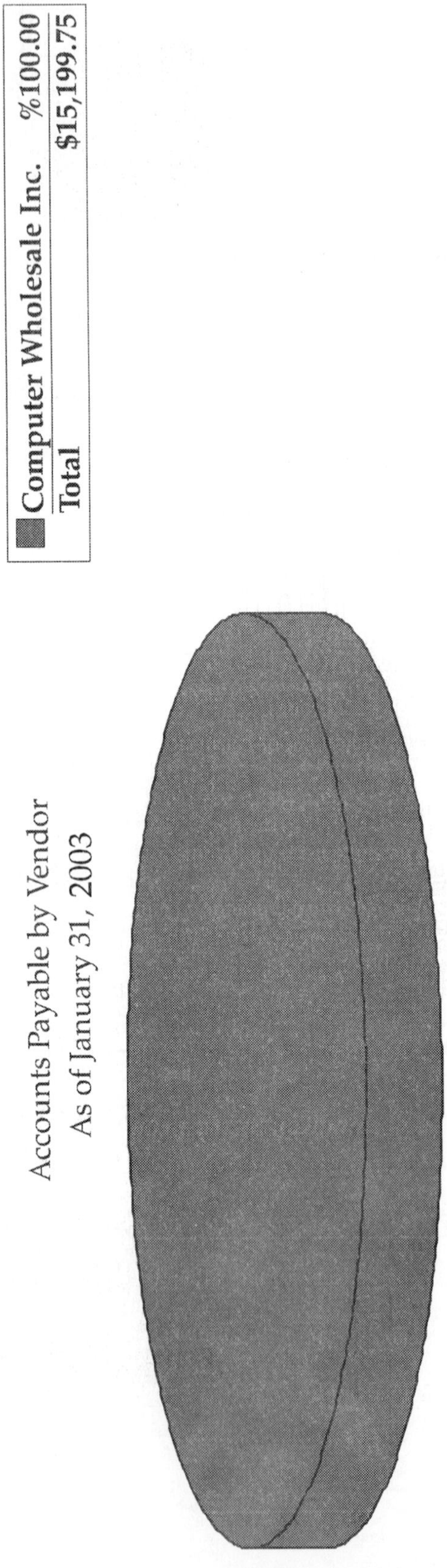
Accounts Payable by Vendor
As of January 31, 2003
Computer Wholesale Inc. %100.00
Total $15,199.75

Figure 7.16

Central Coast Cellular
Income Statement
January 2003

	Jan 03	% of Income
Ordinary Income/Expense		
Income		
Commissions	1,750	9%
Consulting	7,600	39%
Phone Sales	10,375	53%
Total Income	19,725	100%
Cost of Goods Sold		
Cost of Goods Sold	6,875	35%
Total COGS	6,875	35%
Gross Profit	12,850	65%
Expense		
Bank Service Charges	80	0%
Depreciation Expense	1,500	8%
Interest Expense		
Loan Interest	950	5%
Payroll Expenses	9,812	50%
Rent	3,000	15%
Total Expense	15,342	78%
Net Ordinary Income	-2,492	-13%
Net Income	**-2,492**	**-13%**

Figure 7.17

Central Coast Cellular

Income Statement

January 2003

	A	B	C	D	E	F	G	H
1						Jan 03		% of Income
2		Ordinary Income/Expense						
3				Income				
4					Commissions	1,750		9%
5					Consulting	7,600		39%
6					Phone Sales	10,375		53%
7				Total Income		19,725		100%
8			Cost of Goods Sold					
9					Cost of Goods Sold	6,875		35%
10				Total COGS		6,875		35%
11			Gross Profit			12,850		65%
12				Expense				
13					Bank Service Charges	80		0%
14					Depreciation Expense	1,500		8%
15					Interest Expense			
16					Loan Interest	950		5%
17					Total Interest Expense	950		5%
18					Payroll Expenses	9,812		50%
19					Rent	3,000		15%
20				Total Expense		15,342		78%
21		Net Ordinary Income				-2.492		-13%
22	Net Income					-2,492		-13%

Figure 7.18

Central Coast Cellular
Balance Sheet
As of January 31, 2003

	Jan 31, 03		% of Column
ASSETS			
Current Assets			
Checking/Savings			
Checking	130,393		37%
Total Checking/Savings	130,393		37%
Accounts Receivable			
Accounts Receivable	13,878		4%
Total Accounts Receivable	13,878		4%
Other Current Assets			
Store Supplies	3,000		1%
Inventory Asset	14,750		4%
Short-term Investments	75,000		21%
Total Other Current Assets	92,750		26%
Total Current Assets	237,021		67%
Fixed Assets			
Equipment			
Cost	95,000	27%	
Accumulated Depreciation	-1000	-0%	
Total Equipment	94,000		27%
Office Furniture			
Cost	20,000	6%	
Accumulated Depreciation	-500	-0%	
Total Office Furniture	19,500		6%
Total Fixed Assets	113,500		32%
Other Assets			
Security Deposit	3,000		1%
Total Other Assets	3,000		1%
TOTAL ASSETS	353,521		100%
LIABILITIES & EQUITY			
Liabilities			
Current Liabilities			
Accounts Payable			
Accounts Payable	15,125		4%
Total Accounts Payable	15,125		4%
Other Current Liabilities			
Unearned Revenue	10,000		3%
Interest Payable	950		0%
Payroll Liabilities	3,360		1%
Sales Tax Payable	1,578		0%
Total Other Current Liabilities	15,888		4%
Total Current Liabilities	31,013		9%
Long Term Liabilities			
Notes Payable	125,000		35%
Total Long Term Liabilities	125,000		35%
Total Liabilities	156,013		44%
Equity			
Common Stock	200,000		57%
Net Income	-2,492		-1%
Total Equity	197,508		56%
TOTAL LIABILITIES & EQUITY	353,521		100%

Figure 7.19   **Central Coast Cellular**
                                      Balance Sheet
                                     As of January 31, 2003

	A	B	C	D	E	F	G	H
1								
2						Jan 31, '03		% of Column
3	ASSETS							
4		Current Assets						
5			Checking/Savings					
6				Checking		130,393		37%
7			Total Checking/Savings			130,393		37%
8			Accounts Receivable					
9				Accounts Receivable		13,878		4%
10			Total Accounts Receivable			13,878		4%
11			Other Current Assets					
12				Store Supplies		3,000		1%
13				Inventory Asset		14,750		4%
14				Short-term Investments		75,000		21%
15			Total Other Current Assets			92,750		26%
16		Total Current Assets				237,021		67%
17		Fixed Assets						
18			Equipment					
19				Cost		95,000		27%
20				Accumulated Depreciation		-1,000		-0%
21			Total Equipment			94,000		27%
22			Office Furniture					
23				Cost		20,000		6%
24				Accumulated Depreciation		-500		-0%
25			Total Office Furniture			19,500		6%
26		Total Fixed Assets				113,500		32%
27		Other Assets						
28			Security Deposit			3,000		1%
29		Total Other Assets				3,000		1%
30	TOTAL ASSETS					353,521		100%
31	LIABILITIES & EQUITY							
32		Liabilities						
33			Current Liabilities					
34				Accounts Payable				
35					Accounts Payable	15,125		4%
36				Total Accounts Payable		15,125		4%

Figure 7.19 (Concluded)   **Central Coast Cellular**
Balance Sheet
As of January 31, 2003

	A	B	C	D	E	F	G	H
1								
2						Jan 31, '03		% of Column
37					**Other Current Liabilities**			
38					**Interest Payable**	950		0%
39					**Unearned Revenue**	10,000		3%
40					**Payroll Liabilities**	3,360		1%
41					**Sales Tax Payable**	1,578		0%
42					**Total Other Current Liabilities**	15,888		4%
43					**Total Current Liabilities**	31,013		9%
44					**Long Term Liabilities**			
45					**Notes Payable**	125,000		35%
46					**Total Long-Term Liabilities**	125,000		35%
47			**Total Liabilities**			156,013		44%
48		**Equity**						
49			**Common Stock**			200,000		57%
50			**Net Income**			-2,492		-1%
51		**Total Equity**				197,508		56%
52	**TOTAL LIABILITIES & EQUITY**					353,521		100%

Figure 7.20

Central Coast Cellular
Profit & Loss Budget vs. Actual
January 2003

	Jan 03	Budget	$ Over Budget	% of Budget
Ordinary Income/Expense				
Income				
Commissions	1,750	2,000	-250	88%
Consulting	7,600	8,000	-400	95%
Phone Sales	10,375	15,000	-4,625	69%
Total Income	19,725	25,000	-5,275	79%
Cost of Goods Sold				
Cost of Goods Sold	6,875	8,000	-1,125	86%
Total COGS	6,875	8,000	-1,125	86%
Gross Profit	12,850	17,000	-4,150	76%
Expense				
Bank Service Charges	80	80	0	100%
Depreciation Expense	1,500	1,500	0	100%
Interest Expense				
Loan Interest	950	1,000	-50	95%
Total Interest Expense	950	1,000	-50	95%
Payroll Expenses	9,812	10,000	-188	98%
Rent	3,000	3,000	0	100%
Telephone	0	500	-500	0%
Utilities				
Gas and Electric	0	300	-300	0%
Total Utilities	0	300	-300	0%
Total Expense	15,342	16,380	-1,038	94%
Net Ordinary Income	-2,492	620	-3,112	-402%
Net Income	**-2,492**	**620**	**-3,112**	**-402%**

Figure 7.21

Central Coast Cellular
Balance Sheet Budget vs. Actual
As of January 31, 2003

	Jan 31, 03	Budget	$ Over Budget	% of Budget
ASSETS				
Current Assets				
Checking/Savings				
Checking	130,393	125,500	4,893	104%
Total Checking/Savings	130,393	125,500	4,893	104%
Accounts Receivable				
Accounts Receivable	13,878	15,000	-1,122	93%
Total Accounts Receivable	13,878	15,000	-1,122	93%
Other Current Assets				
Store Supplies	3,000	3,000	0	100%
Inventory Asset	14,750	15,000	-250	98%
Short-term Investments	75,000	75,000	0	100%
Total Other Current Assets	92,750	93,000	-250	100%
Total Current Assets	237,021	233,500	3,521	102%
Fixed Assets				
Equipment	94,000	94,000	0	100%
Office Furniture	19,500	19,500	0	100%
Total Fixed Assets	113,500	113,500	0	100%
Other Assets				
Security Deposit	3,000	3,000	0	100%
Total Other Assets	3,000	3,000	0	100%
TOTAL ASSETS	353,521	350,000	3,521	101%
LIABILITIES & EQUITY				
Liabilities				
Current Liabilities				
Accounts Payable				
Accounts Payable	15,125	18,380	-3,255	82%
Total Accounts Payable	15,125	18,380	-3,255	82%
Other Current Liabilities				
Interest Payable	950	1,000	-50	95%
Unearned Revenue	10,000			
Payroll Liabilities	3,360	3,500	-140	96%
Sales Tax Payable	1,578	1,500	78	105%
Total Other Current Liabilities	15,888	6,000	9,888	265%
Total Current Liabilities	31,013	24,380	6,633	127%
Long Term Liabilities				
Notes Payable	125,000	125,000	0	100%
Total Long Term Liabilities	125,000	125,000	0	100%
Total Liabilities	156,013	149,380	6,633	104%
Equity				
Common Stock	200,000	200,000	0	100%
Retained Earnings	0	620	-620	0%
Net Income	-2,492	0	-2,492	100%
Total Equity	197,508	200,620	-3,112	98%
TOTAL LIABILITIES & EQUITY	353,521	350,000	3,521	101%

Figure 7.22

Central Coast Cellular
Inventory Valuation Summary
As of January 31, 2003

Item Description	On Hand	Avg Cost	Asset Value	% of Tot Asset	Sales Price	Retail Value	% of Tot Retail
Ericsson LX588	15	50	750	5%	85	1,275	6%
Ericsson T19LX	60	75	4,500	31%	100	6,000	28%
Nokia 3285	25	200	5,000	34%	300	7,500	35%
Nokia 8290	30	150	4,500	31%	225	6,750	31%
Nokia 8890	0	175	0	0%	250	0	0%
TOTAL	**130**		**14,750**	**100%**		**21,525**	**100%**

Figure 7.23

Ocean View Flowers
Profit & Loss Budget vs. Actual
January through February 2004

	Jan - Feb 04	Budget	$ Over Budget	% of Budget
Ordinary Income/Expense				
Income				
Sales				
Anthuriums	35,500.00	30,000.00	5,500.00	118.3%
Daylilies	37,800.00	45,000.00	-7,200.00	84.0%
Total Sales	73,300.00	75,000.00	-1,700.00	97.7%
Total Income	73,300.00	75,000.00	-1,700.00	97.7%
Cost of Goods Sold				
Cost of Goods Sold	38,400.00	40,000.00	-1,600.00	96.0%
Total COGS	38,400.00	40,000.00	-1,600.00	96.0%
Gross Profit	34,900.00	35,000.00	-100.00	99.7%
Expense				
Bank Service Charges	100.00			
Depreciation Expense	3,100.00			
Insurance				
Liability Insurance	200.00			
Total Insurance	200.00			
Payroll Expenses	39,769.62	40,000.00	-230.38	99.4%
Professional Fees				
Legal Fees	2,500.00	1,000.00	1,500.00	250.0%
Total Professional Fees	2,500.00	1,000.00	1,500.00	250.0%
Rent	3,000.00	6,000.00	-3,000.00	50.0%
Subscriptions	60.00			
Telephone	650.00	800.00	-150.00	81.3%
Utilities	800.00	600.00	200.00	133.3%
Gas and Electric	800.00			
Utilities – Other	0.00	600.00	-600.00	0.0%
Total Utilities	800.00	600.00	200.00	133.3%
Total Expense	50,179.62	48,400.00	1,779.62	103.7%
Net Ordinary Income	-15,279.62	-13,400.00	-1,879.62	114.0%
Other Income/Expense				
Other Income				
Interest Revenue	1,175.00			
Total Other Income	1,175.00			
Net Other Income	1,175.00			
Net Income	**-14,104.62**	**-13,400.00**	**-704.62**	**105.3%**

Figure 7.24

Ocean View Flowers
Balance Sheet Budget vs. Actual
As of February 29, 2004

	Feb 29, 04	Budget	$ Over Budget	% of Budget
ASSETS				
Current Assets				
Checking/Savings				
Union Checking	29,442.06	46,300.00	-16,857.94	63.6%
Short-term Investments	20,800.00	25,000.00	-4,200.00	83.2%
Total Checking/Savings	50,242.06	71,300.00	-21,057.94	70.5%
Accounts Receivable				
Accounts Receivable	30,500.00	15,000.00	15,500.00	203.3%
Total Accounts Receivable	30,500.00	15,000.00	15,500.00	203.3%
Other Current Assets				
Prepaid Insurance	2,300.00	1,000.00	1,300.00	230.0%
Undeposited Funds	9,000.00			
Office Supplies	1,500.00	1,500.00	0.00	100.0%
Inventory Asset	43,900.00	30,000.00	13,900.00	146.3%
Total Other Current Assets	56,700.00	32,500.00	24,200.00	174.5%
Total Current Assets	137,442.06	118,800.00	18,642.06	115.7%
Fixed Assets				
Land	50,000.00	50,000.00	0.00	100.0%
Building				
Cost	250,000.00	250,000.00	0.00	100.0%
Accumulated Depreciation	-2,000.00			
Total Building	248,000.00	250,000.00	-2,000.00	99.2%
Computer Equipment				
Cost	15,000.00	16,000.00	-1,000.00	93.8%
Accumulated Depreciation	-600.00			
Total Computer Equipment	14,400.00	16,000.00	-1,600.00	90.00%
Office Equipment				
Cost	20,000.00	21,000.00	-1,000.00	95.2%
Accumulated Depreciation	-500.00			
Total Office Equipment	19,500.00	21,000.00	-1,500.00	92.9%
Total Fixed Assets	331,900.00	337,000.00	-5,100.00	98.5%
TOTAL ASSETS	**469,342.06**	**455,800.00**	**13,542.06**	**103.0%**
LIABILITIES & EQUITY				
Liabilities				
Current Liabilities				
Accounts Payable				
Accounts Payable	47,860.00	35,000.00	12,860.00	136.7%
Total Accounts Payable	47,860.00	35,000.00	12,860.00	136.7%
Other Current Liabilities				
Legal fees payable	2,500.00			
Payroll Liabilities	14,086.68	14,000.00	86.68	100.6%
Total Other Current Liabilities	16,586.68	14,000.00	2,586.68	118.5%
Total Current Liabilities	64,446.68	49,000.00	15,446.68	131.5%

Figure 7.24 (Concluded)

Long Term Liabilities				
Long-Term Note Payable	319,000.00	320,000.00	-1,000.00	99.7%
Total Long Term Liabilities	319,000.00	320,000.00	-1,000.00	99.7%
Total Liabilities	383,446.68	369,000.00	14,446.68	103.9%
Equity				
Common Stock	100,000.00	100,000.00	0.00	100.0%
Retained Earnings	0.00	-13,200.00	13,200.00	0.0%
Net Income	-14,104.62	0.00	-14,104.62	100.0%
Total Equity	85,895.38	86,800.00	-904.62	99.0%
TOTAL LIABILITIES & EQUITY	**469,342.06**	**455,800.00**	**13,542.06**	**103.0%**

Figure 7.25

Ocean View Flowers
Balance Sheet Budget vs. Actual
As of February 29, 2004

	A	B	C	D	E	F	G	H	I	J	K	L
1												
2						Feb 29, 04		Budget		$ Over Budget		% of Budget
3	ASSETS											
4		Current Assets										
5			Checking/Savings									
6				Union Checking		29,442.06		46,300.00		-16,857.94		63.59%
7				Short-term Investments		20,800.00		25,000.00		-4,200.00		83.2%
8			Total Checking/Savings			50,242.06		71,300.00		-21,057.94		70.47%
9			Accounts Receivable									
10				Accounts Receivable		30,500.00		15,000.00		15,500.00		203.33%
11			Total Accounts Receivable			30,500.00		15,000.00		15,500.00		203.33%
12			Other Current Assets									
13				Prepaid Insurance		2,300.00		1,000.00		1,300.00		230.0%
14				Undeposited Funds		9,000.00						
15				Office Supplies		1,500.00		1,500.00		0.00		100.0%
16				Inventory Asset		43,900.00		30,000.00		13,900.00		146.33%
17			Total Other Current Assets			56,700.00		32,500.00		24,200.00		174.46%
18		Total Current Assets				137,442.06		118,800.00		18,642.06		115.69%
19		Fixed Assets										
20			Land			50,000.00		50,000.00		0.00		100.0%
21			Building									
22				Cost		250,000.00		250,000.00		0.00		100.0%
23				Accumulated Depreciation		-2,000.00						
24			Total Building			248,000.00		250,000.00		-2,000.00		99.2%
25			Computer Equipment									
26				Cost		15,000.00		16,000.00		-1,000.00		93.75%
27				Accumulated Depreciation		-600.00						
28			Total Computer Equipment			14,400.00		16,000.00		-1,600.00		90.0%
29			Office Equipment									
30				Cost		20,000.00		21,000.00		-1,000.00		95.24%
31				Accumulated Depreciation		-500.00						
32			Total Office Equipment			19,500.00		21,000.00		-1,500.00		92.86%

Figure 7.25 (Concluded)

Ocean View Flowers
Balance Sheet Budget vs. Actual
As of February 29, 2004

	A	B	C	D	E	F	G	H	I	J	K	L
1												
2						Feb 29, 04		Budget		$ Over Budget		% of Budget
33			Total Fixed Assets			331,900.00		337,000.00		-5,100.00		98.49%
34	TOTAL ASSETS					469.342.06		455,800.00		13,542.06		102.97%
35	LIABILITIES & EQUITY											
36		Liabilities										
37			Current Liabilities									
38				Accounts Payable								
39					Accounts Payable	47,860.00		35,000.00		12,860.00		136.74%
40				Total Accounts Payable		47,860.00		35,000.00		12,860.00		136.74%
41				Other Current Liabilities								
42					Legal Fees Payable	2,500.00						
43					Payroll Liabilities	14,086.68		14,000.00		86.68		100.62%
44				Total Other Current Liabilities		16,586.68		14,000.00		2,586.68		118.48%
45			Total Current Liabilities			64,446.68		49,000.00		15,446.68		131.52%
46			Long Term Liabilities									
47				Long-Term Note Payable		319,000.00		320,000.00		-1,000.00		99.69%
48				Total Long-Term Note Payable		319,000.00		320,000.00		-1,000.00		99.69%
49			Total Liabilities			383,446.68		369,000.00		14,446.68		103.92%
50		Equity										
51			Common Stock			100,000.00		100,000.00		0.00		100.0%
52			Retained Earnings			0.00		-13,200.00		13,200.00		0.0%
53			Net Income			-14,104.62		0.00		-14,104.62		100.0%
54		Total Equity				85,895.38		86,800.00		-904.62		98.96%
55	TOTAL LIABILITIES & EQUITY					469,342.06		455,800.00		13,542.06		102.97%

Figure 7.26

Ocean View Flowers
Sales by Customer Summary
January through February 2004

	Jan - Feb 04
California Beauties	25,000.00
Eastern Scents	22,200.00
FTD	10,500.00
Latin Ladies	9,000.00
Valley Florists	6,600.00
TOTAL	**73,300.00**

Figure 7.27

Ocean View Flowers
Inventory Stock Status by Item
January through February 2004

Item Description	Pref Vendor	Reorder	On Hand	Order	On Order	Next Deliv	Sales/Week
Almond Puff - Daylilies	Brophy Bros. Farms		300		0		81.7
Bright Red - Anthuriums	Vordale Farms		400		0		35
Calistoga Sun - Daylilies	Brophy Bros. Farms		15,000		0		58.3
Caribbean Pink Sands - Dayl	Brophy Bros. Farms		0		0		58.3
Peach - Anthuriums	Vordale Farms		800		0		0
White - Anthuriums	Vordale Farms		100		0		58.3

| Almond Puffs |
| Bright Red |
| Calistoga Sun |
| Caribbean Pink |
| Peach |
| White |

Figure 7.28

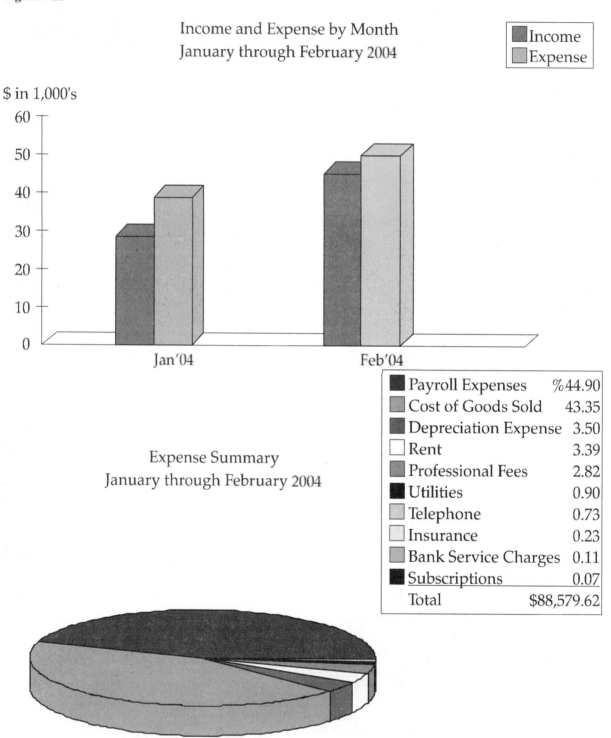

Income and Expense by Month
January through February 2004

Income
Expense

$ in 1,000's

Payroll Expenses	%44.90
Cost of Goods Sold	43.35
Depreciation Expense	3.50
Rent	3.39
Professional Fees	2.82
Utilities	0.90
Telephone	0.73
Insurance	0.23
Bank Service Charges	0.11
Subscriptions	0.07
Total	$88,579.62

Expense Summary
January through February 2004

By Account

Figure 7.29

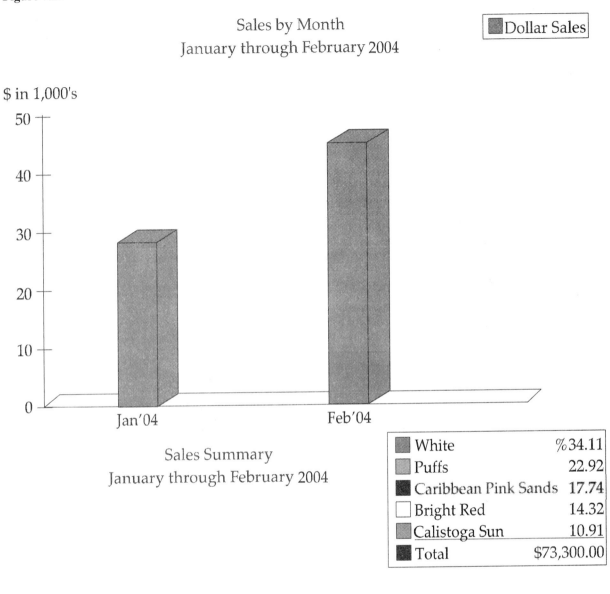

Sales by Month
January through February 2004

Dollar Sales

$ in 1,000's

Sales Summary
January through February 2004

White	%	34.11
Puffs		22.92
Caribbean Pink Sands		17.74
Bright Red		14.32
Calistoga Sun		10.91
Total		$73,300.00

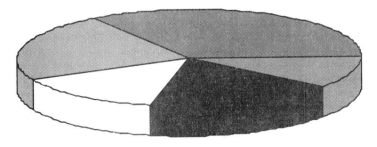

By Item

Figure 7.30

Jennings & Associates (KJ07cp)
Profit & Loss
For the three Months Ended March 31, 2004

		Jan - Mar 04
Ordinary Income/Expense		
Income		
Fee Income		
Film	965	
Magazine	12,100	
Press Release	975	
Promotion	12,350	
Radio	2,178	
Television	21,175	
Total Fee Income		49,743
Total Income		49,743
Gross Profit		49,743
Expense		
Bank Service Charges		270
Depreciation Expense		943
Equipment Rental		75
Film expenses		632
Insurance		
Liability Insurance	775	
Total Insurance		775
Interest Expense		
Loan Interest	80	
Total Interest Expense		80
Office Supplies		101
Payroll Expenses		29,024
Postage and Delivery		109
Practice Development		35
Printing and Reproduction		25
Professional Fees		
Legal Fees	650	
Total Professional Fees		650
Radio Spots		0
Rent		2,100
Repairs		
Computer Repairs	95	
Total Repairs		95
Telephone		249
TV Commercial Spots		10,000
Utilities		
Gas and Electric	295	
Water	217	
Total Utilities		512
Total Expense		45,675
Net Ordinary Income		4,067
Other Income/Expense		
Other Income		
Interest Revenue		500
Other Income		500
Total Other Income		1,000
Net Other Income		1,000
Net Income		**5,067**

Figure 7.31

Jennings & Associates (KJ07cp)
Balance Sheet
As of March 31, 2004

	Mar 31, 04
ASSETS	
Current Assets	
Checking/Savings	
First Valley Savings & Loan	52,722
Union Bank Checking	4,081
Total Checking/Savings	56,803
Accounts Receivable	
Accounts Receivable	24,938
Total Accounts Receivable	24,938
Other Current Assets	
Interest Receivable	41
Inventory Asset	1,760
Prepaid Insurance	1,800
Short-term investments	2,459
Total Other Current Assets	6,060
Total Current Assets	87,801
Fixed Assets	
Computer Equipment	
Cost	14,000
Accumulated Depreciation	-1,518
Total Computer Equipment	12,482
Furniture	
Cost	2,500
Accumulated Depreciation	-625
Total Furniture	1,875
Vehicles	
Cost	18,500
Accumulated Depreciation	-300
Total Vehicles	18,200
Total Fixed Assets	32,557
TOTAL ASSETS	**120,358**
LIABILITIES & EQUITY	
Liabilities	
Current Liabilities	
Accounts Payable	
Accounts Payable	8,770
Total Accounts Payable	8,770
Other Current Liabilities	
Payroll Liabilities	2,676
Short-term note payable	8,000
Unearned Revenue	1,425
Total Other Current Liabilities	12,101
Total Current Liabilities	20,871
Long Term Liabilities	
Vehicle loan	18,580
Total Long Term Liabilities	18,580
Total Liabilities	39,451

Figure 7.31 (Concluded)

Jennings & Associates (KJ07cp)
Balance Sheet
As of March 31, 2004

	Mar 31, 04
Equity	
Capital Stock	70,000
Opening Bal Equity	3,590
Retained Earnings	2,250
Net Income	5,067
Total Equity	80,907
TOTAL LIABILITIES & EQUITY	**120,358**

Figure 7.32

Jennings & Associates (KJ07cp)
Balance Sheet Budget vs. Actual
As of March 31, 2004

	Mar 31, 04	Budget	$ Over Budget	% of Budget
ASSETS				
Current Assets				
Checking/Savings				
First Valley Savings & Loan	52,722	45,000	7,722	117%
Union Bank Checking	4,081	29,227	-25,146	14%
Total Checking/Savings	56,803	74,227	-17,424	77%
Accounts Receivable				
Accounts Receivable	24,938	15,053	9,885	166%
Total Accounts Receivable	24,938	15,053	9,885	166%
Other Current Assets				
Interest Receivable	41			
Inventory Asset	1,760	2,500	-740	70%
Prepaid Insurance	1,800			
Short-term investments	2,459			
Total Other Current Assets	6,060	2,500	3,560	242%
Total Current Assets	87,801	91,780	-3,979	96%
Fixed Assets				
Computer Equipment				
Cost	14,000	14,000	0	100%
Accumulated Depreciation	-1,518	-1,350	-168	112%
Total Computer Equipment	12,482	12,650	-168	99%
Furniture				
Cost	2,500	2,500	0	100%
Accumulated Depreciation	-625	-550	-75	114%
Total Furniture	1,875	1,950	-75	96%
Vehicles				
Cost	18,500			
Accumulated Depreciation	-300			
Total Vehicles	18,200			
Total Fixed Assets	32,557	14,600	17,957	223%
TOTAL ASSETS	**120,358**	**106,380**	**13,978**	**113%**
LIABILITIES & EQUITY				
Liabilities				
Current Liabilities				
Accounts Payable				
Accounts Payable	8,770	10,000	-1,230	88%
Total Accounts Payable	8,770	10,000	-1,230	88%
Other Current Liabilities				
Payroll Liabilities	2,676	10,000	-7,324	27%
Sales Tax Payable	0			
Short-term note payable	8,000			
Unearned Revenue	1,425			
Total Other Current Liabilities	12,101	10,000	2,101	121%
Total Current Liabilities	20,871	20,000	871	104%
Long Term Liabilities				
Bank of San Martin	0	5,000	-5,000	0%
Vehicle loan	18,580			
Total Long Term Liabilities	18,580	5,000	13,580	372%
Total Liabilities	39,451	25,000	14,451	158%

Figure 7.32 (Concluded)

	Mar 31, 04	Budget	$ Over Budget	% of Budget
Equity				
Capital Stock	70,000	73,590	-3,590	95%
Opening Bal Equity	3,590			
Retained Earnings	2,250	7,790	-5,540	29%
Net Income	5,067	0	5,067	100%
Total Equity	80,907	81,380	-473	99%
TOTAL LIABILITIES & EQUITY	120,358	106,380	13,978	113%

Figure 7.33

Jennings & Associates (KJ07cp)
Profit & Loss Budget vs. Actual
January through March 2004

	Jan - Mar 04	Budget	$ Over Budget	% of Budget
Ordinary Income/Expense				
Income				
Fee Income				
Film	965.00			
Magazine	12,100.00			
Press Release	975.00			
Promotion	12,350.00			
Radio	2,177.50			
Television	21,175.00			
Fee Income - Other	0.00	46,340.00	-46,340.00	0.0%
Total Fee Income	49,742.50	46,340.00	3,402.50	107.3%
Total Income	49,742.50	46,340.00	3,402.50	107.3%
Gross Profit	49,742.50	46,340.00	3,402.50	107.3%
Expense				
Bank Service Charges	270.00			
Depreciation Expense	943.34	600.00	343.34	157.2%
Equipment Rental	75.00			
Film expenses	632.21			
Insurance				
Liability Insurance	775.00			
Total Insurance	775.00			
Interest Expense				
Loan Interest	80.00			
Total Interest Expense	80.00			
Office Supplies	101.00			
Payroll Expenses	29,023.83	38,000.00	-8,976.17	76.4%
Postage and Delivery	109.00			
Practice Development	35.00			
Printing and Reproduction	25.00			
Professional Fees				
Legal Fees	650.00			
Total Professional Fees	650.00			
Radio Spots	0.00			
Rent	2,100.00	1,200.00	900.00	175.0%
Repairs				
Computer Repairs	95.00			
Total Repairs	95.00			
Telephone	249.00			
TV Commercial Spots	10,000.00			
Utilities				
Gas and Electric	295.00			
Water	217.00			
Total Utilities	512.00			
Total Expense	45,675.38	39,800.00	5,875.38	114.8%
Net Ordinary Income	4,067.12	6,540.00	-2,472.88	62.2%
Other Income/Expense				
Other Income				
Interest Revenue	500.17			
Other Income	500.00			
Total Other Income	1,000.17			
Net Other Income	1,000.17			
Net Income	5,067.29	6,540.00	-1,472.71	77.5%

Figure 7.34

Jennings & Associates (KJ07cp)
Profit & Loss Budget vs. Actual
January through March 2004

	A	B	C	D	E	F	G	H	I	J	K	L	M
1													
2							Jan - Mar 04		Budget		$ Over Budget		% of Budget
3						Ordinary Income/Expense							
4						Income							
5						Fee Income							
6						Film	965.00						
7						Magazine	12,100.00						
8						Press Release	975.00						
9						Promotion	12,350.00						
10						Radio	2,177.50						
11						Television	21,175.00						
12						Fee Income - Other	0.00		46,340.00		-46,340.00		0.0%
13						Total Fee Income	49,742.50		46,340.00		3,402.50		107.34%
14						Total Income	49,742.50		46,340.00		3,402.50		107.34%
15						Gross Profit	49,742.50		46,340.00		3,402.50		107.34%
16						Expense							
17						Bank Service Charges	270.00						
18						Depreciation Expense	943.34		600.00		343.34		157.22%
19						Equipment Rental	75.00						
20						Film expenses	632.21						
21						Insurance							
22						Liability Insurance	775.00						
23						Total Insurance	775.00						
24						Interest Expense							
25						Loan Interest	80.00						
26						Total Interest Expense	80.00						
27						Office Supplies	101.00						
28						Payroll Expenses	29,023.83		38,000.00		-8,976.17		76.38%
29						Postage and Delivery	109.00						
30						Practice Development	35.00						
31						Printing and Reproduction	25.00						
32						Professional Fees							
33						Legal Fees	650.00						
34						Total Professional Fees	650.00						

Figure 7.34 (Concluded)

	A	B	C	D	E	F	G	H	I	J	K	L	M
1													
2							**Jan - Mar 04**		**Budget**		**$ Over Budget**		**% of Budget**
35						Radio Spots	0.00						
36						Rent	2,100.00		1,200.00		900.00		175.0%
37						Repairs							
38						Computer Repairs	95.00						
39						Total Repairs	95.00						
40						Telephone	249.00						
41						TV Commercial Spots	10,000.00						
42						Utilities							
43						Gas and Electric	295.00						
44						Water	217.00						
45						Total Utilities	512.00						
46						Total Expense	45,675.38		39,800.00		5,875.38		114.76%
47						Net Ordinary Income	4,067.12		6,540.00		-2,472.88		62.19%
48						Other Income/Expense							
49						Other Income							
50						Interest Revenue	500.17						
51						Other Income	500.00						
52						Total Other Income	1,000.17						
53						Net Other Income	1,000.17						
54		**Net Income**					**5,067.29**		**6,540.00**		**-1,472.71**		**77.48%**

Figure 7.35

Jennings & Associates (KJ07cp)
Sales by Customer Summary
January through March 2004

	Jan - Mar 04
AAA Appliance	7,825
Big 10	16,075
Bob and Mary Schultz	875
Evelyn Walker Real Estate	4,865
Fancy Yogurt Co.	6,438
Paulson	1,950
Ray's Chevron	650
Sally's Fabrics	3,238
Yaskar Farms	5,328
TOTAL	**47,243**

Figure 7.36

Jennings & Associates (KJ07cp)
Sales by Item Summary
January through March 2004

				Jan - Mar 04				
	Qty	Amount	% of Sales	Avg Price	COGS	Avg COGS	Gross Margin	Gross Margin%
Inventory								
Film	102	765	2%	8	512	5	253	33%
Film HQ	8	200	0%	25	120	15	80	40%
Total Inventory		965	2%		632		333	34%
Service								
Magazine	121	12,100	26%	100				
Press	20	975	2%	50				
Promotion	130	12,350	26%	95				
Radio	34	2,178	5%	65				
Television	249	18,675	40%	75				
Total Service		46,278	98%					
TOTAL		**47,243**	**100%**					

Figure 7.37

Jennings & Associates (KJ07cp)
A/R Aging Summary
As of March 31, 2004

	Current	1 - 30	31 - 60	61 - 90	> 90	TOTAL
Big 10	15,750.00	0.00	0.00	0.00	0.00	15,750.00
Bob and Mary Schultz	1,425.00	0.00	-1,425.00	0.00	0.00	0.00
Fancy Yogurt Co.	5,625.00	0.00	0.00	0.00	0.00	5,625.00
Paulson	0.00	1,950.00	0.00	0.00	0.00	1,950.00
Sally's Fabrics	500.00	0.00	862.50	0.00	0.00	1,363.50
Yaskar Farms	250.00	0.00	0.00	0.00	0.00	250.00
TOTAL	**23,550.00**	**1,950.00**	**-562.50**	**0.00**	**0.00**	**24,937.50**

Figure 7.38

Jennings & Associates (KJ07cp)
A/P Aging Summary
As of March 31,2004

	Current	1 - 30	31 - 60	61 - 90	> 90	TOTAL
Frank Mendez Properties	700.00	0.00	0.00	0.00	0.00	700.00
KCOY TV	7,500.00	0.00	0.00	0.00	0.00	7,500.00
Owen & Owen	375.00	0.00	0.00	0.00	0.00	375.00
Pacific Electric Co.	135.00	60.00	0.00	0.00	0.00	195.00
TOTAL	**8,710.00**	**60.00**	**0.00**	**0.00**	**0.00**	**8,770.00**

Figure 7.39

Jennings & Associates (KJ07cp)
Inventory Valuation Summary
As of March 31, 2004

Item Description	On Hand	Avg Cost	Asset Value	% of Tot Asset	Sales Price	Retail Value	% of Tot Retail
Film	198	5	980	56%	8	1,485	53%
Film HQ — High Quality Film	52	15	780	44%	25	1,300	47%
TOTAL	**250**		**1,760**	**100%**		**2,785**	**100%**

Figure 7.40

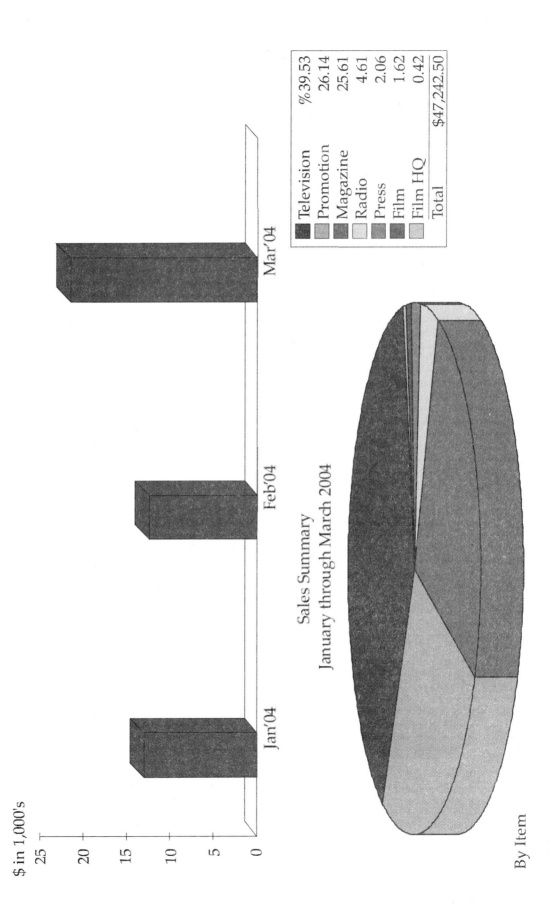

Sales by Month
January through March 2004

$ in 1,000's

25
20
15
10
5
0

Jan'04   Feb'04   Mar'04

	%
Television	39.53
Promotion	26.14
Magazine	25.61
Radio	4.61
Press	2.06
Film	1.62
Film HQ	0.42
Total	$47,242.50

Sales Summary
January through March 2004

By Item

Figure 7.41

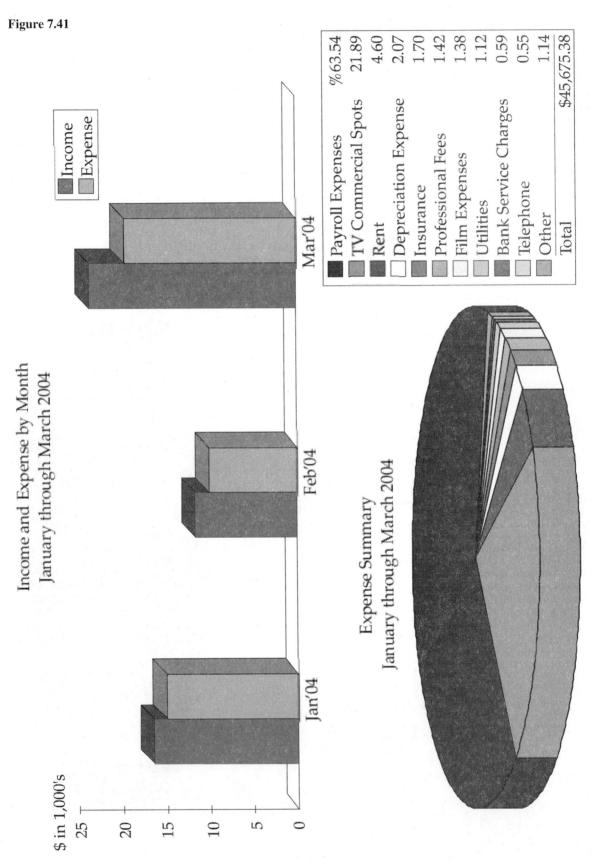

Income and Expense by Month
January through March 2004

$ in 1,000's

	%
Payroll Expenses	63.54
TV Commercial Spots	21.89
Rent	4.60
Depreciation Expense	2.07
Insurance	1.70
Professional Fees	1.42
Film Expenses	1.38
Utilities	1.12
Bank Service Charges	0.59
Telephone	0.55
Other	1.14
Total	$45,675.38

Expense Summary
January through March 2004

By Account

Figure 7.42

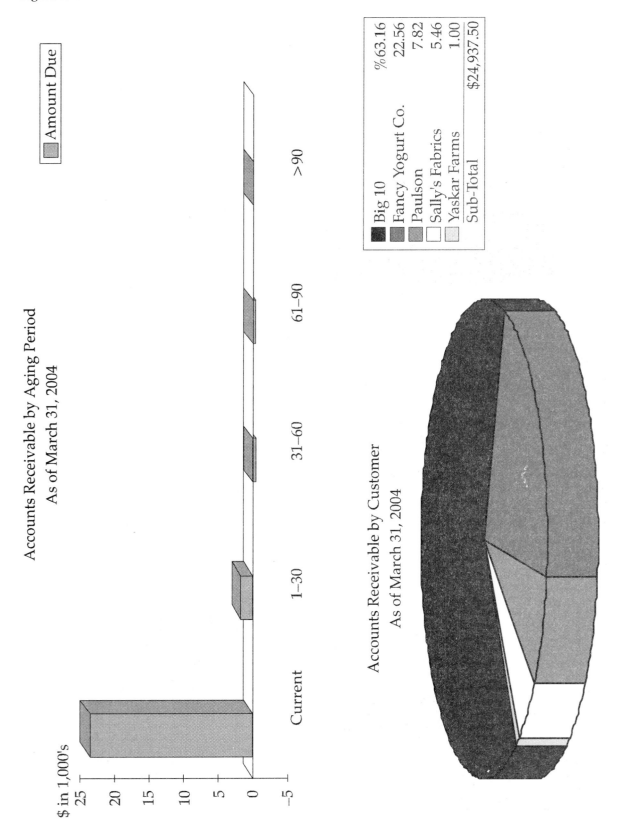

Accounts Receivable by Aging Period
As of March 31, 2004

Accounts Receivable by Customer
As of March 31, 2004

	%
Big 10	63.16
Fancy Yogurt Co.	22.56
Paulson	7.82
Sally's Fabrics	5.46
Yaskar Farms	1.00
Sub-Total	$24,937.50

Figure 7.43

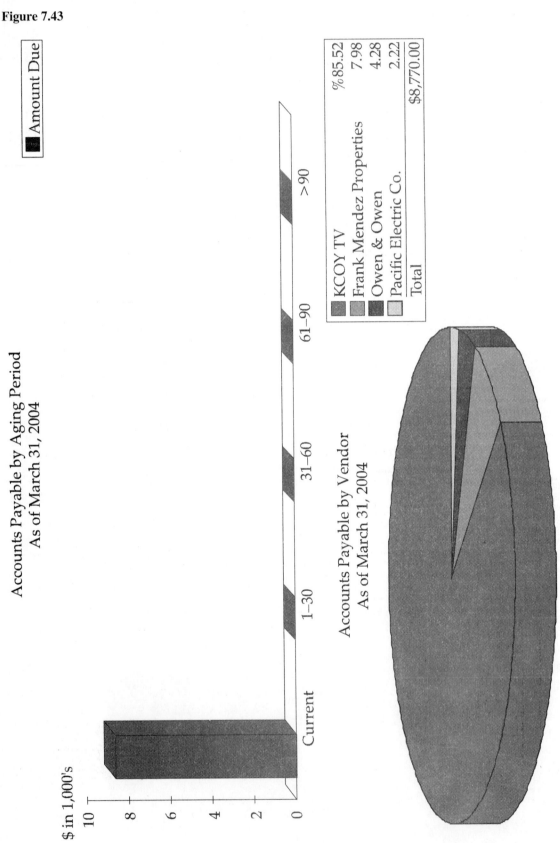

Accounts Payable by Aging Period
As of March 31, 2004

$ in 1,000's

Amount Due

Current   1–30   31–60   61–90   >90

Accounts Payable by Vendor
As of March 31, 2004

	%
KCOY TV	85.52
Frank Mendez Properties	7.98
Owen & Owen	4.28
Pacific Electric Co.	2.22
Total	$8,770.00

Figure 7.44 Comprehensive Problem 1, Custom Transaction Detail Report, page 1

Sports City
Custom Transaction Detail Report
April 2004

Type	Date	Num	Name	Memo	Account	Clr	Split	Amount	Balance
Apr 04									
Deposit	4/1/2004		Scott Szulczewski	Deposit	Mid State Bank	X	Common Stock	40,000.00	40,000.00
Deposit	4/1/2004			Deposit	Common Stock		Mid State Bank	-40,000.00	0.00
Check	4/1/2004	1	Office Max		Mid State Bank	X	Cost	-15,000.00	-15,000.00
Check	4/1/2004	1	Office Max		Cost		Mid State Bank	15,000.00	0.00
Check	4/1/2004	2	Wiser Realty		Mid State Bank	X	Prepaid Rent	-6,000.00	-6,000.00
Check	4/1/2004	2	Wiser Realty		Prepaid Rent		Mid State Bank	6,000.00	0.00
Invoice	4/1/2004	1	Lompoc High School	Soccer balls	Accounts Receivable		-SPLIT-	1,215.00	1,215.00
Invoice	4/1/2004	1	Lompoc High School	Soccer balls	Sales		Accounts Rec...	-1,125.00	90.00
Invoice	4/1/2004	1	Lompoc High School	Soccer balls	Inventory Asset		Accounts Rec...	-585.00	-495.00
Invoice	4/1/2004	1	Lompoc High School	Soccer balls	Cost of Goods Sold		Accounts Rec...	585.00	90.00
Invoice	4/1/2004	1	State Board of Equ...	Sales Tax	Sales Tax Payable		Accounts Rec...	-90.00	0.00
Check	4/2/2004	3	Pro Sports Supply		Mid State Bank	X	-SPLIT-	-6,300.00	-6,300.00
Check	4/2/2004	3	Pro Sports Supply	Pro Footballs	Inventory Asset		Mid State Bank	1,700.00	-4,600.00
Check	4/2/2004	3	Pro Sports Supply	Pro Basketba...	Inventory Asset		Mid State Bank	1,000.00	-3,600.00
Check	4/2/2004	3	Pro Sports Supply	Soccer balls	Inventory Asset		Mid State Bank	2,600.00	-1,000.00
Check	4/2/2004	3	Pro Sports Supply	Volley balls	Inventory Asset		Mid State Bank	1,000.00	0.00
Invoice	4/2/2004	2	Cabrillo High School		Accounts Receivable		-SPLIT-	761.40	761.40
Invoice	4/2/2004	2	Cabrillo High School	Volley balls	Sales		Accounts Rec...	-705.00	56.40
Invoice	4/2/2004	2	Cabrillo High School	Volley balls	Inventory Asset		Accounts Rec...	-375.00	-318.60
Invoice	4/2/2004	2	Cabrillo High School	Volley balls	Cost of Goods Sold		Accounts Rec...	375.00	56.40
Invoice	4/2/2004	2	State Board of Equ...	Sales Tax	Sales Tax Payable		Accounts Rec...	-56.40	0.00
Bill	4/2/2004		Southern Cal Edison		Accounts Payable		Utilities	-219.00	-219.00
Bill	4/2/2004		Southern Cal Edison		Utilities		Accounts Pay...	219.00	0.00
Bill	4/2/2004		Verizon		Telephone		Accounts Pay...	-75.00	-75.00
Bill	4/2/2004		Verizon		Accounts Payable		Telephone	75.00	0.00
Bill	4/2/2004		Gas Company		Utilities		Accounts Pay...	-50.00	-50.00
Bill	4/2/2004		Gas Company		Accounts Payable		Utilities	50.00	0.00
Payment	4/6/2004		Arroyo Grande High...		Mid State Bank	X	Accounts Rec...	1,000.00	1,000.00
Payment	4/6/2004		Arroyo Grande High...		Accounts Receivable		Mid State Bank	-1,000.00	0.00
Sales Receipt	4/8/2004	1	Village Hills Youth ...	Pro Basketba...	Mid State Bank	X	-SPLIT-	2,160.00	2,160.00
Sales Receipt	4/8/2004	1	Village Hills Youth ...	Pro Basketba...	Sales		Mid State Bank	-2,000.00	160.00
Sales Receipt	4/8/2004	1	Village Hills Youth ...	Pro Basketba...	Inventory Asset		Mid State Bank	-1,000.00	-840.00
Sales Receipt	4/8/2004	1	Village Hills Youth ...	Pro Basketba...	Cost of Goods Sold		Mid State Bank	1,000.00	160.00
Sales Receipt	4/8/2004	1	State Board of Equ...	Sales Tax	Sales Tax Payable		Mid State Bank	-160.00	0.00
Sales Receipt	4/11/2004	2	Vandeberg Youth F...	Pro Footballs	Mid State Bank	X	-SPLIT-	756.00	756.00
Sales Receipt	4/11/2004	2	Vandeberg Youth F...	Pro Footballs	Sales		Mid State Bank	-700.00	56.00
Sales Receipt	4/11/2004	2	Vandeberg Youth F...	Pro Footballs	Inventory Asset		Mid State Bank	-340.00	-284.00
Sales Receipt	4/11/2004	2	Vandeberg Youth F...	Pro Footballs	Cost of Goods Sold		Mid State Bank	340.00	56.00
Sales Receipt	4/11/2004	2	State Board of Equ...	Sales Tax	Sales Tax Payable		Mid State Bank	-56.00	0.00
Paycheck	4/15/2004		Kelly Flowers		Mid State Bank	X	-SPLIT-	-960.40	-960.40
Paycheck	4/15/2004		Kelly Flowers		Payroll Expenses		Mid State Bank	1,250.00	289.60
Paycheck	4/15/2004		Kelly Flowers		Payroll Liabilities		Mid State Bank	-147.00	142.60
Paycheck	4/15/2004		Kelly Flowers		Payroll Expenses		Mid State Bank	77.50	220.10
Paycheck	4/15/2004		Kelly Flowers		Payroll Liabilities		Mid State Bank	-77.50	142.60
Paycheck	4/15/2004		Kelly Flowers		Payroll Liabilities		Mid State Bank	-77.50	65.10
Paycheck	4/15/2004		Kelly Flowers		Payroll Expenses		Mid State Bank	18.13	83.23
Paycheck	4/15/2004		Kelly Flowers		Payroll Liabilities		Mid State Bank	-18.13	65.10
Paycheck	4/15/2004		Kelly Flowers		Payroll Liabilities		Mid State Bank	-18.13	46.97

Figure 7.44 Comprehensive Problem 1, Custom Transaction Detail Report, page 2

Sports City
Custom Transaction Detail Report
April 2004

Type	Date	Num	Name	Memo	Account	Clr	Split	Amount	Balance
Paycheck	4/15/2004		Kelly Flowers		Payroll Expenses		Mid State Bank	10.00	56.97
Paycheck	4/15/2004		Kelly Flowers		Payroll Liabilities		Mid State Bank	-10.00	46.97
Paycheck	4/15/2004		Kelly Flowers		Payroll Liabilities		Mid State Bank	-40.72	6.25
Paycheck	4/15/2004		Kelly Flowers		Payroll Liabilities		Mid State Bank	-6.25	0.00
Paycheck	4/15/2004		Kelly Flowers		Payroll Expenses		Mid State Bank	0.63	0.63
Paycheck	4/15/2004		Kelly Flowers		Payroll Liabilities		Mid State Bank	-0.63	0.00
Paycheck	4/15/2004		Kelly Flowers		Payroll Expenses		Mid State Bank	1.25	1.25
Paycheck	4/15/2004		Kelly Flowers		Payroll Liabilities		Mid State Bank	-1.25	0.00
Paycheck	4/15/2004		Sam Snead		Mid State Bank	X	-SPLIT-	-1,038.08	-1,038.08
Paycheck	4/15/2004		Sam Snead		Payroll Expenses		Mid State Bank	1,458.33	420.25
Paycheck	4/15/2004		Sam Snead		Payroll Liabilities		Mid State Bank	-244.00	176.25
Paycheck	4/15/2004		Sam Snead		Payroll Expenses		Mid State Bank	90.42	266.67
Paycheck	4/15/2004		Sam Snead		Payroll Liabilities		Mid State Bank	-90.42	176.25
Paycheck	4/15/2004		Sam Snead		Payroll Liabilities		Mid State Bank	-90.42	85.83
Paycheck	4/15/2004		Sam Snead		Payroll Expenses		Mid State Bank	21.15	106.98
Paycheck	4/15/2004		Sam Snead		Payroll Liabilities		Mid State Bank	-21.15	85.83
Paycheck	4/15/2004		Sam Snead		Payroll Liabilities		Mid State Bank	-21.15	64.68
Paycheck	4/15/2004		Sam Snead		Payroll Expenses		Mid State Bank	11.67	76.35
Paycheck	4/15/2004		Sam Snead		Payroll Liabilities		Mid State Bank	-11.67	64.68
Paycheck	4/15/2004		Sam Snead		Payroll Liabilities		Mid State Bank	-57.39	7.29
Paycheck	4/15/2004		Sam Snead		Payroll Liabilities		Mid State Bank	-7.29	0.00
Paycheck	4/15/2004		Sam Snead		Payroll Expenses		Mid State Bank	0.73	0.73
Paycheck	4/15/2004		Sam Snead		Payroll Liabilities		Mid State Bank	-0.73	0.00
Paycheck	4/15/2004		Sam Snead		Payroll Expenses		Mid State Bank	1.46	1.46
Paycheck	4/15/2004		Sam Snead		Payroll Liabilities		Mid State Bank	-1.46	0.00
Bill	4/16/2004		Office Max		Accounts Payable		Office	-250.00	-250.00
Bill	4/16/2004		Office Max		Office		Accounts Pay...	250.00	0.00
Payment	4/16/2004		Cabrillo High School		Undeposited Funds	X	Accounts Rec...	400.00	400.00
Payment	4/16/2004		Cabrillo High School		Accounts Receivable		Undeposited F...	-400.00	0.00
Bill	4/17/2004		Nike		Accounts Payable		-SPLIT-	-12,625.00	-12,625.00
Bill	4/17/2004		Nike	Pro Running ...	Inventory Asset		Accounts Pay...	3,250.00	-9,375.00
Bill	4/17/2004		Nike	Basketball sh...	Inventory Asset		Accounts Pay...	9,375.00	0.00
Bill	4/18/2004		Wilson Sporting Go...		Accounts Payable		-SPLIT-	-6,025.00	-6,025.00
Bill	4/18/2004		Wilson Sporting Go...	Sports Bag	Inventory Asset		Accounts Pay...	625.00	-5,400.00
Bill	4/18/2004		Wilson Sporting Go...	Shorts	Inventory Asset		Accounts Pay...	1,800.00	-3,600.00
Bill	4/18/2004		Wilson Sporting Go...	Shirts	Inventory Asset		Accounts Pay...	3,600.00	0.00
Invoice	4/21/2004		Buena Vista Eleme...		Accounts Receivable		-SPLIT-	2,673.00	2,673.00
Invoice	4/21/2004	3	Buena Vista Eleme...	Shirts	Sales		Accounts Rec...	-2,300.00	373.00
Invoice	4/21/2004	3	Buena Vista Eleme...	Shirts	Inventory Asset		Accounts Rec...	-1,800.00	-1,427.00
Invoice	4/21/2004	3	Buena Vista Eleme...		Cost of Goods Sold		Accounts Rec...	1,800.00	373.00
Invoice	4/21/2004	3	Buena Vista Eleme...	Pro Footballs	Sales		Accounts Rec...	-175.00	198.00
Invoice	4/21/2004	3	Buena Vista Eleme...	Pro Footballs	Inventory Asset		Accounts Rec...	-85.00	113.00
Invoice	4/21/2004	3	Buena Vista Eleme...		Cost of Goods Sold		Accounts Rec...	85.00	198.00
Invoice	4/21/2004		State Board of Equ...	Sales Tax	Sales Tax Payable		Accounts Rec...	-198.00	0.00
Payment	4/22/2004		Lompoc High School		Undeposited Funds	X	Accounts Rec...	600.00	600.00
Payment	4/22/2004		Lompoc High School		Accounts Receivable		Undeposited F...	-600.00	0.00
Deposit	4/24/2004			Deposit	Mid State Bank	X	Short-term No...	10,000.00	10,000.00
Deposit	4/24/2004		Mid-State Bank	Deposit	Short-term Notes P...		Mid State Bank	-10,000.00	0.00
Bill Pmt -Check	4/25/2004	4	Gas Company		Mid State Bank	X	Accounts Pay...	-50.00	-50.00

Figure 7.44 Comprehensive Problem 1, Custom Transaction Detail Report, page 3

Sports City
Custom Transaction Detail Report
April 2004

Type	Date	Num	Name	Memo	Account	Clr	Split	Amount	Balance
Bill Pmt -Check	4/25/2004	4	Gas Company		Accounts Payable		Mid State Bank	50.00	0.00
Bill Pmt -Check	4/25/2004	5	Nike		Mid State Bank	X	Accounts Pay...	-12,625.00	-12,625.00
Bill Pmt -Check	4/25/2004	5	Nike		Accounts Payable		Mid State Bank	12,625.00	0.00
Bill Pmt -Check	4/25/2004	6	Office Max		Mid State Bank	X	Accounts Pay...	-250.00	-250.00
Bill Pmt -Check	4/25/2004	6	Office Max		Accounts Payable		Mid State Bank	250.00	0.00
Bill Pmt -Check	4/25/2004	7	Southern Cal Edison		Mid State Bank	X	Accounts Pay...	-219.00	-219.00
Bill Pmt -Check	4/25/2004	7	Southern Cal Edison		Accounts Payable		Mid State Bank	219.00	0.00
Bill Pmt -Check	4/25/2004	8	Verizon		Mid State Bank	X	Accounts Pay...	-75.00	-75.00
Bill Pmt -Check	4/25/2004	8	Verizon		Accounts Payable		Mid State Bank	75.00	0.00
Bill Pmt -Check	4/25/2004	9	Wilson Sporting Go...		Mid State Bank	X	Accounts Pay...	-6,025.00	-6,025.00
Bill Pmt -Check	4/25/2004	9	Wilson Sporting Go...		Accounts Payable		Mid State Bank	6,025.00	0.00
Deposit	4/29/2004		Cabrillo High School	Deposit	Mid State Bank		-SPLIT-	1,000.00	1,000.00
Deposit	4/29/2004		Lompoc High School	Deposit	Undeposited Funds	X	Mid State Bank	-400.00	600.00
Deposit	4/30/2004			Deposit	Undeposited Funds	X	Mid State Bank	-600.00	0.00
General Journal	4/30/2004				Accumulated Depre...		Depreciation E...	-2,000.00	-2,000.00
General Journal	4/30/2004				Depreciation Expense		Accumulated ...	2,000.00	0.00
Paycheck	4/30/2004	10	Anne Franks		Mid State Bank		-SPLIT-	-470.44	-470.44
Paycheck	4/30/2004	10	Anne Franks		Payroll Expenses		Mid State Bank	600.00	129.56
Paycheck	4/30/2004	10	Anne Franks		Payroll Liabilities		Mid State Bank	-73.00	56.56
Paycheck	4/30/2004	10	Anne Franks		Payroll Expenses		Mid State Bank	37.20	93.76
Paycheck	4/30/2004	10	Anne Franks		Payroll Liabilities		Mid State Bank	-37.20	56.56
Paycheck	4/30/2004	10	Anne Franks		Payroll Liabilities		Mid State Bank	-37.20	19.36
Paycheck	4/30/2004	10	Anne Franks		Payroll Expenses		Mid State Bank	8.70	28.06
Paycheck	4/30/2004	10	Anne Franks		Payroll Liabilities		Mid State Bank	-8.70	19.36
Paycheck	4/30/2004	10	Anne Franks		Payroll Liabilities		Mid State Bank	-8.70	10.66
Paycheck	4/30/2004	10	Anne Franks		Payroll Expenses		Mid State Bank	4.80	15.46
Paycheck	4/30/2004	10	Anne Franks		Payroll Liabilities		Mid State Bank	-4.80	10.66
Paycheck	4/30/2004	10	Anne Franks		Payroll Liabilities		Mid State Bank	-7.66	3.00
Paycheck	4/30/2004	10	Anne Franks		Payroll Liabilities		Mid State Bank	-3.00	0.00
Paycheck	4/30/2004	10	Anne Franks		Payroll Expenses		Mid State Bank	0.30	0.30
Paycheck	4/30/2004	10	Anne Franks		Payroll Liabilities		Mid State Bank	-0.30	0.00
Paycheck	4/30/2004	10	Anne Franks		Payroll Expenses		Mid State Bank	0.60	0.60
Paycheck	4/30/2004	10	Anne Franks		Payroll Liabilities		Mid State Bank	-0.60	0.00
Paycheck	4/30/2004	11	Kelly Flowers		Mid State Bank		-SPLIT-	-960.41	-960.41
Paycheck	4/30/2004	11	Kelly Flowers		Payroll Expenses		Mid State Bank	1,250.00	289.59
Paycheck	4/30/2004	11	Kelly Flowers		Payroll Liabilities		Mid State Bank	-147.00	142.59
Paycheck	4/30/2004	11	Kelly Flowers		Payroll Expenses		Mid State Bank	77.50	220.09
Paycheck	4/30/2004	11	Kelly Flowers		Payroll Liabilities		Mid State Bank	-77.50	142.59
Paycheck	4/30/2004	11	Kelly Flowers		Payroll Liabilities		Mid State Bank	-77.50	65.09
Paycheck	4/30/2004	11	Kelly Flowers		Payroll Expenses		Mid State Bank	18.12	83.21
Paycheck	4/30/2004	11	Kelly Flowers		Payroll Liabilities		Mid State Bank	-18.12	65.09
Paycheck	4/30/2004	11	Kelly Flowers		Payroll Liabilities		Mid State Bank	-18.12	46.97
Paycheck	4/30/2004	11	Kelly Flowers		Payroll Expenses		Mid State Bank	10.00	56.97
Paycheck	4/30/2004	11	Kelly Flowers		Payroll Liabilities		Mid State Bank	-10.00	46.97
Paycheck	4/30/2004	11	Kelly Flowers		Payroll Liabilities		Mid State Bank	-40.72	6.25
Paycheck	4/30/2004	11	Kelly Flowers		Payroll Liabilities		Mid State Bank	-6.25	0.00
Paycheck	4/30/2004	11	Kelly Flowers		Payroll Expenses		Mid State Bank	0.62	0.62
Paycheck	4/30/2004	11	Kelly Flowers		Payroll Liabilities		Mid State Bank	-0.62	0.00
Paycheck	4/30/2004	11	Kelly Flowers		Payroll Expenses		Mid State Bank	1.25	1.25

Figure 7.44 Comprehensive Problem 1, Custom Transaction Detail Report, page 4

Sports City
Custom Transaction Detail Report
April 2004

Type	Date	Num	Name	Memo	Account	Clr	Split	Amount	Balance
Paycheck	4/30/2004	11	Kelly Flowers		Payroll Liabilities		Mid State Bank	-1.25	0.00
Paycheck	4/30/2004	12	Sam Snead		Mid State Bank		-SPLIT-	-1,038.10	-1,038.10
Paycheck	4/30/2004	12	Sam Snead		Payroll Expenses		Mid State Bank	1,458.33	420.23
Paycheck	4/30/2004	12	Sam Snead		Payroll Liabilities		Mid State Bank	-244.00	176.23
Paycheck	4/30/2004	12	Sam Snead		Payroll Expenses		Mid State Bank	90.41	266.64
Paycheck	4/30/2004	12	Sam Snead		Payroll Liabilities		Mid State Bank	-90.41	176.23
Paycheck	4/30/2004	12	Sam Snead		Payroll Liabilities		Mid State Bank	-90.41	85.82
Paycheck	4/30/2004	12	Sam Snead		Payroll Expenses		Mid State Bank	21.14	106.96
Paycheck	4/30/2004	12	Sam Snead		Payroll Liabilities		Mid State Bank	-21.14	85.82
Paycheck	4/30/2004	12	Sam Snead		Payroll Liabilities		Mid State Bank	-21.14	64.68
Paycheck	4/30/2004	12	Sam Snead		Payroll Expenses		Mid State Bank	11.66	76.34
Paycheck	4/30/2004	12	Sam Snead		Payroll Liabilities		Mid State Bank	-11.66	64.68
Paycheck	4/30/2004	12	Sam Snead		Payroll Liabilities		Mid State Bank	-57.39	7.29
Paycheck	4/30/2004	12	Sam Snead		Payroll Liabilities		Mid State Bank	-7.29	0.00
Paycheck	4/30/2004	12	Sam Snead		Payroll Expenses		Mid State Bank	0.73	0.73
Paycheck	4/30/2004	12	Sam Snead		Payroll Liabilities		Mid State Bank	-0.73	0.00
Paycheck	4/30/2004	12	Sam Snead		Payroll Expenses		Mid State Bank	1.46	1.46
Paycheck	4/30/2004	12	Sam Snead		Payroll Liabilities		Mid State Bank	-1.46	0.00
General Journal	4/30/2004				Prepaid Rent		Rent	-3,000.00	-3,000.00
General Journal	4/30/2004				Rent		Prepaid Rent	3,000.00	0.00
General Journal	4/30/2004		Arroyo Grande High...	To reclassify ...	Unearned Revenue		Accounts Rec...	-1,000.00	-1,000.00
General Journal	4/30/2004		Arroyo Grande High...	To reclassify ...	Accounts Receivable		Unearned Rev...	1,000.00	0.00
Check	4/30/2004			Service Charge	Mid State Bank	X	Bank Service ...	-40.00	-40.00
Check	4/30/2004			Service Charge	Bank Service Charg...		Mid State Bank	40.00	0.00
Apr 04								**0.00**	**0.00**

Figure 7.45 Comprehensive Problem 1, Balance Sheet

Sports City
Balance Sheet
As of April 30, 2004

	Apr 30, 04	% of Column
ASSETS		
Current Assets		
Checking/Savings		
Mid State Bank	3,864.57	8.7%
Total Checking/Savings	3,864.57	8.7%
Accounts Receivable		
Accounts Receivable	3,649.40	8.2%
Total Accounts Receivable	3,649.40	8.2%
Other Current Assets		
Inventory Asset	20,765.00	46.9%
Prepaid Rent	3,000.00	6.8%
Total Other Current Assets	23,765.00	53.7%
Total Current Assets	31,278.97	70.6%
Fixed Assets		
Furniture & Fixtures		
Cost	15,000.00	33.9%
Accumulated Depreciation	-2,000.00	-4.5%
Total Furniture & Fixtures	13,000.00	29.4%
Total Fixed Assets	13,000.00	29.4%
TOTAL ASSETS	44,278.97	100.0%
LIABILITIES & EQUITY		
Liabilities		
Current Liabilities		
Other Current Liabilities		
Payroll Liabilities	2,066.66	4.7%
Sales Tax Payable	560.40	1.3%
Short-term Notes Payable	10,000.00	22.6%
Unearned Revenue	1,000.00	2.3%
Total Other Current Liabilities	13,627.06	30.8%
Total Current Liabilities	13,627.06	30.8%
Total Liabilities	13,627.06	30.8%
Equity		
Common Stock	40,000.00	90.3%
Net Income	-9,348.09	-21.1%
Total Equity	30,651.91	69.2%
TOTAL LIABILITIES & EQUITY	44,278.97	100.0%

Figure 7.46 Comprehensive Problem 1, Profit & Loss Statement

Sports City
Profit & Loss
April 2004

	Apr 04	% of Income
Ordinary Income/Expense		
Income		
Sales	7,005.00	100.0%
Total Income	7,005.00	100.0%
Cost of Goods Sold		
Cost of Goods Sold	4,185.00	59.7%
Total COGS	4,185.00	59.7%
Gross Profit	2,820.00	40.3%
Expense		
Bank Service Charges	40.00	0.6%
Depreciation Expense	2,000.00	28.6%
Payroll Expenses	6,534.09	93.3%
Rent	3,000.00	42.8%
Supplies		
Office	250.00	3.6%
Total Supplies	250.00	3.6%
Telephone	75.00	1.1%
Utilities	269.00	3.8%
Total Expense	12,168.09	173.7%
Net Ordinary Income	-9,348.09	-133.4%
Net Income	**-9,348.09**	**-133.4%**

Figure 7.47 Comprehensive Problem 1, Statement of Cash Flows

Sports City
Statement of Cash Flows
April 2004

	Apr 04
OPERATING ACTIVITIES	
Net Income	-9,348.09
Adjustments to reconcile Net Income	
to net cash provided by operations:	
Accounts Receivable	-3,649.40
Inventory Asset	-20,765.00
Prepaid Rent	-3,000.00
Furniture & Fixtures:Accumulated Depreciation	2,000.00
Payroll Liabilities	2,066.66
Sales Tax Payable	560.40
Short-term Notes Payable	10,000.00
Unearned Revenue	1,000.00
Net cash provided by Operating Activities	-21,135.43
INVESTING ACTIVITIES	
Furniture & Fixtures:Cost	-15,000.00
Net cash provided by Investing Activities	-15,000.00
FINANCING ACTIVITIES	
Common Stock	40,000.00
Net cash provided by Financing Activities	40,000.00
Net cash increase for period	3,864.57
Cash at end of period	**3,864.57**

Figure 7.48 Comprehensive Problem 1, Profit & Loss Budget vs. Actual

Sports City
Profit & Loss Budget vs. Actual
April 2004

	Apr 04	Budget	$ Over Budget	% of Budget
Ordinary Income/Expense				
Income				
Sales	7,005.00	10,000.00	-2,995.00	70.1%
Total Income	7,005.00	10,000.00	-2,995.00	70.1%
Cost of Goods Sold				
Cost of Goods Sold	4,185.00	6,000.00	-1,815.00	69.8%
Total COGS	4,185.00	6,000.00	-1,815.00	69.8%
Gross Profit	2,820.00	4,000.00	-1,180.00	70.5%
Expense				
Bank Service Charges	40.00			
Depreciation Expense	2,000.00	2,000.00	0.00	100.0%
Payroll Expenses	6,534.09	6,500.00	34.09	100.5%
Rent	3,000.00	3,000.00	0.00	100.0%
Supplies				
Office	250.00			
Total Supplies	250.00			
Telephone	75.00	100.00	-25.00	75.0%
Utilities	269.00	200.00	69.00	134.5%
Total Expense	12,168.09	11,800.00	368.09	103.1%
Net Ordinary Income	-9,348.09	-7,800.00	-1,548.09	119.8%
Net Income	-9,348.09	-7,800.00	-1,548.09	119.8%

Figure 7.49 Comprehensive Problem 1, Profit & Loss Budget Overview

Sports City
Profit & Loss Budget Overview
April through June 2004

	Apr 04	May 04	Jun 04	TOTAL Apr - Jun 04
Ordinary Income/Expense				
Income				
Sales	10,000.00	11,500.00	13,225.00	34,725.00
Total Income	10,000.00	11,500.00	13,225.00	34,725.00
Cost of Goods Sold				
Cost of Goods Sold	6,000.00	6,900.00	7,935.00	20,835.00
Total COGS	6,000.00	6,900.00	7,935.00	20,835.00
Gross Profit	4,000.00	4,600.00	5,290.00	13,890.00
Expense				
Depreciation Expense	2,000.00	2,000.00	2,000.00	6,000.00
Payroll Expenses	6,500.00	7,000.00	7,500.00	21,000.00
Rent	3,000.00	3,000.00	3,000.00	9,000.00
Telephone	100.00	105.00	110.25	315.25
Utilities	200.00	210.00	220.50	630.50
Total Expense	11,800.00	12,315.00	12,830.75	36,945.75
Net Ordinary Income	-7,800.00	-7,715.00	-7,540.75	-23,055.75
Net Income	**-7,800.00**	**-7,715.00**	**-7,540.75**	**-23,055.75**

Figure 7.50 Comprehensive Problem 1, Reconciliation Summary

Sports City
Reconciliation Summary
Mid State Bank, Period Ending 04/30/04

	Apr 30, 04
Beginning Balance	5,333.52
Cleared Transactions	
Checks and Payments - 1 item	-40.00
Deposits and Credits - 1 item	40.00
Total Cleared Transactions	0.00
Cleared Balance	**5,333.52**
Uncleared Transactions	
Checks and Payments - 3 items	-2,468.95
Deposits and Credits - 1 item	1,000.00
Total Uncleared Transactions	-1,468.95
Register Balance as of 04/30/04	**3,864.57**
Ending Balance	3,864.57

Figure 7.51 Comprehensive Problem 1, Balance Sheet, page 1

Sports City
Balance Sheet
As of April 30, 2004

				Apr 30, 04	% of Column
ASSETS					
	Current Assets				
		Checking/Savings			
			Mid State Bank	3,864.57	8.73%
		Total Checking/Savings		3,864.57	8.73%
		Accounts Receivable			
			Accounts Receivable	3,649.40	8.24%
		Total Accounts Receivable		3,649.40	8.24%
		Other Current Assets			
			Inventory Asset	20,765.00	46.9%
			Prepaid Rent	3,000.00	6.78%
		Total Other Current Assets		23,765.00	53.67%
	Total Current Assets			31,278.97	70.64%
	Fixed Assets				
		Furniture & Fixtures			
			Cost	15,000.00	33.88%
			Accumulated Depreciation	-2,000.00	-4.52%
		Total Furniture & Fixtures		13,000.00	29.36%
	Total Fixed Assets			13,000.00	29.36%
TOTAL ASSETS				44,278.97	100.0%
LIABILITIES & EQUITY					
	Liabilities				
		Current Liabilities			
			Other Current Liabilities		
			Payroll Liabilities	2,066.66	4.67%
			Sales Tax Payable	560.40	1.27%
			Short-term Notes Payable	10,000.00	22.58%
			Unearned Revenue	1,000.00	2.26%
			Total Other Current Liabilities	13,627.06	30.78%
		Total Current Liabilities		13,627.06	30.78%

Figure 7.51 Comprehensive Problem 1, Balance Sheet, page 2

Sports City
Balance Sheet
As of April 30, 2004

		Apr 30, 04	% of Column
Total Liabilities		13,627.06	30.78%
Equity			
Common Stock		40,000.00	90.34%
Opening Bal Equity		40.00	0.09%
Retained Earnings		-40.00	-0.09%
Net Income		-9,348.09	-21.11%
Total Equity		30,651.91	69.23%
TOTAL LIABILITIES & EQUITY		44,278.97	100.0%

Figure 7.52

Pacific Brew, Inc.
Custom Transaction Detail Report
January 17-31, 2006

Type	Date	Num	Name	Memo	Account	Cir	Split	Amount	Balance
Jan 17-31, 06									
Bill	1/17/2006		Staples		Accounts Payable		Office Supplies	-2,500.00	-2,500.00
Bill	1/17/2006		Staples		Office Supplies		Accounts Payable	2,500.00	0.00
Bill	1/17/2006		Lost Coast		Accounts Payable		-SPLIT-	-4,725.00	-4,725.00
Bill	1/17/2006		Lost Coast	Lost Coast Pa...	Inventory Asset		Accounts Paya...	1,575.00	-3,150.00
Bill	1/17/2006		Lost Coast	Lost Coast St...	Inventory Asset		Accounts Paya...	1,875.00	-1,275.00
Bill	1/17/2006		Lost Coast	Lost Coast A...	Inventory Asset		Accounts Paya...	1,275.00	0.00
Invoice	1/20/2006	7001	Bon Jovi's		Accounts Receivable		-SPLIT-	4,575.00	4,575.00
Invoice	1/20/2006	7001	Bon Jovi's	Mad River Pal...	Sales		Accounts Rece...	-1,800.00	2,775.00
Invoice	1/20/2006	7001	Bon Jovi's	Mad River Pal...	Inventory Asset		Accounts Rece...	-1,000.00	1,775.00
Invoice	1/20/2006	7001	Bon Jovi's	Mad River Pal...	Cost of Good Sold		Accounts Rece...	1,000.00	2,775.00
Invoice	1/20/2006	7001	Bon Jovi's	Mad River Stout	Sales		Accounts Rece...	-1,575.00	1,200.00
Invoice	1/20/2006	7001	Bon Jovi's	Mad River Stout	Inventory Asset		Accounts Rece...	-900.00	300.00
Invoice	1/20/2006	7001	Bon Jovi's	Mad River Stout	Cost of Goods Sold		Accounts Rece...	900.00	1,200.00
Invoice	1/20/2006	7001	Bon Jovi's	Humboldt Re...	Sales		Accounts Rece...	-1,200.00	0.00
Invoice	1/20/2006	7001	Bon Jovi's	Humboldt Re...	Inventory Asset		Accounts Rece...	-700.00	-700.00
Invoice	1/20/2006	7001	Bon Jovi's	Humboldt Re...	Cost of Goods Sold		Accounts Rece...	700.00	0.00
Invoice	1/20/2006	7002	Ocean Grove		Accounts Receivable		-SPLIT-	2,625.00	2,625.00
Invoice	1/20/2006	7002	Ocean Grove	Mad River Pal...	Sales		Accounts Rece...	-900.00	1,725.00
Invoice	1/20/2006	7002	Ocean Grove	Mad River Pal...	Inventory Asset		Accounts Rece	-500.00	1,225.00
Invoice	1/20/2006	7002	Ocean Grove	Mad River Pal...	Cost of Goods Sold		Accounts Rece...	500.00	1,725.00
Invoice	1/20/2006	7002	Ocean Grove	Mad River Am...	Sales		Accounts Rece...	-750.00	975.00
Invoice	1/20/2006	7002	Ocean Grove	Mad River Am...	Inventory Asset		Accounts Rece...	-400.00	575.00
Invoice	1/20/2006	7002	Ocean Grove	Mad River Am...	Cost of Goods Sold		Accounts Rece...	400.00	975.00
Invoice	1/20/2006	7002	Ocean Grove	Mad River Por...	Sales		Accounts Rece...	-975.00	0.00
Invoice	1/20/2006	7002	Ocean Grove	Mad River Por...	Inventory Asset		Accounts Rece...	-550.00	-550.00
Invoice	1/20/2006	7002	Ocean Grove	Mad River Por...	Cost of Goods Sold		Accounts Receivable	550.00	0.00
Invoice	1/23/2006	7003	Avalon Bistro		Accounts Receivable		-SPLIT-	4,950.00	4,950.00
Invoice	1/23/2006	7003	Avalon Bistro	Humboldt Pal...	Sales		Accounts Rece...	-1,462.50	3,487.50
Invoice	1/23/2006	7003	Avalon Bistro	Humboldt Pal...	Inventory Asset		Accounts Rece...	-825.00	2,662.50
Invoice	1/23/2006	7003	Avalon Bistro	Humboldt Pal...	Cost of Goods Sold		Accounts Rece...	825.00	3,487.50
Invoice	1/23/2006	7003	Avalon Bistro	Humboldt IPA	Sales		Accounts Rece...	-1,687.50	1,800.00
Invoice	1/23/2006	7003	Avalon Bistro	Humboldt IPA	Inventory Asset		Accounts Rece...	-975.00	825.00
Invoice	1/23/2006	7003	Avalon Bistro	Humboldt IPA	Cost of Goods Sold		Accounts Rece...	975.00	1,800.00
Invoice	1/23/2006	7003	Avalon Bistro	Humboldt Re...	Sales		Accounts Rece...	-1,800.00	0.00
Invoice	1/23/2006	7003	Avalon Bistro	Humboldt Re...	Inventory Asset		Accounts Rece...	-1,050.00	-1,050.00
Invoice	1/23/2006	7003	Avalon Bistro	Humboldt Re...	Cost of Good Sold		Accounts Rece...	1,050.00	0.00
Bill	1/24/2006		Verizon		Accounts Payable		Telephone	-500.00	-500.00
Bill	1/24/2006		Verizon		Telephone		Accounts Paya...	500.00	0.00
Bill	1/24/2006		City of Arcata		Accounts Payable		Gas and Electric	-1,500.00	-1,500.00
Bill	1/24/2006		City of Arcata		Gas and Electric		Accounts Paya...	1,500.00	0.00
Payment	1/24/2006		Bon Jovi's		Accounts Receivable	X	Undeposited Funds	4,575.00	4,575.00
Payment	1/24/2006		Bon Jovi's		Undeposited Funds		Accounts Rece...	-4,575.00	0.00
Payment	1/24/2006		River House		Accounts Receivable	X	Undeposited F...	1,200.00	1,200.00
Payment	1/24/2006		River House		Undeposited Funds		Accounts Receivable	-1,200.00	0.00
Deposit	1/27/2006			Deposit	Wells Fargo		-SPLIT-	5,775.00	5,775.00
Deposit	1/27/2006		Bon Jovi's	Deposit	Undeposited Funds	X	Wells Fargo	-4,575.00	1,200.00
Deposit	1/27/2006		River House	Deposit	Undeposited Funds	X	Wells Fargo	-1,200.00	0.00

Figure 7.52 (Continued)

Pacific Brew, Inc.
Custom Transaction Detail Report
January 17-31, 2006

Type	Date	Num	Name	Memo	Account	Cir	Split	Amount	Balance
Bill	1/27/2006		Lost Coast		Accounts Payable		-SPLIT-	-23,125.00	-23,125.00
Bill	1/27/2006		Lost Coast	Lost Coast Pa...	Inventory Asset		Accounts Pay...	5,250.00	-17,875.00
Bill	1/27/2006		Lost Coast	Lost Coast St....	Inventory Asset		Accounts Pay...	9,375.00	-8,500.00
Bill	1/27/2006		Lost Coast	Lost Coast A....	Inventory Asset		Accounts Paya...	8,500.00	0.00
Bill	1/27/2006		Mad River		Accounts Payable		-SPLIT-	-15,375.00	-15,375.00
Bill	1/27/2006		Mad River	Mad River Pal...	Inventory Asset		Accounts Paya...	3,750.00	-11,625.00
Bill	1/27/2006		Mad River	Mad River Stout	Inventory Asset		Accounts Paya...	4,500.00	-7,125.00
Bill	1/27/2006		Mad River	Mad River Am...	Inventory Asset		Accounts Paya...	3,000.00	-4,125.00
Bill	1/27/2006		Mad River	Mad River Por...	Inventory Asset		Accounts Paya...	4,125.00	0.00
Bill Pmt-Check	1/30/2006	110	City of Arcata		Accounts Payable		Wells Fargo	-1,500.00	-1,500.00
Bill Pmt-Check	1/30/2006	110	City of Arcata		Accounts Payable		Wells Fargo	1,500.00	0.00
Bill Pmt-Check	1/30/2006	111	Staples		Wells Fargo		Accounts Paya...	-2,500.00	-2,500.00
Bill Pmt-Check	1/30/2006	111	Staples		Accounts Payable		Wells Fargo	2,500.00	0.00
Bill Pmt-Check	1/30/2006	112	Verizon		Wells Fargo		Accounts Paya...	-500.00	-500.00
Bill Pmt-Check	1/30/2006	112	Verizon		Accounts Payable		Wells Fargo	500.00	0.00
Paycheck	1/30/2006	113	Emilio Duarte		Wells Fargo		-SPLIT-	-663.28	-663.28
Paycheck	1/30/2006	113	Emilio Duarte		Payroll Expenses		Wells Fargo	913.00	249.72
Paycheck	1/30/2006	113	Emilio Duarte		Payroll Expenses		Wells Fargo	0.91	250.63
Paycheck	1/30/2006	113	Emilio Duarte		Payroll Liabilities		Wells Fargo	-0.91	249.72
Paycheck	1/30/2006	113	Emilio Duarte		Payroll Liabilities		Wells Fargo	-125.08	124.64
Paycheck	1/30/2006	113	Emilio Duarte		Payroll Expenses		Wells Fargo	56.61	181.25
Paycheck	1/30/2006	113	Emilio Duarte		Payroll Liabilities		Wells Fargo	-56.61	124.64
Paycheck	1/30/2006	113	Emilio Duarte		Payroll Liabilities		Wells Fargo	-56.61	68.03
Paycheck	1/30/2006	113	Emilio Duarte		Payroll Expenses		Wells Fargo	13.24	81.27
Paycheck	1/30/2006	113	Emilio Duarte		Payroll Liabilities		Wells Fargo	-13.24	68.03
Paycheck	1/30/2006	113	Emilio Duarte		Payroll Liabilities		Wells Fargo	-13.24	54.79
Paycheck	1/30/2006	113	Emilio Duarte		Payroll Expenses		Wells Fargo	7.30	62.09
Paycheck	1/30/2006	113	Emilio Duarte		Payroll Liabilities		Wells Fargo	-7.30	54.79
Paycheck	1/30/2006	113	Emilio Duarte		Payroll Liabilities		Wells Fargo	-50.22	4.57
Paycheck	1/30/2006	113	Emilio Duarte		Payroll Liabilities		Wells Fargo	-4.57	0.00
Paycheck	1/30/2006	113	Emilio Duarte		Payroll Expenses		Wells Fargo	27.39	27.39
Paycheck	1/30/2006	113	Emilio Duarte		Payroll Liabilities		Wells Fargo	-27.39	0.00
Paycheck	1/30/2006	114	Michael Patrick		Wells Fargo		-SPLIT-	-1,513.53	-1,513.53
Paycheck	1/30/2006	114	Michael Patrick		Payroll Expenses		Wells Fargo	2,083.33	569.80
Paycheck	1/30/2006	114	Michael Patrick		Payroll Expenses		Wells Fargo	2.08	571.88
Paycheck	1/30/2006	114	Michael Patrick		Payroll Liabilities		Wells Fargo	-2.08	569.80
Paycheck	1/30/2006	114	Michael Patrick		Payroll Liabilities		Wells Fargo	-285.42	284.38
Paycheck	1/30/2006	114	Michael Patrick		Payroll Expenses		Wells Fargo	129.17	413.55
Paycheck	1/30/2006	114	Michael Patrick		Payroll Liabilities		Wells Fargo	-129.17	284.38
Paycheck	1/30/2006	114	Michael Patrick		Payroll Liabilities		Wells Fargo	-129.17	155.21
Paycheck	1/30/2006	114	Michael Patrick		Payroll Expenses		Wells Fargo	30.21	185.42
Paycheck	1/30/2006	114	Michael Patrick		Payroll Liabilities		Wells Fargo	-30.21	155.21
Paycheck	1/30/2006	114	Michael Patrick		Payroll Liabilities		Wells Fargo	-30.21	125.00
Paycheck	1/30/2006	114	Michael Patrick		Payroll Expenses		Wells Fargo	16.67	141.67
Paycheck	1/30/2006	114	Michael Patrick		Payroll Liabilities		Wells Fargo	-16.67	125.00
Paycheck	1/30/2006	114	Michael Patrick		Payroll Liabilities		Wells Fargo	-114.58	10.42
Paycheck	1/30/2006	114	Michael Patrick		Payroll Liabilities		Wells Fargo	-10.42	0.00
Paycheck	1/30/2006	114	Michael Patrick		Payroll Expenses		Wells Fargo	62.50	62.50

Figure 7.52 (Concluded)

Pacific Brew, Inc.
Custom Transaction Detail Report
JANUARY 17-31, 2006

Type	Date	Num	Name	Memo	Account	Clr	Split	Amount	Balance
Paycheck	1/30/2006	114	Michael Patrick		Payroll Liabilities		Wells Fargo	-62.50	0.00
Paycheck	1/30/2006	115	Shawn Lopez		Wells Fargo		-SPLIT-	-688.74	-688.74
Paycheck	1/30/2006	115	Shawn Lopez		Payroll Expenses		Wells Fargo	948.00	259.26
Paycheck	1/30/2006	115	Shawn Lopez		Payroll Expenses		Wells Fargo	0.95	260.21
Paycheck	1/30/2006	115	Shawn Lopez		Payroll Liabilities		Wells Fargo	-0.95	259.26
Paycheck	1/30/2006	115	Shawn Lopez		Payroll Liabilities		Wells Fargo	-129.88	129.38
Paycheck	1/30/2006	115	Shawn Lopez		Payroll Expenses		Wells Fargo	58.78	188.16
Paycheck	1/30/2006	115	Shawn Lopez		Payroll Liabilities		Wells Fargo	-58.78	129.38
Paycheck	1/30/2006	115	Shawn Lopez		Payroll Liabilities		Wells Fargo	-58.75	70.63
Paycheck	1/30/2006	115	Shawn Lopez		Payroll Expenses		Wells Fargo	13.75	84.38
Paycheck	1/30/2006	115	Shawn Lopez		Payroll Liabilities		Wells Fargo	-13.75	70.63
Paycheck	1/30/2006	115	Shawn Lopez		Payroll Liabilities		Wells Fargo	-13.75	56.88
Paycheck	1/30/2006	115	Shawn Lopez		Payroll Expenses		Wells Fargo	7.58	64.46
Paycheck	1/30/2006	115	Shawn Lopez		Payroll Liabilities		Wells Fargo	-7.58	56.88
Paycheck	1/30/2006	115	Shawn Lopez		Payroll Expenses		Wells Fargo	-52.14	4.74
Paycheck	1/30/2006	115	Shawn Lopez		Payroll Liabilities		Wells Fargo	-4.74	0.00
Paycheck	1/30/2006	115	Shawn Lopez		Payroll Expenses		Wells Fargo	28.44	28.44
Paycheck	1/30/2006	115	Shawn Lopez		Payroll Liabilities		Wells Fargo	-28.44	0.00
General Journal	1/31/2006	1			Depreciation Expense		-SPLIT-	800.00	800.00
General Journal	1/31/2006	1			Accumulated Deprec...		Depreciation E...	-500.00	300.00
General Journal	1/31/2006	1			Accumulated Deprec...		Depreciation E...	-300.00	0.00
General Journal	1/31/2006	2			Office		Office Supplies	400.00	400.00
General Journal	1/31/2006	2			Office Supplies		Office	-400.00	0.00
General Journal	1/31/2006	3	River House		Accounts Receivable		Unearned Rev...	1,000.00	1,000.00
General Journal	1/31/2006	3	River House		Unearned Revenue		Accounts Rece...	-1,000.00	0.00
General Journal	1/31/2006	4			Short-Term Investm...		Interest Income	2,000.00	2,000.00
General Journal	1/31/2006	4			Interest Income		Short-Term Inv...	-2,000.00	0.00
General Journal	1/31/2006	5			Interest Expense		Notes Payable	2,600.00	2,600.00
General Journal	1/31/2006	5			Notes Payable		Interest Expense	-2,600.00	0.00
Sales Receipt	1/31/2006	5007	Hole in the Wall		Wells Fargo		-SPLIT-	7,032.50	7,032.50
Sales Receipt	1/31/2006	5007	Hole in the Wall	Mad River Stout	Sales		Wells Fargo	-2,625.00	4,407.50
Sales Receipt	1/31/2006	5007	Hole in the Wall	Mad River Stout	Inventory Asset		Wells Fargo	-1,500.00	2,907.50
Sales Receipt	1/31/2006	5007	Hole in the Wall	Mad River Stout	Cost of Goods Sold		Wells Fargo	1,500.00	4,407.50
Sales Receipt	1/31/2006	5007	Hole in the Wall	Mad River Por...	Sales		Wells Fargo	-2,437.50	1,970.00
Sales Receipt	1/31/2006	5007	Hole in the Wall	Mad River Por...	Inventory Asset		Wells Fargo	-1,375.00	595.00
Sales Receipt	1/31/2006	5007	Hole in the Wall	Mad River Por...	Cost of Goods Sold		Wells Fargo	1,375.00	1,970.00
Sales Receipt	1/31/2006	5007	Hole in the Wall	Lost Coast A...	Sales		Wells Fargo	-1,970.00	0.00
Sales Receipt	1/31/2006	5007	Hole in the Wall	Lost Coast A...	Inventory Asset		Wells Fargo	-1,062.50	-1,062.50
Sales Receipt	1/31/2006	5007	Hole in the Wall	Lost Coast A...	Cost of Goods Sold		Wells Fargo	1,062.50	0.00
								0.00	0.00

Figure 7.53

Pacific Brew, Inc.
Balance Sheet
As of January 31, 2006

	Jan 31, 06
ASSETS	
Current Assets	
Checking/Savings	
Wells Fargo	35,340
Total Checking/Savings	35,340
Accounts Receivable	
Accounts Receivable	7,375
Total Accounts Receivable	7,375
Other Current Assets	
Inventory Asset	46,483
Office Supplies	2,100
Prepaid Rent	2,500
Short-Term Investments	32,000
Total Other Current Assets	83,083
Total Current Assets	125,798
Fixed Assets	
Equipment	
Cost	13,200
Accumulated Depreciation	-500
Total Equipment	12,700
Furniture/Fixtures	
Cost	5,000
Accumulated Depreciation	-300
Total Furniture/Fixtures	4,700
Total Fixed Assets	17,400
TOTAL ASSETS	**143,198**
LIABILITIES AND EQUITIES	
Liabilities	
Current Liabilities	
Accounts Payable	
Accounts Payable	43,225
Total Accounts Payable	43,225
Other Current Liabilities	
Unearned Revenue	1,000
Payroll Liabilities	3,037
Total Other Current Liabilities	4,037
Total Current Liabilities	47,262
Long Term Liabilities	
Notes Payable	42,600
Total Long Term Liabilities	42,600
Total Liabilities	89,862
Equity	
Common Stock	50,000
Net Income	3,336
Total Equity	53,336
TOTAL LIABILITIES AND EQUITY	**143,198**

Figure 7.54

Pacific Brew, Inc.
Profit and Loss
January 2006

	Jan 06	% of Income
Ordinary Income/Expense		
Income		
Consulting Revenue	9,350	28%
Sales	23,588	72%
Total Income	32,938	100%
Cost of Goods Sold		
Cost of Goods Sold	14,593	44%
Total COGS	14,593	44%
Gross Profit	18,345	56%
Expense		
Depreciation Expense	800	2%
Interest Expense	2,600	8%
Payroll Expenses	8,709	26%
Rent	2,500	8%
Supplies		
Office	400	1%
Total Supplies	400	1%
Telephone	500	2%
Utilities		
Gas and Electric	1,500	5%
Total Utilities	1,500	5%
Total Expense	17,009	52%
Net Ordinary Income	1,336	4%
Other Income/Expense		
Other Income		
Interest Income	2,000	6%
Total Other Income	2,000	6%
Net Other Income	2,000	6%
Net Income	3,336	10%

Figure 7.55

Pacific Brew, Inc.
Statement of Cash Flows
January 2006

	Jan 06
OPERATING ACTIVITIES	
Net Income	3,336
Adjustments to reconcile Net Income	
to net cash provided by operations:	
Accounts Receivable	-7,375
Inventory Asset	-46,483
Office Supplies	-2,100
Prepaid Rent	-2,500
Short-Term Investments	-32,000
Equipment: Accumulated Depreciation	500
Furniture/Fixtures:Accumulated Depreciation	300
Accounts Payable	43,225
Unearned Revenue	1,000
Payroll Liabilities	3,037
Net cash provided by Operating Activities	-39,060
INVESTING ACTIVITIES	
Equipment:Cost	-13,200
Furniture/Fixtures:Cost	-5,000
Net cash provided by Investing Activities	-18,200
FINANCING ACTIVITIES	
Notes Payable	42,600
Common Stock	50,000
Net cash provided by Financing Activities	92,600
Net cash increase for period	35,340
Cash at end of period	**35,340**

Figure 7.56

Pacific Brew, Inc.
Profit and Loss Budget vs. Actual
January 2006

	Jan 06	Budget	$ Over Budget	% of Budget
Ordinary Income/Expense				
Income				
Consulting Revenue	9,350.00	15,000.00	-5,650.00	62.3%
Sales	23,587.50	20,000.00	3,587.50	117.9%
Total Income	32,937.50	35,000.00	-2,062.50	94.1%
Cost of Goods Sold				
Cost of Goods Sold	14,592.50	15,000.00	-407.50	97.3%
Total COGS	14,592.50	15,000.00	-407.50	97.3%
Gross Profit	18,345.00	20,000.00	-1655.00	91.7%
Expense				
Depreciation Expense	800.00	1,000.00	-200.00	80.0%
Interest Expense	2,600.00	2,000.00	600.00	130.0%
Payroll Expenses	8,709.46	8,500.00	209.46	102.5%
Rent	2,500.00	2,500.00	0.00	100.0%
Supplies				
Office	400.00	500.00	-100.00	80.0%
Total Supplies	400.00	500.00	-100.00	80.0%
Telephone	500.00	450.00	50.00	111.1%
Utilities				
Gas and Electric	1,500.00	1,200.00	300.00	125.0%
Total Utilities	1,500.00	1,200.00	300.00	125.0%
Total Expenses	17,009.46	16,150.00	869.46	105.3%
Net Ordinary Income	1,335.54	3,850.00	-2,514.46	34.7%
Other Income/Expense				
Other Income				
Interest Income	2,000.00	1,500.00	500.00	133.3%
Total Other Income	2,000.00	1,500.00	500.00	133.3%
Net Other Income	2,000.00	1,500.00	500.00	133.3%
Net Income	3,335.54	5,350.00	-2,014.46	62.3%

Figure 7.57

Pacific Brew, Inc.
Profit and Loss Budget Overview
January through March 2006

	Jan 06	Feb 06	Mar 06	Total Jan-Mar 06
Ordinary Income/Expense				
Income				
Consulting Revenue	15,000.00	15,000.00	15,000.00	45,000.00
Sales	20,000.00	25,000.00	30,000.00	75,000.00
Total Income	35,000.00	40,000.00	45,000.00	120,000.00
Cost of Goods Sold				
Cost of Goods Sold	15,000.00	17,500.00	20,000.00	52,500.00
Total COGS	15,000.00	17,500.00	20,000.00	52,500.00
Gross Profit	20,000.00	22,500.00	25,000.00	67,500.00
Expense				
Depreciation Expense	1,000.00	1,000.00	1,000.00	3,000.00
Interest Expense	2,000.00	2,000.00	2,000.00	6,000.00
Payroll Expenses	8,500.00	8,500.00	10,000.00	27,000.00
Rent	2,500.00	2,500.00	2,500.00	7,500.00
Supplies				
Office	500.00	500.00	500.00	1,500.00
Total Supplies	500.00	500.00	500.00	1,500.00
Telephone	450.00	500.00	550.00	1,500.00
Utilities				
Gas and Electric	1,200.00	1,260.00	1,323.00	3,783.00
Total Utilities	1,200.00	1,260.00	1,323.00	3,783.00
Total Expenses	16,150.00	16,260.00	17,873.00	50,283.00
Net Ordinary Income	3,850.00	6,240.00	7,127.00	17,217.00
Other Income/Expense				
Other Income				
Interest Income	1,500.00	1,500.00	1,500.00	4,500.00
Total Other Income	1,500,00	1,500.00	1,500.00	4,500.00
Net Other Income	1,500.00	1,500.00	1,500.00	4,500.00
Net Income	**5,350.00**	**7,740.00**	**8,627.00**	**21,717.00**

Figure 7.58

Pacific Brew, Inc.
Reconciliation Summary
Wells Fargo, Period Ending 01/31/2006

	Jan 31, 06
Beginning Balance	0.00
Cleared Transactions	
Checks and Payments – 9 items	-73,856.70
Deposits and Credits – 9 items	109.530.00
Total Cleared Transactions	35,673.30
Cleared Balance	**35,673.30**
Uncleared Transactions	
Checks and Payments – 6 items	-7,365.55
Deposits and Credits – 1 item	7,032.50
Total Uncleared Transactions	-333.05
Register Balance as of 01/31/2006	**35,340.25**
Ending Balance	35,340.25

Figure 7.59

Pacific Brew, Inc.
Profit and Loss
January 2006

	A	B	C	D	E	F	G	H	I
1									
2							Jan 06		% of Income
3		Ordinary Income/Expense							
4				Income					
5					Consulting Revenue		9,350		28%
6					Sales		23,588		72%
7				Total Income			32,938		100%
8				Cost of Goods Sold					
9					Cost of Goods Sold		14,593		44%
10				Total COGS			14,593		44%
11			Gross Profit				18,345		56%
12				Expense					
13					Depreciation Expense		800		2%
14					Interest Expense		2,600		8%
15					Payroll Expenses		8,709		26%
16					Rent		2,500		8%
17					Supplies				
18						Office	400		1%
19					Total Supplies		400		1%
20					Telephone		500		2%
21					Utilities				
22						Gas and Electric	1,500		5%
23					Total Utilities		1,500		5%
24				Total Expense			17,009		52%
25		Net Ordinary Income					1,336		4%
26		Other Income/Expense							
27			Other Income						
28				Interest Income			2,000		6%
29			Total Other Income				2,000		6%
30		Net Other Income					2,000		6%
31	Net Income						3,336		10%

Figure 7.60

Pacific Brew, Inc.
Sales by Customer Summary
January 2006

	Jan 06
Avalon Bistro	5,852.50
Bon Jovi's	5,362.50
Hole in the Wall	7,032.50
Michael's Brew House	6,250.00
Ocean Grove	3,340.00
River House	5,100.00
TOTAL	**32,937.50**

Figure 7.61

Pacific Brew, Inc.
Custom Transaction Detail Report
JANUARY 2006

	Qty	Amount	% of Sales	Avg Price	COGS	Avg COGS	Gross Margin	Gross Margin %
Inventory								
302	480	3,780.00	11.5%	7.88	2,400.00	5.00	1,380.00	36.5%
303	400	4,200.00	12.8%	10.50	2,400.00	6.00	1,800.00	42.9%
304	130	900.00	2.7%	6.92	520.00	4.00	380.00	42.2%
305	475	4,225.00	12.8%	8.89	2,612.50	5.50	1,612.50	38.2%
404	250	1,970.00	6.0%	7.88	1,062.50	4.25	907.50	46.1%
502	200	1,787.50	5.4%	8.94	1,100.00	5.50	687.50	38.5%
506	315	2,925.00	8.9%	9.29	2,047.50	6.50	877.50	30.0%
507	350	3,800.00	11.5%	10.86	2,450.00	7.00	1,350.00	35.5%
Total Inventory		23,587.50	71.6%		14,592.50		8,995.00	38.1%
Service								
100	110	9,350.00	28.4%	85.00				
Total Service		9,350.00	28.4%					
TOTAL		32,937.50	100.0%					

Figure 7.62

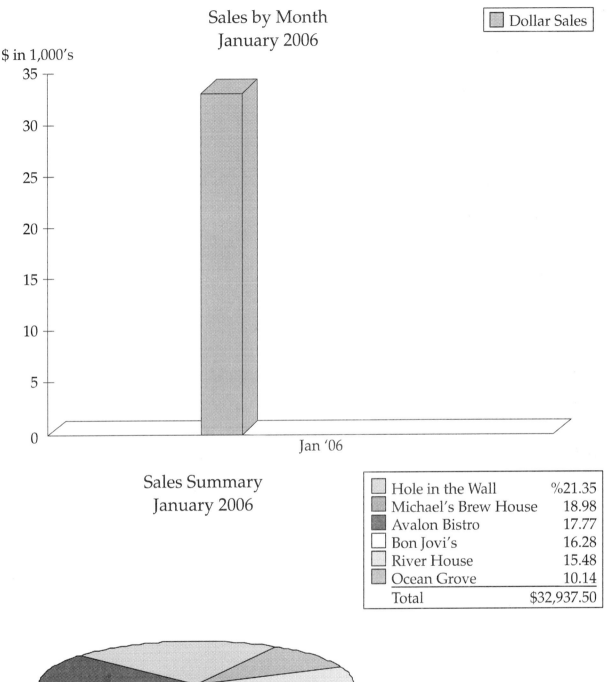

Figure 7.63

Pacific Brew, Inc.
Inventory Stock Status by Item
January 2006

Inventory	Item Description	Pref Vendor	Reorder Pt	On Hand	Order	On Purchases Order	Next Deliv	Sales/Week
302	Mad River Pale Ale	Mad River		770		0		108.4
303	Mad River Stout	Mad River		850		0		90.3
304	Mad River Amber Ale	Mad River		1,120		0		29.4
305	Mad River Porter	Mad River		775		0		107.3
402	Lost Coast Pale Ale	Lost Coast		1,300		0		0
403	Lost Coast Stout	Lost Coast		1,800		0		0
404	Lost Coast Amber Ale	Lost Coast		2,050		0		56.5
502	Humboldt Pale Ale	Humboldt		200		500	1/19/2006	45.2
506	Humboldt IPA	Humboldt		85		500	1/19/2006	71.1
507	Humboldt Red Nectar	Humboldt		50		500	1/19/2006	79

Figure 7.64

Chart of Accounts

Account	**Type**
Checking	Bank
Accounts Receivable	Accounts Receivable
Inventory Asset	Other Current Asset
Prepaid Insurance	Other Current Asset
Short-Term Investments	Other Current Asset
Undeposited Funds	Other Current Asset
Equipment	Fixed Asset
Cost	Fixed Asset
Accumulated Depreciation	Fixed Asset
Furniture/Fixtures	Fixed Asset
Cost	Fixed Asset
Accumulated Depreciation	Fixed Asset
Prepaid Rent	Other Asset
Accounts Payable	Accounts Payable
Unearned Revenue	Other Current Liability
Accrued Interest Payable	Other Current Liability
Payroll Liabilities	Other Current Liability
Sales Tax Payable	Other Current Liability
Note Payable	Long Term Liability
Common Stock	Equity
Opening Bal Equity	Equity
Retained Earnings	Equity
Cash Discrepancies	Income
Overages	Income
Shortages	Income
Sales	Income
Consignment Sales	Income
Discounts Given	Income
Merchandise	Income
Service	Income
Shipping and Handling	Income
Cost of Goods Sold	Cost of Goods Sold
Purchase Discounts	Cost of Goods Sold
Purchases	Cost of Goods Sold
Automobile Expense	Expense
Bad Debt Expense	Expense
Bank Service Charges	Expense
Charitable Contributions	Expense
Depreciation Expense	Expense
Dues and Subscriptions	Expense
Equipment Rental	Expense
Franchise Fees	Expense

Figure 7.64 (Continued)

Chart of Accounts

Account	Type
Insurance	Expense
Health Insurance	Expense
Liability Insurance	Expense
Interest Expense	Expense
Licenses and Permits	Expense
Marketing & Advertising	Expense
Merchant Fees	Expense
Miscellaneous	Expense
Office Expenses	Expense
Office Supplies	Expense
Postage and Delivery	Expense
Printing and Reproduction	Expense
Payroll Expenses	Expense
Professional Fees	Expense
Accounting	Expense
Legal Fees	Expense
Rent	Expense
Repairs	Expense
Building Repairs	Expense
Computer Repairs	Expense
Equipment Repairs	Expense
Taxes	Expense
Telephone	Expense
Travel & Ent	Expense
Entertainment	Expense
Meals	Expense
Travel	Expense
Utilities	Expense
Interest Income	Other Income
Other Income	Other Income
Other Expenses	Other Expenses
Purchase Orders	Non-Posting

Figure 7.65

Employee List

Employee	Bryan Christopher		**SS No.**	556-95-4789
Type	Regular			
Phone	858-555-1264			
Address	Bryan Christopher		**Hired**	01/01/2007
	12 Mesa Way			
	Del Mar, CA 92014		**Salary**	60,000.00

Accrual	**Rate**	**Accrued**	**Limit**	**Used**	**By Year/Period**	**Reset Hrs**
Sick	0:00	0:00		0:00	Y	N
Vacation	0:00	0:00		0:00	Y	N

	FUTA:	**Soc. Sec.:**	**Medicare:**	**SDI:**	**SUI:**	**AEIC:**
Subject To	Y	Y	Y	Y	Y	N

Withholding	**Allowances**	**Extra**	**Status**	**State Lived**	**State Worked**
Federal	0	0.00	Married		
State	0	0.00	Married (one income)	CA	CA

Earnings

Name	**Hourly/Annual Rate**
Salary	60,000.00

Addition, Deduction, Commission, Company Contributions

Name	**Amount**	**Limit**

Employee	Loriel Sanchez		**SS No.**	475-54-8746
Type	Regular			
Phone	858-555-3365			
Address	Loriel Sanchez		**Hired**	09/15/2004
	2342 Court			
	Del Mar, CA 92014			

Accrual	**Rate**	**Accrued**	**Limit**	**Used**	**By Year/Period**	**Reset Hrs**
Sick	0:00	0:00		0:00	Y	N
Vacation	0:00	0:00		0:00	Y	N

	FUTA:	**Soc. Sec.:**	**Medicare:**	**SDI:**	**SUI:**	**AEIC:**
Subject To	Y	Y	Y	Y	Y	N

Withholding	**Allowances**	**Extra**	**Status**	**State Lived**	**State Worked**
Federal	0	0.00	Married		
State	0	0.00	Married (one income)	CA	CA

Earnings

Name	**Hourly/Annual Rate**
Hourly Rate	13.00

Addition, Deduction, Commission, Company Contributions

Name	**Amount**	**Limit**

Figure 7.65 (Continued)

Employee List

Employee	Sharon Lee	**SS No.**	125-58-8452

Type Regular

Phone 858-555-9874

Address Sharon Lee   **Hired** 09/15/2004
323 Ridgefield Pl.
Del Mar, CA 92014

Accrual	Rate	Accrued	Limit	Used	By Year/Period	Reset Hrs
Sick	0:00	0:00		0:00	Y	N
Vacation	0:00	0:00		0:00	Y	N

	FUTA:	Soc. Sec.:	Medicare:	SDI:	SUI:	AEIC:
Subject To	Y	Y	Y	Y	Y	N

Withholding	Allowances	Extra	Status	State Lived	State Worked
Federal	0	0.00	Single		
State	0	0.00	Single	CA	CA

Earnings

Name	Hourly/Annual Rate
Hourly Rate	12.00

Addition, Deduction, Commission, Company Contributions

Name	Amount	Limit

Employee	Walton Perez	**SS No.**	323-99-2394

Type Regular

Address Walton Perez   **Hired** 02/01/2007
530 Miramar Rd. Apt 230
San Diego, CA 92145

Accrual	Rate	Accrued	Limit	Used	By Year/Period	Reset Hrs
Sick	0:00	0:00		0:00	Y	N
Vacation	0:00	0:00		0:00	Y	N

	FUTA:	Soc. Sec.:	Medicare:	SDI:	SUI:	AEIC:
Subject To	Y	Y	Y	Y	Y	N

Withholding	Allowances	Extra	Status	State Lived	State Worked
Federal	0	0.00	Single		
State	0	0.00	Single	CA	CA

Earnings

Name	Hourly/Annual Rate
Hourly Rate	9.00

Addition, Deduction, Commission, Company Contributions

Name	Amount	Limit

Figure 7.66

Customer Job List

Customer	J's Landscaping		
Company	J's Landscaping	**Phone**	858-555-1348
Bill To	J's Landscaping	**Ship To**	J's Landscaping
	12 Bones Way		12 Bones Way
	San Diego, CA 92345		San Diego, CA 92345
Balance	0.00		
		Pmt Terms	Due on receipt
		Sales Tax Code	Tax

Customer	Kristen's Spa Resort		
Bill To	Kristen's Spa Resort		
Balance	0.00		
		Sales Tax Code	Tax

Customer	Landmark Landscaping		
Bill To	Loriel Angel	**Ship to**	Loriel Angel
	Landmark Landscaping		Landmark Landscaping
	8500 Ridgefield Place		8500 Ridgefield Place
	San Diego, CA 92129		San Diego, CA 92129
Balance	11,612.50		
		Pmt Terms	Net 15
		Sales Tax Code	Tax

Customer	Marriott Hotels		
Company	Marriott Hotels	**Phone**	858-555-7407
Bill To	Marriott Hotels	**Ship To**	Marriott Hotels
	97444 Miramar		97444 Miramar
	San Diego, CA 92145		San Diego, CA 92145
Balance	21,446.25		
		Pmt Terms	Net 15
		Sales Tax Code	Tax

Customer	Pam's Designs		
Company	Pam's Designs	**Phone**	707-555-5748
Bill To	Pam's Designs	**Ship To**	Pam's Designs
	5144 Union		5144 Union
	San Diego, CA 92129		San Diego, CA 92129
Balance	59,535.00		
		Pmt Terms	Net 15
		Sales Tax Code	Tax

Figure 7.67

Sunset Spas
Custom Transaction Detail Report
January 1-16, 2007

Jan 17-31, 07

Type	Date	Num	Name	Memo	Account	Cir	Split	Amount	Balance
Bill	1/17/2007		Staples		Accounts Payable		Office Supplies	-500.00	-500.00
Bill	1/17/2007		Staples		Office Supplies		Accounts Pay...	500.00	0.00
Check	1/17/2007	110	Hartford Insurance		Prepaid Insurance	X	Prepaid Insura...	-18,000.00	-18,000.00
Check	1/17/2007	110	Hartford Insurance		Checking		Checking	18,000.00	0.00
Invoice	1/18/2007	10001	Landmark Landsca...		Accounts Receivable		-SPLIT-	16,612.50	16,612.50
Invoice	1/18/2007	10001	Landmark Landsca...	Ultimate	Merchandise		Accounts Rec...	-15,000.00	1,612.50
Invoice	1/18/2007	10001	Landmark Landsca...	Ultimate	Inventory Asset		Accounts Rec...	-11,000.00	-9,387.50
Invoice	1/18/2007	10001	Landmark Landsca...	Ultimate	Cost of Goods Sold		Accounts Rec...	11,000.00	1,612.50
Invoice	1/18/2007	10001	Landmark Landsca...	Installation	Service		Accounts Rec...	-450.00	1,162.50
Invoice	1/18/2007	10001	State Board of Equa...	Sales Tax	Sales Tax Payable		Accounts Rec...	-1,162.50	0.00
Invoice	1/19/2007	10002	Marriott Hotels		Accounts Receivable		-SPLIT-	26,446.25	26,446.25
Invoice	1/19/2007	10002	Marriott Hotels	Optima	Merchandise		Accounts Rec...	-16,000.00	10,446.25
Invoice	1/19/2007	10002	Marriott Hotels	Optima	Inventory Asset		Accounts Rec...	-12,000.00	-1,553.75
Invoice	1/19/2007	10002	Marriott Hotels	Optima	Cost of Goods Sold		Accounts Rec...	12,000.00	10,446.25
Invoice	1/19/2007	10002	Marriott Hotels	Ultimate	Merchandise		Accounts Rec...	-7,500.00	2,946.25
Invoice	1/19/2007	10002	Marriott Hotels	Ultimate	Inventory Asset		Accounts Rec...	-5,500.00	-2,553.75
Invoice	1/19/2007	10002	Marriott Hotels	Ultimate	Cost of Goods Sold		Accounts Rec...	5,500.00	2,946.25
Invoice	1/19/2007	10002	Marriott Hotels	Installation	Service		Accounts Rec...	-1,125.00	1,821.25
Invoice	1/19/2007	10002	State Board of Equa...	Sales Tax	Sales Tax Payable		Accounts Rec...	-1,821.25	0.00
Bill	1/21/2007		Outlet Tool Supply		Accounts Payable		Cost	-25,000.00	-25,000.00
Bill	1/21/2007		Outlet Tool Supply		Cost		Accounts Payable	25,000.00	0.00
Deposit	1/22/2007		Kristen's Spa Resort	Deposit	Checking	X	Unearned Rev...	3,500.00	3,500.00
Deposit	1/22/2007		City of San Diego	Deposit	Unearned Revenue		Checking	-3,500.00	0.00
Bill	1/23/2007		City of San Diego		Accounts Payable		Licenses and ...	-23,000.00	-23,000.00
Bill	1/23/2007		City of San Diego		Licenses and Permits		Accounts Pay...	23,000.00	0.00
Invoice	1/24/2007	10003	Pam's Designs		Accounts Receivable		-SPLIT-	59,535.00	59,535.00
Invoice	1/24/2007	10003	Pam's Designs	Cameo	Merchandise		Accounts Rec...	-54,000.00	5,535.00
Invoice	1/24/2007	10003	Pam's Designs	Cameo	Inventory Asset		Accounts Rec...	-42,000.00	-36,465.00
Invoice	1/24/2007	10003	Pam's Designs	Cameo	Cost of Goods Sold		Accounts Rec...	42,000.00	5,535.00
Invoice	1/24/2007	10003	Pam's Designs	Installation	Service		Accounts Rec...	-1,350.00	4,185.00
Invoice	1/24/2007	10003	State Board of Equa...	Sales Tax	Sales Tax Payable		Accounts Rec...	-4,185.00	0.00
Bill	1/25/2007		Verizon		Accounts Payable		Telephone	-1,400.00	-1,400.00
Bill	1/25/2007		Verizon		Telephone		Accounts Pay...	1,400.00	0.00
Bill	1/25/2007		Cal Spas	Galaxy	Accounts Payable		-SPLIT-	-17,500.00	-17,500.00
Bill	1/25/2007		Cal Spas	Ultimate	Inventory Asset		Accounts Pay...	4,500.00	-13,000.00
Bill	1/25/2007		Cal Spas	Aqua	Inventory Asset		Accounts Pay...	5,500.00	-7,500.00
Bill	1/25/2007		Landmark Landsca...		Inventory Asset		Accounts Pay...	7,500.00	0.00
Payment	1/27/2007		Landmark Landsca...		Checking		Accounts Rec...	5,000.00	5,000.00
Payment	1/27/2007		Landmark Landsca...		Accounts Receivable		Checking	-5,000.00	0.00
Bill Pmt -Check	1/30/2007	111	City of San Diego		Checking	X	Accounts Pay...	-23,000.00	-23,000.00
Bill Pmt -Check	1/30/2007	111	City of San Diego		Accounts Payable		Checking	23,000.00	0.00
Bill Pmt -Check	1/30/2007	112	Verizon		Checking	X	Accounts Pay...	-1,400.00	-1,400.00
Bill Pmt -Check	1/30/2007	112	Verizon		Accounts Payable		Checking	1,400.00	0.00
General Journal	1/31/2007	1			Prepaid Insurance		Prepaid Insura...	1,500.00	1,500.00
General Journal	1/31/2007	1			Liability Insurance		Liability Insura...	-1,500.00	0.00
General Journal	1/31/2007	2			Depreciation Expense		-SPLIT-	1,750.00	1,750.00
General Journal	1/31/2007	2			Accumulated Depre...		Depreciation E...	-1,500.00	250.00
General Journal	1/31/2007	2			Accumulated Depre...		Depreciation E...	-250.00	0.00

Figure 7.67 (Continued)

Sunset Spas
Custom Transaction Detail Report
January 1-16, 2007

Type	Date	Num	Name	Cir	Account	Split	Amount	Balance
General Journal	1/31/2007	3			Interest Expense	Accrued Intere...	1,000.00	1,000.00
General Journal	1/31/2007	3			Accrued Interest Pa...	Interest Expen...	-1,000.00	0.00
General Journal	1/31/2007	4			Short-term investme...	Interest Income	75.00	75.00
General Journal	1/31/2007	4			Interest Income	Short-term inv...	-75.00	0.00
Paycheck	1/31/2007	113	Bryan Christopher		Checking	-SPLIT-	-1,816.25	-1,816.25
Paycheck	1/31/2007	113	Bryan Christopher		Payroll Expenses	Checking	2,500.00	683.75
Paycheck	1/31/2007	113	Bryan Christopher		Payroll Expenses	Checking	2.50	686.25
Paycheck	1/31/2007	113	Bryan Christopher		Payroll Liabilities	Checking	-2.50	683.75
Paycheck	1/31/2007	113	Bryan Christopher		Payroll Expenses	Checking	-342.50	341.25
Paycheck	1/31/2007	113	Bryan Christopher		Payroll Liabilities	Checking	155.00	496.25
Paycheck	1/31/2007	113	Bryan Christopher		Payroll Liabilities	Checking	-155.00	341.25
Paycheck	1/31/2007	113	Bryan Christopher		Payroll Liabilities	Checking	-155.00	186.25
Paycheck	1/31/2007	113	Bryan Christopher		Payroll Expenses	Checking	36.25	222.50
Paycheck	1/31/2007	113	Bryan Christopher		Payroll Liabilities	Checking	-36.25	186.25
Paycheck	1/31/2007	113	Bryan Christopher		Payroll Liabilities	Checking	-36.25	150.00
Paycheck	1/31/2007	113	Bryan Christopher		Payroll Expenses	Checking	20.00	170.00
Paycheck	1/31/2007	113	Bryan Christopher		Payroll Liabilities	Checking	-20.00	150.00
Paycheck	1/31/2007	113	Bryan Christopher		Payroll Liabilities	Checking	-137.50	12.50
Paycheck	1/31/2007	113	Bryan Christopher		Payroll Liabilities	Checking	-12.50	0.00
Paycheck	1/31/2007	113	Bryan Christopher		Payroll Expenses	Checking	6.25	6.25
Paycheck	1/31/2007	113	Bryan Christopher		Payroll Liabilities	Checking	-6.25	0.00
Paycheck	1/31/2007	114	Loriel Sanchez		Checking	-SPLIT-	-793.35	-793.35
Paycheck	1/31/2007	114	Loriel Sanchez		Payroll Expenses	Checking	1,092.00	298.65
Paycheck	1/31/2007	114	Loriel Sanchez		Payroll Expenses	Checking	1.09	299.74
Paycheck	1/31/2007	114	Loriel Sanchez		Payroll Liabilities	Checking	-1.09	298.65
Paycheck	1/31/2007	114	Loriel Sanchez		Payroll Liabilities	Checking	-149.60	149.05
Paycheck	1/31/2007	114	Loriel Sanchez		Payroll Expenses	Checking	67.70	216.75
Paycheck	1/31/2007	114	Loriel Sanchez		Payroll Liabilities	Checking	-67.70	149.05
Paycheck	1/31/2007	114	Loriel Sanchez		Payroll Expenses	Checking	-67.70	81.35
Paycheck	1/31/2007	114	Loriel Sanchez		Payroll Expenses	Checking	15.83	97.18
Paycheck	1/31/2007	114	Loriel Sanchez		Payroll Liabilities	Checking	-15.83	81.35
Paycheck	1/31/2007	114	Loriel Sanchez		Payroll Liabilities	Checking	-15.83	65.52
Paycheck	1/31/2007	114	Loriel Sanchez		Payroll Expenses	Checking	8.74	74.26
Paycheck	1/31/2007	114	Loriel Sanchez		Payroll Liabilities	Checking	-8.74	65.52
Paycheck	1/31/2007	114	Loriel Sanchez		Payroll Expenses	Checking	-60.06	5.46
Paycheck	1/31/2007	114	Loriel Sanchez		Payroll Liabilities	Checking	-5.46	0.00
Paycheck	1/31/2007	114	Loriel Sanchez		Payroll Liabilities	Checking	2.73	2.73
Paycheck	1/31/2007	114	Loriel Sanchez		Payroll Liabilities	Checking	-2.73	0.00
Paycheck	1/31/2007	115	Sharon Lee		Checking	-SPLIT-	-584.10	-584.10
Paycheck	1/31/2007	115	Sharon Lee		Payroll Expenses	Checking	804.00	219.90
Paycheck	1/31/2007	115	Sharon Lee		Payroll Expenses	Checking	0.80	220.70
Paycheck	1/31/2007	115	Sharon Lee		Payroll Liabilities	Checking	-0.80	219.90
Paycheck	1/31/2007	115	Sharon Lee		Payroll Liabilities	Checking	-110.15	109.75
Paycheck	1/31/2007	115	Sharon Lee		Payroll Expenses	Checking	49.85	159.60
Paycheck	1/31/2007	115	Sharon Lee		Payroll Liabilities	Checking	-49.85	109.75
Paycheck	1/31/2007	115	Sharon Lee		Payroll Liabilities	Checking	-49.85	59.90
Paycheck	1/31/2007	115	Sharon Lee		Payroll Expenses	Checking	11.66	71.56
Paycheck	1/31/2007	115	Sharon Lee		Payroll Liabilities	Checking	-11.66	59.90
Paycheck	1/31/2007	115	Sharon Lee		Payroll Liabilities	Checking	-11.66	48.24

Figure 7.67 (Concluded)

Sunset Spas
Custom Transaction Detail Report
January 1-16, 2007

Type	Date	Num	Name	Memo	Account	Clr	Split	Amount	Balance
Paycheck	1/31/2007	115	Sharon Lee		Payroll Expenses		Checking	6.43	54.67
Paycheck	1/31/2007	115	Sharon Lee		Payroll Liabilities		Checking	-6.43	48.24
Paycheck	1/31/2007	115	Sharon Lee		Payroll Liabilities		Checking	-44.22	4.02
Paycheck	1/31/2007	115	Sharon Lee		Payroll Liabilities		Checking	-4.02	0.00
Paycheck	1/31/2007	115	Sharon Lee		Payroll Expenses		Checking	2.01	2.01
Paycheck	1/31/2007	115	Sharon Lee		Payroll Liabilities		Checking	-2.01	0.00
Jan 17 - 31, 07								0.00	0.00

Figure 7.68

Sunset Spas
Balance Sheet
As of January 31, 2007

	Jan 31, 07	% of Column
ASSETS		
Current Assets		
Checking/Savings		
Checking	27,700	8%
Total Checking/Savings	27,700	8%
Accounts Receivable		
Accounts Receivable	92,594	25%
Total Accounts Receivable	92,594	25%
Other Current Assets		
Inventory Asset	158,500	43%
Prepaid Insurance	16,500	4%
Short-term investments	30,075	8%
Total Other Current Assets	205,075	56%
Total Current Assets	325,368	88%
Fixed Assets		
Equipment		
Cost	37,400	10%
Accumulated Depreciation	-1,500	-0%
Total Equipment	35,900	10%
Furniture/Fixtures		
Cost	4,500	1%
Accumulated Depreciation	-250	-0%
Total Furniture/Fixtures	4,250	1%
Total Fixed Assets	40,150	11%
Other Assets		
Prepaid Rent	3,000	1%
Total Other Assets	3,000	1%
TOTAL ASSETS	**368,518**	**100%**
LIABILITIES & EQUITY		
Liabilities		
Current Liabilities		
Accounts Payable		
Accounts Payable	43,000	12%
Total Accounts Payable	43,000	12%
Other Current Liabilities		
Unearned Revenue	3,500	1%
Accrued Interest Payable	1,000	0%
Payroll Liabilities	3,205	1%
Sales Tax Payable	13,170	4%
Total Other Current Liabilities	20,876	6%
Total Current Liabilities	63,876	17%
Long Term Liabilities		
Note Payable	200,000	54%
Total Long Term Liabilities	200,000	54%
Total Liabilities	263,876	72%
Equity		
Common Stock	100,000	27%
Net Income	4,643	1%
Total Equity	104,643	28%
TOTAL LIABILITIES & EQUITY	**368,518**	**100%**

Figure 7.69

Sunset Spas
Profit & Loss
January 2007

	Jan - Mar 04
Ordinary Income/Expense	
Income	
Sales	
Merchandise	168,500
Service	4,365
Total Sales	172,865
Total Income	172,865
Cost of Goods Sold	
Cost of Goods Sold	126,500
Total COGS	126,500
Gross Profit	46,365
Expense	
Depreciation Expense	1,750
Insurance	
Liability Insurance	1,500
Total Insurance	1,500
Interest Expense	1,000
Licenses and Permits	23,000
Office Expenses	
Office Supplies	500
Total Office Expenses	500
Payroll Expenses	9,647
Rent	3,000
Telephone	1,400
Total Expense	41,797
Net Ordinary Income	4,568
Other Income/Expense	
Other Income	
Interest Income	75
Total Other Income	75
Net Other Income	75
Net Income	**4,643**

Figure 7.70

Sunset Spas
Statement of Cash Flows
January 2006

	Jan 07
OPERATING ACTIVITIES	
Net Income	4,643
Adjustments to reconcile Net Income	
to net cash provided by operations:	
Accounts Receivable	-92,594
Inventory Asset	-158,500
Prepaid Insurance	-16,500
Short-term investments	-30,075
Equipment:Accumulated Depreciation	1,500
Furniture/Fixtures:Accumulated Depreciation	250
Accounts Payable	43,000
Unearned Revenue	3,500
Accrued Interest Payable	1,000
Payroll Liabilities	3,205
Sales Tax Payable	13,170
Net cash provided by Operating Activities	-227,400
INVESTING ACTIVITIES	
Equipment:Cost	-37,400
Furniture/Fixtures:Cos	-4,500
Prepaid Rent	-3,000
Net cash provided by Investing Activities	-44,900
FINANCING ACTIVITIES	
Note Payable	200,000
Common Stock	100,000
Net cash provided by Financing Activities	300,000
Net cash increase for period	27,700
Cash at end of period	**27,700**

Figure 7.71

Sunset Spas
Profit & Loss Budget vs. Actual
January 2007

	Jan 07	Budget	$ Over Budget	% of Budget
Ordinary Income/Expense				
Income				
Sales				
Merchandise	168,500	170,000	-1,500	99%
Service	4,365	10,000	-5,635	44%
Total Sales	172,865	180,000	-7,135	96%
Total Income	172,865	180,000	-7,135	96%
Cost of Goods Sold				
Cost of Goods Sold	126,500	127,500	-1,000	99%
Total COGS	126,500	127,500	-1,000	99%
Gross Profit	46,365	52,500	-6,135	88%
Expense				
Depreciation Expense	1,750	1,800	-50	97%
Insurance				
Liability Insurance	1,500	1,500	0	100%
Total Insurance	1,500	1,500	0	100%
Interest Expense	1,000	1,000	0	100%
Licenses and Permits	23,000	20,000	3,000	115%
Office Expenses				
Office Supplies	500	500	0	100%
Total Office Expenses	500	500	0	100%
Payroll Expenses	9,647	10,000	-353	96%
Rent	3,000	3,000	0	100%
Telephone	1,400	1,500	-100	93%
Total Expense	41,797	39,300	2,497	106%
Net Ordinary Income	4,568	13,200	-8,632	35%
Other Income/Expense				
Other Income				
Interest Income	75			
Total Other Income	75			
Net Other Income	75			
Net Income	4,643	13,200	-8,557	35%

Figure 7.72

Sunset Spas
Profit & Loss Budget Overview
January through March 2007

	Jan 07	Feb 07	Mar 07	TOTAL Jan - Mar 07
Ordinary Income/Expense				
Income				
Sales				
Merchandise	170,000	180,000	190,000	540,000
Service	10,000	11,000	12,000	33,000
Total Sales	180,000	191,000	202,000	573,000
Total Income	180,000	191,000	202,000	573,000
Cost of Goods Sold				
Cost of Goods Sold	127,500	135,000	142,500	405,000
Total COGS	127,500	135,000	142,500	405,000
Gross Profit	52,500	56,000	59,500	168,000
Expense				
Depreciation Expense	1,800	1,800	1,800	5,400
Insurance				
Liability Insurance	1,500	1,500	1,500	4,500
Total Insurance	1,500	1,500	1,500	4,500
Interest Expense	1,000	1,000	1,000	3,000
Licenses and Permits	20,000			20,000
Office Expenses				
Office Supplies	500	500	500	1,500
Total Office Expenses	500	500	500	1,500
Payroll Expenses	10,000	10,000	10,000	30,000
Rent	3,000	3,000	3,000	9,000
Telephone	1,500	1,500	1,500	4,500
Total Expense	39,300	19,300	19,300	77,900
Net Ordinary Income	13,200	36,700	40,200	90,100
Net Income	**13,200**	**36,700**	**40,200**	**90,100**

Figure 7.73

Sunset Spas
Reconciliation Summary
Checking, Period Ending 01/31/2007

	Jan 31, 07	
Beginning Balance		0.00
Cleared Transactions		
Checks and Payments - 11 items	-357,148.17	
Deposits and Credits - 8 items	391,941.60	
Total Cleared Transactions	34,793.43	
Cleared Balance		**34,793.43**
Uncleared Transactions		
Checks and Payments - 4 items	-12,093.70	
Deposits and Credits - 1 item	5,000.00	
Total Uncleared Transactions	-7,093.70	
Register Balance as of 01/31/2007		27,699.73
Ending Balance		**27,699.73**

Figure 7.74

	A	B	C	D	E	F	G
1							**Jan 07**
2		Ordinary Income/Expense					
3				Income			
4					Sales		
5						Merchandise	168500
6						Service	4365
7					Total Sales		172865
8				Total Income			172865
9				Cost of Goods Sold			
10					Cost of Goods Sold		126500
11				Total COGS			126500
12			Gross Profit				46365
13				Expense			
14					Depreciation Expense		1750
15					Insurance		
16						Liability Insurance	1500
17					Total Insurance		1500
18					Interest Expense		1000
19					Licenses and Permits		23000
20					Office Expenses		
21						Office Supplies	500
22					Total Office Expenses		500
23					Payroll Expenses		9647
24					Rent		3000
25					Telephone		1400
26				Total Expense			41797
27		Net Ordinary Income					4568
28		Other Income/Expense					
29			Other Income				
30				Interest Income			75
31			Total Other Income				75
32		Net Other Income					75
33	Net Income						**4643**

Figure 7.75

Sunset Spas
Sales by Customer Detail Report
January 2007

Type	Date	Num	Memo	Name	Item	Qty	Sales Price	Amount	Balance
J's Landscaping									
Sales Receipt	1/11/2007	7001	Consulting se...	J's Landscaping	101	10	80	800	800
Sales Receipt	1/16/2007	7004	Maxus	J's Landscaping	201	3	7,000	21,000	21,800
Sales Receipt	1/16/2007	7004	Cameo	J's Landscaping	203	2	9,000	18,000	39,800
Total J's Landscaping								39,800	39,800
Landmark Landscaping									
Invoice	1/18/2007	10001	Ultimate	Landmark Landsca...	302	2	7,500	15,000	15,000
Invoice	1/18/2007	10001	Installation	Landmark Landsca...	100	6	75	450	15,450
Total Landmark Landscaping								15,450	15,450
Marriott Hotels									
Sales Receipt	1/15/2007	7003	Consulting se...	Marriott Hotels	101	8	80	640	640
Invoice	1/19/2007	10002	Optima	Marriott Hotels	202	2	8,000	16,000	16,640
Invoice	1/19/2007	10002	Ultimate	Marriott Hotels	302	1	7,500	7,500	24,140
Invoice	1/19/2007	10002	Installation	Marriott Hotels	100	15	75	1,125	25,265
Total Marriott Hotels								25,265	25,265
Pam's Designs									
Sales Receipt	1/15/2007	7002	Galaxy	Pam's Designs	301	3	6,500	19,500	19,500
Sales Receipt	1/15/2007	7002	Optima	Pam's Designs	202	1	8,000	8,000	27,500
Sales Receipt	1/15/2007	7002	Aqua	Pam's Designs	303	1	9,500	9,500	37,000
Invoice	1/24/2007	10003	Cameo	Pam's Designs	203	6	9,000	54,000	91,000
Invoice	1/24/2007	10003	Installation	Pam's Designs	100	18	75	1,350	92,350
Total Pam's Designs								92,350	92,350
TOTAL								**172,865**	**172,865**

Figure 7.76

Sunset Spas
Sales by Item Summary
January 2007

	Qty	Amount	% of Sales	Jan - Mar 04 Avg Price	COGS	Avg COGS	Gross Margin	Gross Margin%
Inventory								
201	3	21,000	12%	7,000	15,000	5,000	6,000	29%
202	3	24,000	14%	8,000	18,000	6,000	6,000	25%
203	8	72,000	42%	9,000	56,000	7,000	16,000	22%
301	3	19,500	11%	6,500	13,500	4,500	6,000	31%
302	3	22,500	13%	7,500	16,500	5,500	6,000	27%
303	1	9,500	5%	9,500	7,500	7,500	2,000	21%
Total Inventory		168,500	97%		126,500		42,000	25%
Service								
100	39	2,925	2%	75				
101	18	1,400	1%	80				
Total Service		4,365	3%					
TOTAL		172,865	100%					

Figure 7.77

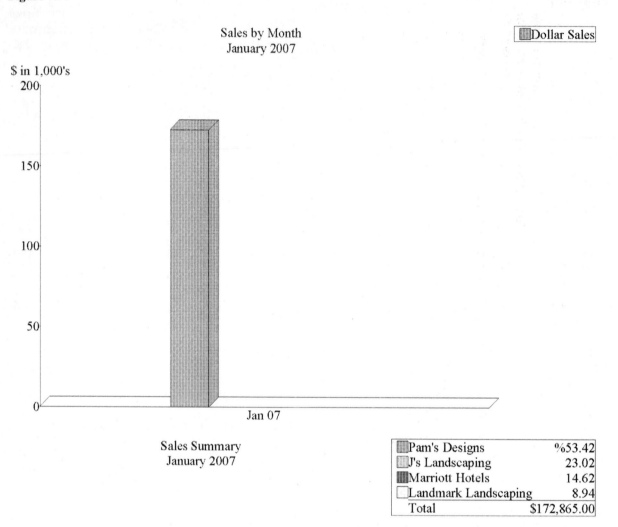

Sales by Month
January 2007

Dollar Sales

$ in 1,000's

Jan 07

Sales Summary
January 2007

Pam's Designs	%53.42
J's Landscaping	23.02
Marriott Hotels	14.62
Landmark Landscaping	8.94
Total	$172,865.00

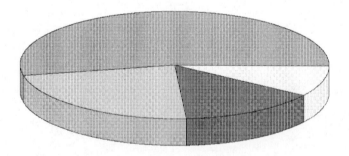

By Customer

Figure 7.78

Sunset Spas
Inventory Stock Status by Item
January 2007

Inventory	Item Description	Pref Vendor	Reorder Pt	On Hand	Order	On Purchase Order	Next Deliv	Sales/Week
201	Maxus	Sundance Spas		7		0		0.7
202	Optima	Sundance Spas		7		0		0.7
203	Cameo	Sundance Spas		2		0		1.8
301	Galaxy	Cal Spas		3		0		0.7
302	Ultimate	Cal Spas		3		0		0.7
303	Aqua	Cal Spas		5		0		0.2

Traditional Accounting Records

In the Appendix, students see that they can use QuickBooks with or without debits and credits. The integrity of QuickBooks's data is maintained using registers (similar to general ledger accounts) without using the terms debit and credit. Instructors wishing to emphasize debits and credits might assign this chapter early in the course.

Appendix Questions

1. QuickBooks lists accounts in the trial balance report in this order: assets, liabilities, equity, revenue, and expense.

2. QuickBooks's QuickZoom feature allows you to access supporting accounts or journals when viewing the trial balance. QuickZoom refers to the "magnifying glass" symbol that appears in reports and graphs. When the QuickZoom symbol appears over a number in a report or an item in a graph, you can double-click it to bring up more detail about that number or item.

3. When you double-click an amount on the trial balance, the QuickZoom feature brings up more detail about that number. Specifically, a Transactions by Account report appears that identifies all transactions affecting that account during the period specified in the original trial balance report.

4. A transaction recorded through an account register also creates a general journal entry. This provides a source for the transaction recorded. Thus, if after the transaction has been recorded through the account register you want to examine the source of an increase or decrease in an account, the journal entry would be that source.

5. QuickBooks has a general ledger to satisfy traditional accountants who might feel uncomfortable with an accounting system without one. QuickBooks's style of maintaining transactions in an account register is very similar to a general ledger format.

6. QuickBooks's document-initiated recording method has several advantages over the standard journal entry method. In particular, once you enter a transaction via a document such as an invoice, several steps are completed simultaneously. When you enter information on an invoice for instance, Accounts Receivable is debited and Sales Revenue is credited. If you're selling inventory, the same invoice updates the perpetual inventory record, credits the Inventory account, and debits the Cost of Goods Sold account. Plus, QuickBooks adjusts the customer's account accordingly so you know how much each customer owes and when their amounts are due.

7. When you double-click on an amount in the general ledger the source document is revealed. Double-clicking a deposit opens the Make Deposit window with the specific deposit transaction you clicked on.

8. Journal entries can be used in QuickBooks to record business transactions as in a traditional accounting setting. Within the journal you specify what accounts are debited and credited and by what amounts.

9. The Make Journal Entry menu item in the Company menu is used to access QuickBooks's journal entries.

10. You can access accounts in QuickBooks's general journal entry by clicking once in the account column and either typing an account name or selecting an account from the drop-down list available.

Appendix Assignments

1. Creating a Trial Balance, General Ledger, and Journal Entry for Phoenix Systems, Inc.

   a. The Trial Balance as of February 28, 2003 is shown in Figure A.1.

   b. Page 1 of the General Ledger for the two months ended February 28, 2003 is shown in Figure A.2.

   c. Nothing required.

2. Adding More Information: Central Coast Cellular

   a. The journal entry is shown in Figure A.3

   b. The Trial Balance is shown in Figure A.4

   c. Page 1 of the General Ledger is shown in figure A.5.

3. Internet assignments and related solutions are found at *http://owen.swlearning.com*.

Appendix Case Problems

1. Ocean View Flowers

    a.   The Trial Balance is shown in Figure A.6.

    b.   Page 1 of the General Ledger is shown in Figure A.7.

2. Jennings & Associates—Debits and Credits

    a.   The Trial Balance as of March 31, 2004 is shown in Figure A.8.

    b.   Page 1 of the General Ledger for the quarter ended March 31, 2004 is shown in Figure A.9.

Solution Figures for Appendix

Figure A.1

Phoenix Software 07
Trial Balance
As of February 28, 2003

	Feb 28, 03	
	Debit	Credit
Bank of Cupertino	77,682.10	
Short-term Investments	13,000.00	
Accounts Receivable	22,353.00	
Inventory Asset	39,029.40	
Investments	12,000.00	
Prepaid Insurance	1,384.67	
Prepaid Rent	1,600.00	
Undeposited Funds	0.00	
Computer Equipment: Cost	6,750.00	
Furniture: Cost	3,756.44	
Accounts Payable		45,899.50
Payroll Liabilities		7,992.81
Sales Tax Payable		4,891.12
Short-Term Debt		12,500.00
Long-Term Debt		25,000.00
Capital Stock		75,000.00
Computer Add-ons		2,200.00
Computer Sales		49,450.00
Consulting Income		7,425.00
Maintenance & Repairs		5,990.00
Parts income		149.85
Cost of Goods Sold	35,919.85	
Bank Service Charges	110.00	
Office Supplies	592.56	
Payroll Expenses	22,859.05	
Rent	800.00	
Telephone	252.21	
Utilities: Gas and Electric	409.00	
Investment Income		2,000.00
TOTAL	**238,498.28**	**238,498.28**

Figure A.2

Phoenix Software 07
General Ledger
As of February 28, 2003

Type	Date	Num	Name	Memo	Split	Amount	Balance
Bank of Cupertino							0.00
Deposit	1/2/03			Deposit	Capital Stock	25,000.00	25,000.00
Check	1/7/03	1001	Walker Insurance		Prepaid Insurance	-1,384.67	23,615.33
Check	1/8/03	1002	E-Max Realty	First and last mon...	Prepaid Rent	-1,600.00	22,015.33
Check	1/9/03	1003	Apple Computer Inc.		Inventory Asset	-9,000.00	13,015.33
Deposit	1/10/03			Deposit	Capital Stock	50,000.00	63,015.33
Deposit	1/10/03			Transfer	Short-term Investm...	-8,000.00	55,015.33
Sales Rec...	1/13/03	501	St. Johns Hospital		-SPLIT-	2,015.63	57,030.96
Check	1/13/03	1004	Sky Investments		Investments	-40,000.00	17,030.96
Check	1/14/03	1005	Bengal Drives, Inc		Inventory Asset	-2,250.00	14,780.96
Sales Rec...	1/14/03	502	Jdesign		-SPLIT-	688.00	15,468.96
Payment	1/14/03		Netscape		Accounts Receivable	6,500.00	21,968.96
Check	1/17/03	1006	Office Mart		Cost	-3,756.44	18,212.52
Check	1/17/03				Short-term Investm	2,000.00	20,212.52
Deposit	1/23/03			Deposit	Short-term Debt	12,500.00	32,712.52
Deposit	1/23/03			Deposit	-SPLIT-	35,000.00	67,712.52
Bill Pmt -Check	1/29/03	1007	GTE	408-555-7911	Accounts Payable	-159.65	67,552.87
Bill Pmt -Check	1/29/03	1008	Office Mart		Accounts Payable	-560.00	66,992.87
Bill Pmt -Check	1/29/03	1009	PG&E		Accounts Payable	-230.00	66,762.87
Check	1/31/03		Bank of Cupertino	January bank...	Bank Service ...	-45.00	66,717.87
Paycheck	1/31/03	1010	Casey K. Nicks		-SPLIT-	3,480.39	63,237.48
Paycheck	1/31/03	1011	Kylie W Patrick		-SPLIT-	-955.20	62,282.28
Paycheck	1/31/03	1012	Paul A Gates		-SPLIT-	-3,026.48	59,255.80
Check	2/3/03	1013	Office Mart		Cost	-6,750.00	52,505.80
Check	2/4/03	1014	Sky Investments		Investments	-10,000.00	42,505.80
Deposit	2/14/03			Deposit	-SPLIT-	24,681.84	67,187.64
Sales Rec...	2/21/03	504	TRW		-SPLIT-	13,867.50	81,055.14
Deposit	2/24/03			Deposit	Long-term Debt	25,000.00	106,055.14
Deposit	2/24/03			Transfer	Short-term Investm...	-7,000.00	99,055.14
Check	2/25/03	1015	Bengal Drives, Inc		-SPLIT-	-2,600.00	96,455.14
Deposit	2/25/03			Deposit	-SPLIT-	5,000.00	101,455.14
Paycheck	2/26/03	1021	Casey K. Nicks		-SPLIT-	-3,480.39	97,974.75
Paycheck	2/26/03	1022	Kylie W Patrick		-SPLIT-	-897.31	97,077.44
Paycheck	2/26/03	1023	Paul A Gates		-SPLIT-	-3,026.47	94,050.97
Bill Pmt -Check	2/27/03	1016	Computer Wholesale Inc.	19-85425	Accounts Payable	-15,199.75	78,851.22
Bill Pmt -Check	2/27/03	1017	GTE	408-555-7911	Accounts Payable	-92.56	78,758.66
Bill Pmt -Check	2/27/03	1018	PG&E		Accounts Payable	-179.00	78,579.66
Bill Pmt -Check	2/27/03	1019	E-Max Realty		Accounts Payable	-800.00	77,779.66
Bill Pmt -Check	2/27/03	1020	Office Mart		Accounts Payable	-32.56	77,747.10
Check	2/28/03		Bank of Cupertino	February ban...	Bank Service ...	-65.00	77,682.10
Total Bank of Cupertino						77,682.10	77,682.10
Short-term Investments							0.00
Deposit	1/10/03			Transfer	Bank of Cupertino	8,000.00	8,000.00
Check	1/17/03			Transfer	Bank of Cupertino	-2,000.00	6,000.00
Deposit	2/24/03			Transfer	Bank of Cupertino	7,000.00	13,000.00
Total Short-term Investments						13,000.00	13,000.00
Accounts Receivable							0.00
Invoice	1/13/03	20001	Los Gatos School D...		-SPLIT-	18,409.38	18,409.38
Payment	1/14/03		Netscape		Bank of Cupertino	-6,500.00	11,909.38
Invoice	1/22/03	20002	St. Johns Hospital		-SPLIT-	5,375.00	17,284.38

Figure A.3

Central Coast Cellular
General Journal Transaction
January 31, 2003

Num	Name	Memo	Account	Class	Debit	Credit
4			Gas and Electric		250.00	
	So. Cal Edison		Accounts Payable			250.00
					250.00	250.00
TOTAL					**250.00**	**250.00**

Figure A.4

Central Coast Cellular
Trial Balance
As of January 31, 2003

	Jan 31, '03	
	Debit	Credit
Checking	130,392.87	
Accounts Receivable	13,878.00	
Store Supplies	3,000.00	
Inventory Asset	14,750.00	
Short-term Investments	75,000.00	
Equipment: Cost	95,000.00	
Equipment: Accumulated Depreciation		1,000.00
Office Furniture: Cost	20,000.00	
Office Furniture: Accumulated Depreciation		500.00
Security Deposit	3,000.00	
Accounts Payable		15,375.00
Unearned Revenue		10,000.00
Interest Payable		950.00
Payroll Liabilities		3,360.31
Sales Tax Payable		1,578.00
Notes Payable		125,000.00
Common Stock		200,000.00
Commissions		1,750.00
Consulting		7,600.00
Phone Sales		10,375.00
Cost of Goods Sold	6,875.00	
Bank Service Charges	80.00	
Depreciation Expense	1,500.00	
Interest Expense	950.00	
Payroll Expenses	9,812.44	
Rent	3,000.00	
Utilities: Gas and Electric	250.00	
TOTAL	377,488.31	377,488.31

Figure A.5

Central Coast Cellular
General Ledger
As of January 31, 2003

Type	Date	Num	Name	Memo	Split	Amount	Balance
Checking							0.0
Deposit	1/3/2003			Deposit	Common Stock	200,000.00	200,000.00
Check	1/6/2003		Schwab Investments		Short-term Inve...	-75,000.00	125,000.00
Deposit	1/7/2003			Deposit	Notes Payable	125,000.00	250,000.00
Check	1/8/2003		Russco		Cost	-20,000.00	230,000.00
Check	1/10/2003		Russco		Store Supplies	-3,000.00	227,000.00
Check	1/13/2003		Central Cost Leasing	Rent-Janua...	-SPLIT-	-6,000.00	221,000.00
Payment	1/14/2003		City of San Luis Obispo	Advance Paym	Accounts Recei...	10,000.00	231,000.00
Sales Receipt	1/16/2003	501	Sterling Hotels Corpo...		-SPLIT-	7,425.00	235,220.49
Paycheck	1/17/2003	3005	Alex Rodriguez		-SPLIT-	-1,437.00	229,563.00
Paycheck	1/17/2003	3006	Jay Bruner		-SPLIT-	-1,077.75	228,485.25
Paycheck	1/17/2003	3007	Megan Paulson		-SPLIT-	-689.76	227,795.49
Check	1/22/2003	3008	Kyle Equipment, Inc.		Cost	-95,000.00	140,220.49
Check	1/22/2003	3009	Ericsson, Inc.		Accounts Paya...	-6,500.00	133,720.49
Paycheck	1/31/2003	3010	Alex Rodriguez		-SPLIT-	-1,437.00	132,283.49
Paycheck	1/31/2003	3011	Jay Bruner		-SPLIT-	-1,077.75	131,205.74
Paycheck	1/31/2003	3012	Megan Paulson		-SPLIT-	-732.87	130,472.87
Check	1/31/2003			Service Cha...	Bank Service C...	-80.00	130,392.87
Total Checking						130,392.87	130,392.87
Accounts Receivable							0.00
Payment	1/14/2003		City of San Luis Obispo	Advance paym...	Checking	-10,000.00	-10,000.00
Invoice	1/21/2003	10001	City of San Luis Obispo		-SPLIT	13,878.00	3,878.00
General Journal	1/31/2003	3	City of San Luis Obispo		Unearned Reve...	10,000.00	13,878.00
Total Accounts Receivable						13,878.00	13,878.00
Store Supplies							0.00
Check	1/10/2003	3003	Russco		Checking	3,000.00	3,000.00
Total Store Supplies						3,000.00	3,000.00
Inventory Asset							0.00
Item Receipt	1/15/2003	PO101	Ericsson, Inc.	Ericsson LX588	Accounts Paya...	2,000.00	2,000.00
Item Receipt	1/15/2003	PO101	Ericsson, Inc.	Ericsson T19LX	Accounts Paya...	4,500.00	6,500.00
Sales Receipt	1/16/2003	501	Sterling Hotels Corpo...	Ericsson LX588	Checking	-1,250.00	5,250.00
Bill	1/20/2003		Nokia Mobile Phones	Nokia 3285	Accounts Paya...	5,000.00	10,250.00
Bill	1/20/2003		Nokia Mobile Phones	Nokia 8290	Accounts Paya...	7,500.00	17,750.00
Bill	1/20/2003		Nokia Mobile Phones	Nokia 8890	Accounts Paya...	2,625.00	20,375.00
Invoice	1/21/2003	10001	City of San Luis Obispo	Nokia 8290	Accounts Recei...	-3,000.00	17,375.00
Invoice	1/21/2003	10001	City of San Luis Obispo	Nokia 8890	Accounts Recei...	-2,625.00	14,750.00
Total Inventory Asset						14,750.00	14,750.00
Short-term Investments							0.00
Check	1/6/2003	3001	Schwab Investments		Checking	75,000.00	75,000.00
Total Short-term Investments						75,000.00	75,000.00
Undeposited Funds							0.00
Total Undeposited Funds							0.00
Equipment							0.00
Cost							0.00
Check	1/22/2003	3008	Kyle Equipment, Inc.		Checking	95,000.00	95,000.00
Total Cost						95,000.00	95,000.00
Accumulated Depreciation							0.00
General Journal	1/31/2003	1			Depreciation Ex...	-1,000.00	-1,000.00
Total Accumulated Depreciation						-1,000.00	-1,000.00
Equipment – Other							0.00
Total Equipment – Other							0.00
Total Equipment						94,000.00	94,000.00
Office Furniture							0.00
Cost							0.00
Check	1/8/2003	3002	Russco		Checking	20,000.00	20,000.00
Total Cost						20,000.00	20,000.00
Accumulated Depreciation							0.00
General Journal	1/31/2003	1			Depreciation Ex...	-500.00	-500.00
Total Accumulated Depreciation						-500.00	-500.00

Figure A.6

Ocean View Flowers Appendix
Trial Balance
As of January 31, 2004

	Jan 31, 04	
	Debit	Credit
Union Checking	70,917.94	
Short-term investments	25,000.00	
Accounts Receivable		5,000.00
Office Supplies	1,500.00	
Inventory Asset	20,100.00	
Computer Equipment: Cost	15,000.00	
Office Equipment: Cost	20,000.00	
Payroll Liabilities		7,178.84
Long-Term Note Payable		50,000.00
Common Stock		100,000.00
Sales: Daylilies		28,800.00
Cost of Goods Sold	14,400.00	
Bank Service Charges	45.00	
Payroll Expenses	20,215.90	
Rent	3,000.00	
Telephone	400.00	
Utilities	500.00	
Interest Revenue		100.00
TOTAL	**191,078.84**	**191,078.84**

Figure A.7

Ocean View Flowers Appendix
General Ledger
As of February 29, 2004

Type	Date	Num	Name	Memo	Split	Amount	Balance
Union Checking							0.00
Deposit	1/4/04			Deposit	Common Stock	100,000.00	100,000.00
Deposit	1/6/04			Deposit	Long-Term No...	50,000.00	150,000.00
Check	1/8/04	101	Prudent Investments		Short-term inv...	-25,000.00	125,000.00
Check	1/11/04	102	Stateside Office Su...		Cost	-20,000.00	105,000.00
Check	1/12/04	103	Gateway Computers		Cost	-15,000.00	90,000.00
Paycheck	1/15/04	104	Edward Thomas		-SPLIT-	-1,819.67	88,180.33
Paycheck	1/15/97	105	Kelly Gusland		-SPLIT-	-689.33	87,491.00
Paycheck	1/15/04	106	Margie Coe		-SPLIT-	699.33	86,791.67
Paycheck	1/15/04	107	Marie McAninch		-SPLIT-	-1,740.70	85,050.97
Paycheck	1/15/04	108	Stan Comstock		-SPLIT-	-1,565.67	83,485.30
Check	1/18/04	109	Brophy Bros. Farms		-SPLIT-	-34,500.00	48,985.30
Check	1/20/04	110	Stateside Office Su...		-SPLIT-	-1,500.00	47,485.30
Sales Rec...	1/22/04	1	Valley Florists		Office Supplies	6,600.00	54,085.30
Sales Rec...	1/25/04	2	Eastern Scents		-SPLIT-	22,200.00	76,285.30
Payment	1/28/04		FTD		Accounts Rec...	5,000.00	81,285.30
Check	1/29/04	111	Hawaiian Farms		Rent	-3,000.00	78,285.30
Check	1/29/04	112	Edison Inc.		Utilities	-500.00	77,785.30
Check	1/29/04	113	GTE		Telephone	-400.00	77,385.30
Paycheck	1/29/04	114	Edward Thomas		-SPLIT-	-1,819.65	75,565.65
Paycheck	1/29/04	115	Kelly Gusland		-SPLIT-	-741.90	74,823.75
Paycheck	1/29/04	116	Margie Coe		-SPLIT-	-654.42	74,169.33
Paycheck	1/29/04	117	Marie McAninch		-SPLIT-	-1,740.70	72,428.63
Paycheck	1/29/04	118	Stan Comstock		-SPLIT-	-1,565.69	70,862.94
Check	1/31/04			Service Charge	Bank Service	-45.00	70,817.94
Deposit	1/31/04			Interest	Interest Revenue	100.00	70,917.94
Check	2/1/04	119	Santa Barbara Ban...		Long-Term No...	-1,000.00	69,917.94
Check	2/3/04	120	State Farm Insurance		Prepaid Insura...	-2,500.00	67,417.94
Deposit	2/9/04			Deposit	-SPLIT-	5,200.00	72,617.94
Paycheck	2/15/04	121	Edward Thomas		-SPLIT-	-1,819.66	70,798.28
Paycheck	2/15/04	122	Kelly Gusland		-SPLIT-	-710.28	70,088.00
Paycheck	2/15/04	123	Margie Coe		-SPLIT-	-671.98	69,416.02
Paycheck	2/15/04	124	Marie McAninch		-SPLIT-	-1,740.70	67,675.32
Paycheck	2/15/04	125	Stan Comstock		-SPLIT-	-1,565.68	66,109.64
Bill Pmt -Check	2/24/04	126	Edison Inc.		Accounts Pay...	-300.00	65,809.64
Bill Pmt -Check	2/24/04	127	GTE		Accounts Pay...	-250.00	65,559.64
Check	2/26/04	128	Hawaiian Farms		-SPLIT-	-30,000.00	35,559.64
Paycheck	2/26/04	129	Edward Thomas		-SPLIT-	-1,819.67	33,739.97
Paycheck	2/26/04	130	Kelly Gusland		-SPLIT-	-579.55	33,160.42
Paycheck	2/26/04	131	Margie Coe		-SPLIT-	-431.99	32,728.43
Paycheck	2/26/04	132	Marie McAninch		-SPLIT-	-1,740.70	30,987.73
Paycheck	2/26/04	133	Stan Comstock		-SPLIT-	-1,565.67	29,422.06
Check	2/28/04			Service Charge	Bank Service ...	-55.00	29,367.06
Deposit	2/28/04			Interest	Interest Reven...	75.00	29,442.06
Total Union Checking						29,442.06	29,442.06
Short-term investments							0.00
Check	1/8/04	101	Prudent Investments		Union Checking	25,000.00	25,000.00
Deposit	2/9/04			Deposit	Union Checking	-5,000.00	20,000.00
Deposit	2/28/04				Interest Reven...	800.00	20,800.00
Total Short-term Investments						20,800.00	20,800.00

Figure A.8

Jennings & Associates (KJ07cp)
Trial Balance
As of March 31, 2004

	Mar 31, 04	
	Debit	Credit
First Valley Savings & Loan	52,722.39	
Union Bank Checking	4,080.97	
Accounts Receivable	24,587.50	
Interest Receivable	41.17	
Inventory Asset	1,760.29	
Prepaid Insurance	1,800.00	
Short-term investments	2,459.00	
Computer Equipment:Cost	14,000.00	
Computer Equipment:Accumulated Depreciation		1,518.33
Furniture:Cost	2,500.00	
Furniture:Accumulated Depreciation		625.01
Vehicles:Cost	18,500.00	
Vehicles:Accumulated Depreciation		300.00
Accounts Payable		8,770.00
Payroll Liabilities		2,675.69
Sales Tax Payable	0.00	
Short-term note payable		8,000.00
Unearned Revenue		1,425.00
Bank of San Martin	0.00	
Vehicle loan		18,580.00
Capital Stock		70,000.00
Opening Bal Equity		3,590.00
Retained Earnings		1,900.00
Fee Income:Film		965.00
Fee Income:Magazine		12,100.00
Fee Income:Press Release		975.00
Fee Income:Promotion		12,350.00
Fee Income:Radio		2,177.50
Fee Income:Television		21,175.00
Bank Service Charges	270.00	
Depreciation Expense	943.34	
Equipment Rental	75.00	
Film expenses	632.21	
Insurance:Liability Insurance	775.00	
Interest Expense:Loan Interest	80.00	
Office Supplies	101.00	
Payroll Expenses	29,023.83	
Postage and Delivery	109.00	
Practice Development	35.00	
Printing and Reproduction	25.00	
Professional Fees:Legal Fees	650.00	
Radio Spots	0.00	
Rent	2,100.00	
Repairs:Computer Repairs	95.00	
Telephone	249.00	
TV Commercial Spots	10,000.00	
Utilities:Gas and Electric	295.00	
Utilities:Water	217.00	
Interest Revenue		500.17
Other Income		500.00
TOTAL	**168,476.70**	**168,476.70**

Figure A.9

Jennings & Associates (KJ07cp)
General Ledger
As of March 31, 2004

Type	Date	Num	Name	Memo	Split	Amount	Balance
First Valley Savings & Loan							1,000.00
Payment	1/16/2004		Ray's Chevron		Accounts Receivable	75.00	1,075.00
Check	1/31/2004	1265	First Valley Savings & Loan		Union Bank Checki...	500.00	1,575.00
Check	1/31/2004			Service Charge	Bank Service Char...	-45.00	1,530.00
Deposit	2/1/2004			Deposit	Capital Stock	20,000.00	21,530.00
Check	2/2/2004	1001	Phoenix Computers		Cost	-3,000.00	18,530.00
Check	2/4/2004	1002	Dean Witter		Short-term investm...	-5,000.00	13,530.00
Check	2/10/2004	1003	Rex's Film Supply		Inventory Asset	-150.00	13,380.00
Check	2/10/2004	1004	Bruno's Stationers		Office Supplies	-75.00	13,305.00
Deposit	2/15/2004			Deposit	Capital Stock	50,000.00	63,305.00
Payment	2/27/2004		Evelyn Walker Real Estate		Accounts Receivable	4,275.00	67,580.00
Check	2/28/2004			Service Charge	Bank Service Char...	-45.00	67,535.00
Deposit	3/1/2004		Bank of San Martin	Deposit	Short-term note pa...	8,000.00	75,535.00
Check	3/2/2004	1005	Bank of San Martin		Bank of San Martin	-5,000.00	70,535.00
Deposit	3/2/2004			Deposit	-SPLIT-	3,500.00	74,035.00
Check	3/3/2004	1006	Phoenix Computers		Cost	-7,000.00	67,035.00
Liability Check	3/4/2004	1023	EDD		-SPLIT-	-713.81	66,321.19
Liability Check	3/15/2004	1024	IRS		-SPLIT-	-6,552.30	59,768.89
Payment	3/15/2004		Big 10		Accounts Receivable	325.00	60,093.89
Bill Pmt -Check	3/26/2004	1021	General Telephone		Accounts Payable	-160.00	59,933.89
Bill Pmt -Check	3/27/2004	1022	San Martin Water District		Accounts Payable	-160.00	59,773.89
Payment	3/27/2004		Evelyn Walker Real Estate		Accounts Receivable	200.00	59,973.89
Bill Pmt -Check	3/28/2004	1025	Frank Mendez Properties		Accounts Payable	-700.00	59,273.89
Bill Pmt -Check	3/28/2004	1007	Banks Office Supply		Accounts Payable	-26.00	59,247.89
Bill Pmt -Check	3/29/2004	1008	Federal Express		Accounts Payable	-47.00	59,200.89
Bill Pmt -Check	3/29/2004	1009	Frank Mendez Properties		Accounts Payable	-700.00	58,500.89
Bill Pmt -Check	3/29/2004	1010	General Telephone		Accounts Payable	-89.00	58,411.89
Bill Pmt -Check	3/29/2004	1011	KCOY TV		Accounts Payable	-2,500.00	55,911.89
Bill Pmt -Check	3/29/2004	1012	KCRQ Radio		Accounts Payable	-750.00	55,161.89
Bill Pmt -Check	3/29/2004	1013	On-Time Copy Shop		Accounts Payable	-100.00	55,061.89
Bill Pmt -Check	3/29/2004	1014	Owen & Owen		Accounts Payable	-275.00	54,786.89
Bill Pmt -Check	3/29/2004	1015	Pacific Electric Co.		Accounts Payable	-45.00	54,741.89
Bill Pmt -Check	3/29/2004	1016	Phoenix Computers		Accounts Payable	-95.00	54,646.89
Bill Pmt -Check	3/29/2004	1017	Rex's Film Supply		Accounts Payable	-2,242.50	52,404.39
Bill Pmt -Check	3/29/2004	1018	San Martin Water District		Accounts Payable	-57.00	52,347.39
Bill Pmt -Check	3/29/2004	1019	So. Cal Gas		Accounts Payable	-55.00	52,292.39
Bill Pmt -Check	3/29/2004	1020	Walker Insurance Co.		Accounts Payable	-175.00	52,117.39
Payment	3/29/2004		Ray's Chevron		Accounts Receivable	650.00	52,767.39
Check	3/31/2004			Service Charge	Bank Service Char...	-45.00	52,722.39
Total First Valley Savings & Loan						51,722.39	52,722.39
Union Bank Checking							2,590.00
Payment	1/3/2004	337	AAA Appliance		Accounts Receivable	100.00	2,690.00
Payment	1/6/2004	1002	Fancy Yogurt Co.		Accounts Receivable	500.00	3,190.00
Bill Pmt -Check	1/6/2004	1251	Frank Mendez Properties	Opening balance	Accounts Payable	-700.00	2,490.00
Bill Pmt -Check	1/6/2004	1252	General Telephone	Opening balance	Accounts Payable	-75.00	2,415.00
Bill Pmt -Check	1/15/2004	1253	On-Time Copy Shop	Opening balance	Accounts Payable	-125.00	2,290.00
Payment	1/15/2004	150	Sally's Fabrics		Accounts Receivable	200.00	2,490.00
Payment	1/15/2004	215	Bob and Mary Schultz		Accounts Receivable	800.00	3,290.00
Paycheck	1/15/2004	1258	Cheryl A Boudreau		-SPLIT-	-893.07	2,396.93
Paycheck	1/15/2004	1259	Diane A Murphy		-SPLIT-	-925.07	1,471.86
Paycheck	1/15/2004	1260	Kelly A Jennings		-SPLIT-	-1,381.62	90.24